MAKING
IT HOME

*I Set Out to See the World and Made It
All the Way to Cleveland*

D1591103

R. Mark Giuliano

Black Rose Writing | Texas

First printing

Some names and identifying details have been changed to protect the privacy of individuals.

ISBN: 978-1-68433-878-8
PUBLISHED BY BLACK ROSE WRITING
www.blackrosewriting.com

Printed in the United States of America
Suggested Retail Price (SRP) $20.95

Making It Home is printed in Book Antiqua

*As a planet-friendly publisher, Black Rose Writing does its best to eliminate unnecessary waste to reduce paper usage and energy costs, while never compromising the reading experience. As a result, the final word count vs. page count may not meet common expectations.

For Beth.

We share the journey. You are my home.

MAKING IT HOME

"In America, there are only three great cities: New York, San Francisco, and New Orleans. Everywhere else is Cleveland."
- Tennessee Williams

Re: Purpose

AT THE MOMENT, our home is on fire.

Tomorrow is moving day. The day the movers will arrive to pack up our belongings, load them into a truck and whisk them away. That is, if our belongings aren't soaked or smoked or, worse, blackened by whatever smoldering crisis has presently driven us out of our apartment and down onto the city street four stories below. You might call this "bad timing."

The fact that our building has ignited the day before we're scheduled to move doesn't surprise me, given the challenges we've had with our historic home throughout the last decade in Cleveland where obstacles and discouragement have been common. The work of condo ownership in downtown Cleveland, like the work of the city itself, has been heavy lifting. I chuckle to myself and wonder if we'll ever get out from underneath our condo. Then again, I've speculated, maybe it was precisely what lies beneath our condo that is the problem. Our home on Public Square may have been jinxed from the beginning, cursed for having been built on top of, or mere feet away from, a plot of land that was once home to Cleveland's very first cemetery. They moved the headstones to the Erie Street Cemetery roughly sixty-five years before our nine-story was erected in 1904. But did they really move the bodies?

I wonder, though, if it was more likely that my own ghosts were holding me back, unconsciously willing us to stay in Cleveland. For eleven years, I had invested all that I had and all that I was into making it home. Cleveland, and its historic, city-center church gave me purpose, and passion, and an opportunity to lose myself for a cause. It blessed me with good people of like mind who shared a vision for restoring and repurposing a great American city. The Christian idealist in me believed that if God could raise up Jesus on Easter morning, then God could most certainly raise up a dying city like Cleveland which, quantifiably speaking, in the year 2008 – the year I followed a call to Cleveland, it was. I trusted that along the way God might give me - a wandering preacher who was still searching for his place in this world – a home in Cleveland, or at least the opportunity to make one. And so, I placed my heart upon the altar of the good work that Cleveland offered me until I had very little of my heart left to give.

The afternoon of the fire, I battled with a stubborn three-inch screw that refused to release its grip from the metal wall mount of my floating desk in the study of our condo. My mulish determination to salvage every single piece of hardware necessary to remount the desk elsewhere, and the relentless torque from my power screwdriver slipping from the grooves on the head of the fastener caused the screw to spark. When I finally yanked it free with a pair of pliers – leaving a gaping hole in the wall that would later demand spackling, the screw was hot to the touch. Just ten minutes later, the fire alarm wailed throughout the building. For a brief moment, I panicked. Had I caused that? Did my sparking wall screw ignite the fire that would drive Beth and me, and a dozen friends and neighbors out into the damp-to-the-bone afternoon with puppies, laptops, and other personal items tucked under our arms? The answer to that question was, "no," of course. We would learn later that the root cause of all the smoke was mechanical and located five floors below us and on the other side of the building.

The fact that I thought I might have had something to do with the fire, however, was telling. Was there something still residing within me, a ghost in my heart, that refused to let go of Cleveland? Was I the obstinate piece of hardware, like the screw anchored in the study wall, so invested in my Cleveland home that I could have unconsciously sparked a fire in our own building just so that we wouldn't have to leave? Was I trying to lock in for a few more years in spite of all that was driving us away?

Cleveland isn't an easy city to live in, let alone thrive. For all its treasures, Cleveland can cause you more than a fair share of grief if you happen to love it too much. Which, I did. I loved Cleveland. I loved the city and its tenacious people for the same reason some people love a falling-down century-home with a leaky roof and drafty windows, or a classic car that's always in need of a part that no longer exists, or a favorite fumbling football team that always drops the ball on the one-yard line in the dying seconds of the game that was theirs to lose, because somewhere along the way we discovered that we needed these things as much and, perhaps, even more than these things needed us.

I needed Cleveland.

•　　•　　•

Making It Home is a story about many things: friendships and the goodness of people everywhere - particularly around the Great Lakes region of North America. It's about the rise and fall, and potential rise again, of America's rustbelt cities – particularly, Cleveland. Mostly though, Making It Home is the story about the longing for and the journey toward home. It's the story of how the high calling of our inward journey often compels us toward the challenges of our outward ones, even those ventures that all but destroy us along the way.

In the year 2008, my inward journey led me bumping and thumping, outwardly, along a very real highway toward a city that I hoped and prayed could become my new home – the city of Cleveland, Ohio. Cleveland was very much like the nine-story office-condo-conversion on Public Square that Beth and I would attempt to make our home. Cleveland was ready to be repurposed. And so was I. That made us a good fit for one another.

Once the sixth largest city in the nation, Cleveland enjoyed an impressive history. It had great cultural bones, too, with its well-established and carefully endowed art museum, orchestra and performing arts district, the Rock & Roll Hall of Fame, a hip and growing restaurant scene, and the famed Cleveland Clinic which treated people from near and far with the most innovative and skilled care-givers and cutting-edge technologies. Cleveland also had a celebrated city-center church where I could grow as a pastor and hone my skills as a public speaker and writer, civic leader and new urbanist advocate.

Cleveland would be the place that I would be awakened. My role as the esteemed pastor of a renowned downtown church was not simply to speak, but also to listen. And to listen with my heart. Cleveland would teach me that my role, in part, was the hard work of trying to pry-open the doors of the church and welcome others in the city whose voice needed to be heard more than my own – people of color, women, and young people who, every single day, live with the terrifying risk of being shot to death at school. Amid the city's proud history and grand architecture, cultural amenities and advanced medical systems were also the harsh realities of higher than average hunger and homelessness, gun violence and police shootings, murder, rape, and other forms of violent crimes, practical and systemic racism, failing infrastructure and educational systems that lacked the tax base to modernize them. I discovered in Cleveland just how severely these seemingly insurmountable challenges weaken the spirit of some, and strengthen it in others.

What drew me to Cleveland wasn't that it was broken, but that it was broken and that there were people, good and faithful people, who believed that it could be restored. Clevelanders, I found, were resilient, good humored, and house-proud. I was impressed by their nothing-left-to-lose enterprising spirit and steel-town, never-say-die toughness. Like its sister cities around the lake – Detroit, Toledo, Buffalo, Rochester, and even Hamilton, Ontario to the north, Cleveland was emerging from the dark winter of post-industrial blight and the twentieth-century damages inflicted by the automobile. Cleveland was reimagining itself as a walkable, bike-able, affordable mid-sized city with a thriving live-work-play downtown community and a nationally renowned sports, arts, music, public parks, and food scene. I was hungry to be a part of that kind of urban rebirth.

Tennessee Williams, the great twentieth century playwright, is often (mis)credited for quipping, "In America, there are only three great cities: New York, San Francisco, and New Orleans. Everywhere else is Cleveland." With all due respect to the great cities of New York, San Francisco, and New Orleans, this book is written for Cleveland, and "for everywhere else," and especially for the people who not only live in those everywhere-else-cities but who love their own particular city and are making it home. It's a book for the good people of places like St. Louis and Memphis, for Louisville, Atlanta, and all other cities South. It's for Oakland, Portland, and Seattle on the West Coast, and for Brooklyn, Philly, and Newark on the East. It's for every great city in the middle, too, Rochester, Buffalo, Columbus and Toledo, and for Detroit which is beginning to thrive again - with or without the automobile, and for Flint which, at the time of this writing, still doesn't have safe drinking water, and especially for the city where I spent the fullness of my heart: Cleveland. Making It Home is written for the people of everywhere else in America who are proving that it's not politicians or bureaucrats in Washington D.C. that make America great, but our cities and the gutsy people who, each and every day, from sunrise until the time their heads hit the pillow at night, work and pray for the health, vitality, and prosperity of their hometown. It's for those individuals and their communities who offer up their own unique characteristics, entrepreneurial spirits, and remarkable capacity for rebirth that are making their place a home - even after long and painful decades of decline. Making It Home is written for Cleveland which, in spite of some recent big wins, is still losing ground, and yet, like those everywhere-else-cities in America, knows in its heart of hearts, that a true fixer-upper is the best place in the world to call home.

•   •   •

A sage person once said, "find what you love to do and do it until it kills you." My oldest brother grimly mocks, that's why he smokes. The imperative, though, is a wise word about vocation, about finding and living into our true purpose. There are just some places and some people worth loving even if they can't love us back. Cleveland looked like a good place for me to go and vocationally empty myself. To die with others and, if I worked hard enough, or was lucky enough, or blessed enough, maybe even be raised to new life with them, too.

Those who are familiar with the seminal work of Elisabeth Kübler-Ross will, no doubt, recognize that this book is organized into sections that loosely follow her five stages of grief: denial, anger, bargaining, depression, and meaning and acceptance. In Cleveland, I experienced all five. I knew that there would be grieving ahead; with every death there is. Admittedly, I had entirely miscalculated the degree to which I would grieve, or even how much Beth and I would lose when we began our great Cleveland experiment. Sometimes we grieve for what and whom we have left behind. Other times, I would discover in Cleveland, we grieve those challenges we encounter along the way – the narrowness of vision and sense of hopelessness that diminishes the human spirit. Even so, I was supercharged and ready to plough through old Kübler-Ross's five stages of grief and arrive at my new place of acceptance.

I was coming home. To Cleveland.

Chapter One

I Set out to See the World and Made it All the Way to Cleveland

————————

BEFORE CLEVELAND, there was longing. For home.

·   ·   ·

"Where are you from?" It's one of my least liked questions. Generally, if I can't avoid it, I try to evade it. "Oh, I'm from around," I'll offer a vague response whenever asked, and then quickly pivot, turning the conversation back to its originator with my own cheery question: "Where's home for you?"

It's not that "Where are you from?" isn't a good question. In fact, it's not only good, it's essential. It's one of those questions we ask, universally, when we're trying to get to know someone, or build a relationship with them, or simply enjoy an interesting conversation.

Place of origin tells us a lot about folks, even if only by way of generalization. If you're from Detroit, for example, I assume you know something about cars, and crossing the border at Windsor to go into Canada for a little underage drinking. If you're from Toronto, I figure you love the Leafs or, maybe Les Canadiens and probably got beat up a lot as a kid. If you're from Pittsburg, I'll automatically assume that you love the Steelers and hate the Browns, but that may be getting a little ahead of myself right now. It's about place. And knowing the places folks are from helps us get a handle on them, no matter how small the handle. Or at least we assume it can help us get to know a person.

I think, too, that sometimes we ask people where they're from because we seek connection with others in the vastness of our world. We seek out people with whom we might hold things in common because they help us feel less alone. Having connection to place helps us feel less like strangers to one another.

"Where are you from?" is a good icebreaker, too. One that shows genuine interest and curiosity in others according the guidebooks on etiquette and success. I have a friend from Chicago who is a hugely successful schmoozer. He's one of those pat-on-the-back, yuck-yuck, how-ya-doin' sort of guys who could sell bread to a baker, or New York style pizza outside Lou Malnati's on State Street. He tells me that winning friends and influencing people is still just a simple matter of acquiring two small pieces of information: a person's name and where they are from. Then you stuff those Post It notes of knowledge in your back pocket or stick them on the wall in a favorite room in your memory palace so that you can gently ease those tidbits of information into the conversation the next time you see that person. For example, when we first met, he learned that I had spent a lot of my youth in a suburb outside of Toronto. Next time he saw me, he offered, "Hey Mark, I hear the Leafs might make the playoffs this year!" This is a pretty safe comment to make since every year, every single Toronto fan mistakenly believes that the Leafs are going to make it into the playoffs, until a month before the playoffs when the Leafs find themselves shoveling coal in the cold and dank basement of the National Hockey League. It's why we refer to Leafs fans as the 'Toronto Make Beliefs.' Or the 'Toronto Make-Me-Laughs.' In this particular example, however, my friend's theory backfired completely. He did get my name right. Check. And he did recall that I had spent some time in Canada as a kid. Check. But he missed the fact that I hadn't been a Leafs fan since 1967, the last year the Leafs won the Stanley Cup and just a year after the best hockey player ever, Mr.

Bobby Orr[1], started playing for the Boston Bruins. When I told my friend that I hadn't been a Leafs fan since I was five or six years of age, he just looked at me stupefied, and then broke into the singing of "Oh Canada." I joined in, of course. Then again, so did every other Clevelander in the bar that night.

Still, you get the idea, "Where are you from?" should be an entrée into understanding. Place has a way of defining us. Place is the soil out of which the substantive clay of our lives is formed and it is the kiln in which our identity is fired, calling forth both the brilliant and the nuanced shades of self.

The problem for me is that when people ask me where I'm from, I don't really have an answer. I don't know where my home is. Would I even recognize the soil of home beneath my feet if I was standing on it?

Oh, sentimentally, I get it. Home is where my heart is. My heart, however, is in a lot of places. Philosophically, I also understand that home isn't so much about a place or destination, rather it's about the people and the experiences we encounter along the way. "Every day is a journey, and the journey itself is home," said the wise old Japanese poet, Matsou Basho. Even religiously speaking, I can still hear echoes from my church-going childhood rattling around somewhere in my memory, the voices of my Christian parents reminding me that my home is with God. Sure enough. The older I get, though, the more I wish I could be at home with God and have a permanent address, too.

Don't get me wrong, like most folks, I experience very real, heart-warming feelings about home. My floodgates open wider than the Hoover Dam when I watch Dorothy, that young, displaced girl from Kansas in the old-time movie click the heels of her ruby red slippers together and chant about home in unison with Glinda the Titania-like good witch of the North. "That's right, Dorothy," I whisper under my breath to cheer her on: "There's no place like home! There's no place like home!" I'm just not sure where I would be whisked back to if I clicked my heels together and wished for home.

---

[1] Arguments about who was the greatest hockey player ever – Bobby Orr, Wayne Gretzky and, lately, Sid Crosby will keep the Canadian beer flowing and the neighborhood barstool hot for quite some time to come.

•   •   •

For a long time, I've longed for a place to call home, a certain soil where my roots might go deep enough to anchor me, or at least secure me against the turbulent winds of the day and age in which we live. I like to imagine that if I truly knew where I was from, I might know where and why I stood on important issues of the day. I could share mutual convictions with others of that same place. I might even have certain people to call when life demands that it's not what you know but who you know. Place might help me understand how to better behave, culturally speaking, in at least one setting on this planet, too. Sardonicism, for example, may be fine someplace "up north," but heaven forbid you'd ever try any of that kind of talk in Savannah, Georgia, where bloodletting or character destroying comments happen with much more subtlety and grace.

Place might put me in a context. Place is a unique backdrop for our lives. In contrast, it helps define the shape and detail of who we are, and the personal stories we're living now.

I've ached for home for good reason. In my fifty-eight years on this good earth, I've moved eighteen times. That may not seem like a lot to some of you. I recognize that I am not alone in the new, somewhat strange North American nomadic culture in which it feels like we uproot and move with the seasons. The U.S. Census estimates that we move, roughly, just over eleven times throughout our lifetimes[2] which is much more frequently than most of our European counterparts.[3] My life is part of that statistic. My eighteen moves average out to a move to a new place, and almost always to a new town or city, every 3.22

---

[2] Mona Chalabi, "How Many Times Does The Average Person Move?", *FiveThirtyEight.com* (ABC), January 29, 2015. Accessed June 28, 2018. https://fivethirtyeight.com/features/how-many-times-the-average-person-moves/

[3] Adam Chandler, "Why Do Americans Move So Much More Than Europeans?" *The Atlantic*, October 21, 2016. Accessed June 28, 2018. https://www.theatlantic.com/business/archive/2016/10/us-geographic-mobility/504968/

years. Some moves were within the same state or province, other times a passport was required like when I moved to Savannah, Georgia from London, Ontario.

To make things just a little more confusing, I was born in one country - the United States of America, and raised in another – Canada. And, I've been back and forth across the border so many times that I now experience bouts of patriotic schizophrenia. Is my "home and native land" the "True North strong free" or is it the "land of the free and the home of the brave"? As a dual citizen with pride for both great nations, when I'm at a sporting event, I struggle to sing either national anthem all the way through. Both leave me too welled-up with tears.

My two older brothers are born and raised Canadians. When we were kids, they used to taunt me - their little American brother: "We kicked your ass in the War of 1812!" It made me defensive about my birth nation, even though I had no memory of having lived there or, for that matter, any knowledge about the War of 1812.

The Olympics were a real problem for me, too. I was never sure who to root for, unless it was hockey – the one and only sport that truly interests me, in which case, of course, there was no question: Team Canada. When Americans talk to me about the 1980 "miracle on ice" - the year that Team USA beat "the Russians" for the bronze medal in Olympic hockey at Lake Placid, NY, I get very passionate in my claim that the real miracle on ice happened almost ten years earlier, in 1972 – the year Team Canada beat the Russians in a nail-biting series and final game victory.[4]

These days, having lived in the United States almost as long as I ever lived in Canada, and almost twice as long as an adult, I find myself cheering on Team USA just as much as Team Canada, even in hockey.

_____

[4] 1972 was the year that the Summit Series was played between Canada and the U.S.S.R. So many Canadian kids skipped out of school to watch the games on television that school wheeled in big televisions to watch the games in the classrooms. For the final game – the one where the Russian national police had been called in after Russian refs had tried to rig the game and Paul Henderson scored the game and series winner for Team Canada - many schools simply closed for the day. This was Canada and it was hockey, after all.

Of my eighteen moves, twelve were as an adult. With some of those moves, I stayed put for as short as four months. Other times, like when my kids were in middle and high school, I locked-in for a full eight years. Sometimes I uprooted to go away to college or grad school in exciting places like Montreal and Nashville, or to do an internship in the buggy but adventurous location of Labrador in Canada's chilly sub-arctic. It snowed there on July first! Like a lot of other migrants today, I've relocated for a job here and there, too.

For most of my life, I rather enjoyed living in different places. There was a freedom to being able to move on whenever I felt like it. And there was an excitement about journey, where ever it might lead. For most of my life, I suffered from an itch that only travel could reach. In many ways, I was George Bailey - bags packed and ready to leave Bedford Falls every time I heard a train whistle blow. "Travelling can sometimes feel like falling in love," says the Canadian writer, Anne Thériault. "There's the same sense of giddiness, the same wild curiosity."[5]

Travel blesses us with a deeper appreciation for others and their rich cultures, too. Mark Twain once said, "Travel is the enemy of ignorance." Well, actually, he didn't say that, precisely. What he said, precisely, was that "Travel is fatal to prejudice, bigotry, and narrow-mindedness, and many of our people need it sorely on these accounts. Broad, wholesome, charitable views of men and things cannot be acquired by vegetating in one little corner of the earth all one's lifetime." I think my paraphrase is much easier to remember than Twain's actual quote, though. Either way, the point is strong: our journeys open us up to a more textured understanding of others and ourselves. Social scientists call it, "contact theory," meaning the more we experience people who are different than ourselves the more tolerant, even welcoming of diversity we become. I believed that every time I made a move to a new town or city or country, my worldview

---

[5] Anne Thériault, "Geel, Belgium has a radical approach to mental illness" *Broadview Magazine*, September 5, 2019 https://broadview.org/geel-belgium-mental-health/ accessed 2019 09 06

was pried open just a little wider and the light of awareness within me shone just a little warmer and brighter.

•   •   •

Something strange happened in my early forties. I experienced something foreign - a sense of homelessness. With so many relocations throughout my lifetime, I was overwhelmed by an acute sense of emotional and spiritual dislocation. I had no roots. No history. No significant feelings associated with place. Or just the opposite - I had a lot of feelings associated with too many places. The people with whom I had grown-up - my parents and siblings, had moved far away from the familiar places of my childhood; there was no "going home" to visit. My best friend, Brian, and his wife, Shelley, were settling into their wonderful new life on the opposite side of the country in California. I was long out of touch with former friends from college and seminary, too. Some people wake up one day in their middle years and ask, "Who am I?" I woke up and asked, "Where am I?" Or better yet, "Where is home?"

Of course, there are many good people in this world who have a far greater right to feel homeless than me. A sense of privilege tugs within me when I compare my safe and secure life in North America to others who have been displaced from their homelands because of political strife, violence, and very real threats to their lives and those of their families. I am sensitive to those who are temporarily 'housed' in some of the most unforgiving and dangerous camps before being shipped across oceans as refugees to destinations unknown. I can only imagine the challenges when they arrive in places foreign of everything from language to religion, and climate to culture, if they are fortunate enough to find a nation with courage and compassion enough to welcome them in the first place. Never mind the ongoing bigotry these folks will experience in their new adopted homelands, the needless delays they will run into at airport security - if they are allowed to travel, or the suspicious looks they will garner from their new neighbors and co-workers who have made no bones about the fact that they didn't want refugees in their community in the first place.

Nor am I insensitive to the half-million homeless men, women, and children that the Department of Housing and Urban Development reports live on our city streets here in the United States. Many of those people are veterans, like my cousin, Bobby from Elizabethtown, Kentucky, who served in the United States Air Force. Bobby often lived on the street or in make shift camps until his untimely death from cirrhosis of the liver. The homeless population in America includes many honored troops like Bobby, people we once promised to support, as well as others who struggle each day with very real addictions and mental illnesses but have been short-changed of the help of which they are in desperate need by our very private and very expensive health care system. Their struggle is as real as the cold concrete beneath their feet. My sense of homelessness cannot compare, although it is heightened by the fact that I live in a nation that allows so many of the vulnerable, the least among us, to fall helplessly through the gaping cracks in our staggeringly affluent country. Those kind of values, or should I say "lack thereof," truly make me feel like a stranger in a strange land.

Still, the yearning for home that began to bubble-up for me in my forties was real. It was deep to the core, visceral. Maybe it was my age. A midlife crisis, perhaps. Maybe it had to do with the fact that I was growing weary of old, blue-blooded Savannahians asking me who my people were and me not having a meaningful answer for them. Too often, I felt like an interloper, an imposter in the South. When I first arrived in Savannah, someone "joked", "Hey Mark, what's the difference between a Yankee and a damn Yankee? . . . A Yankee just comes South for a visit." Even so, I loved the Southern people and their culture. Their pace. Their grace and ease. Their overt politeness. Even if some just feigned gentility, I could live with that. The problem for me was that the Southern culture just wasn't my own. It didn't belong to me and I didn't belong to it.

More and more, I started to feel like Roger of Wendover's character, Cartaphilus. In his Flores historiarum, the thirteenth-century monk and chronicler, Roger of Wendover, recounts the apocryphal story of a man – Cartaphilus, who was damned to sojourn the earth, never finding or being at home in the world until Christ's return. It was his punishment for mocking Jesus on his way to the cross. I pray that I've never mocked Christ, but I can certainly identify with the wanderer within, and with the longing and searching for home but never finding it. Maybe we all can. After all, the popularity of journey narratives figures prominently in our cultural mythos. These stories reflect the sojourner spirit in us all. Classical tales from Homer's Odyssey to beloved modern versions such as Jack Kerouac's, On the Road, Elizabeth Gilbert's, Eat, Love, Pray, and Yann Martel's, Life of Pi - to list just a fractional sample from literature, speak to the restless, inner-wanderer within each of us.

We spend a lot of our lifetime puttering about from one place or experience to another. Beneath these busy distractions, for many of us, there lurks a longing and sometimes even an aching for a home that refuses to be found. We encounter wonderful new things as we travel, and we become new people shaped by our many novel experiences. Yet, buried deep within ourselves, we live with a sense of rootlessness. We're tumbleweed being blown from place to place, scraping-up nutrients along the way from whatever dust we may happen upon, or may happen upon us, but never finding good soil in which to set down our roots.

The biblical analogy of Cain may be even more apropos to my journey since Cain specifically tried to resolve his restlessness in the city. Cain was cursed by God as recompense for his fraternal jealously, and for mortally whacking his little brother, Abel. His punishment? Cain was doomed to be a "fugitive and a wanderer on the earth" (Genesis 4:12). You might even go so far as to say that Cain became history's first urban planner, attempting to build an entire city to satisfy his longing for home. I'm not sure it worked for him. I'm not sure it works for us, either.

In her book, The Death and Life of Great American Cities, the legendary urban thinker, Jane Jacobs said that, "The pseudoscience of [urban] planning seems almost neurotic in its determination to imitate empiric failure and ignore empiric success." Biblically speaking, that neurosis and that failure to make a real home for real people in our cities may be connected to that moment when Cain thumbed his nose at God, and thumbed his nose to restless wandering, and built the first city and called it home. Well, he actually called it "Enoch" after his son, but it was also, for better or worse, his home.

Like Cain, I needed my own Enoch. A place where I could build a home for myself and finally put a stop to all my restless wandering. Sure, I knew that I could always be at home with God, just as Dad and Mom had taught me. I just wanted to be at home on earth, too. Not sure if I could have it both ways, I was just foolish enough, or Cain enough, to try.

· · ·

In his song, The Captain, the singer-songwriter-poet, Leonard Cohen envisions a dialogue between a wise captain on his death bed and a soldier who must continue his journey without his Captain. For me, Cohen's song sounds very much like a conversation between God and humanity. At one point in the song the soldier asks where home could be:

"Tell me, Captain, if you know of a decent place to stand."

The captain replies, "There is no decent place to stand in a massacre; but if a woman take your hand, go and stand with her."

In early 2008, I began looking in earnest for a place that would take my hand. For the first time ever, perhaps, I was looking less for exotic destinations with beaches and warm weather, and more for a city that would allow me to invest myself in it – my ministry, my love for cities, and, perhaps, even my heart and a bit of my soul. I had only a few criteria: my beloved, Beth, and I wanted to be in a place a little closer to our active but aging parents. As a pastor with a love for cities, high on my list of priorities was a yearning to serve in a city-center church and, if possible, one that needed two people since Beth and I were already working together and were not quite ready to give that up. Most importantly, wherever we landed, it had to be a place where we could settle in for the long haul. Our kids were now grown and gone, they were off starting lives of their own. It was time for us to follow their lead and leave our Savannah nest so that we could make a home just for ourselves.

Of all the promising opportunities that popped up on our radar, the historic Old Stone Church located right on Public Square in downtown Cleveland held out the greatest potential of fulfilling our short list of requirements, though it was hardly the perfect church, and Cleveland was hardly the perfect city. In fact, the more we scrolled through the pages on the internet and explored the printed material that the church had sent us in the mail, the more we learned that both the Old Stone Church and the city of Cleveland needed a lot of work. They were fixer-uppers which sounded good to me. I needed a challenge.

I needed a place where I wouldn't be expected just to "fit in" to someone else's old narrative, but a place where we might write a new one together. I needed a city like Cleveland where I knew that if I couldn't be a part of its past, I most certainly would be welcomed as a part of its future. If the city was already dying - and, empirically, it was, then I could easily be a part of what would come after: the resurrection of Cleveland, Ohio. And, I believed, a rising was about to happen for this great city by the lake.

Besides, we all know that sometimes the best homes are the ones that started out as fixer-uppers. Just ask Northeast Ohio author, David Giffels whose engaging 2009 book, All the Way Home: Building a Family in a Falling-Down House wonderfully details the joys and pains of restoring a late nineteenth century architectural beauty in the city of Akron, a home for David and his family. Cleveland could be my fixer upper.

Fixer uppers, whether they are houses, churches, or even cities will exhaust you. They'll drain you of your life's savings. They may even break you in the end. For me, Cleveland succeeded in doing all three. Before they do, however, you may discover that you have participated in creating a thing of beauty. A living art piece that is touched with your very fingerprints and dripping with your blood, sweat and tears. You may have made a home.

In the spring of 2008, Beth and I submitted our letters of resignation to the good and faithful leaders of the Montgomery

Presbyterian Church, sold our house on Wilmington Island in Savannah, and then went to 'die' with the good folks of Cleveland and maybe, just maybe, be raised with them to a new place we could call our home.

2008-2010: GRIEF

*"I'm not afraid of death.
I just don't want to be there when it happens."*
- Woody Allen

Chapter Two

Goodbye, Sweet Savannah

"Cosmos Mariner Destination Unknown. Give my love to the world."
**–Epitaph on memorial bench of Conrad Aiken, Bonaventure
Cemetery, Savannah**

INTERRED IN SAVANNAH'S lush Bonaventure Cemetery are the
remains of the acclaimed American poet, Conrad Aiken. Instead of a
traditional gravestone, however, visitors to his famous burial site will
find a granite bench which his beloved, Mary Hoover Aiken, had
selected to memorialize her husband.

It's a Savannah tradition that folks from near and far will sit on the
stone seat that marks Aiken's final resting place. Beneath the cool
shade of live oaks draped in Spanish moss they will enjoy sleepy
breezes that whisper up the hill from the water's edge below, gaze out
across swaying marsh grasses and toward the lazy Wilmington River
as it meanders away from the Savannah River, past Thunderbolt,
Whitemarsh, Wilmington and Skidaway Islands on its way to Wassaw
Sound and the Atlantic Ocean. Perhaps they will share a martini or
glass of wine while celebrating the story of how Aiken, in the golden
years of his retirement, had one morning caught sight of a ship sailing
up the Savannah River. The name that was stenciled along its bow,
"Cosmos Mariner," piqued something in Aiken's imagination, so the
story goes. The "cosmos" was a recurring theme for his poetry, after
all. Visitors sipping their drinks might recall that when Aiken, later

that same day, edged his finger down the columns of the daily shipping news to learn more about this particular vessel – where it had come from, where it was headed, he found only four words printed on the page: "Cosmos Mariner . . . destination unknown."

The phrase, "Cosmos Mariner Destination Unknown" encapsulated for Aiken many of his poetic and lifetime themes: his explorations into modern psychology, his personal struggles with depression – a physiological inheritance from his father, perhaps, who suffered from severe melancholy and eventually took the life of young Conrad's mother just seconds before ending his own, and Aiken's own general sense of alienation, loneliness, and homelessness in the vast space and time of the cosmos. Visitors to his grave will easily locate the epitaph carved in capitalized font into the seat of the backless pew on which they sit: COSMOS MARINER DESTINATION UNKNOWN.[6]

Aiken's epitaph is a sentiment that whispers the story of homelessness and alienation that many of us have known. It speaks to the vague malaise that resides just beneath the surface of our day-to-day busyness, a subtle but very present feeling that we, like Aiken, are whirring through the boundless space and seemingly limitless time of the universe at breakneck speeds, all the while attempting to make peace with the great mystery of our final destination. We console ourselves with the beauty and wonder, the blessings and joys of the journey itself.

August 18th, 2008, I left Aiken's Savannah, and became a Cosmos Mariner, Destination Cleveland.

•   •   •

The car was packed. I was ready to get on the road and on my way to the place that Beth and I would try, come hell or high toxic water, to make our permanent home. I was prepared for everything about the

---

[6] Much of this information is common knowledge. However, I appreciate the input and clarifications from Bonnie Bowen of the Bonaventure Historical Society, as well a variety articles such as the one by Peggy Medeiros, "Poet Conrad Aiken found comfort in New Bedford," *South Coast Today*, posted Nov 9, 2014, accessed April 16, 2020.

move. I had followed the Getting Ready for a Move checklist from the movers to a tee. I had scheduled the shutoff dates with the utility companies, with the cable company, and given the post office our forwarding address – a temporary one for the first few months in Cleveland. "Where's Cleveland?" the postal worker at the Islands post office drawled, looking at me with his deadpan stare as if I was some sort of traitor who would choose North over South. "I thought that was in Tennessee?" he grumbled.

The most important stuff was well in hand, too. We had our daughter, Daryl, and her cello, all settled in at Georgia State University in Atlanta. Our house had been sold. The new owners had moved in weeks earlier and we were comfortably set up in a furnished beach rental out on Tybee Island where we put in time until our final countdown to Cleveland. In those last few weeks before we finally left town, we drove by the old house to see how the old homestead looked. We had to get over the fact that almost immediately the new owners had chopped down the fragrant star jasmine vines that Beth had spent years carefully training along our side fence and up and over the trellised garden gate. "Oh well, we were moving on," I reasoned.

Our little pound puppy, Scout, was booked-in for a long-term stay with our friends and their three boys on their half acre Talahi Island property. We needed a temporary home for Scout for a few months while construction on our 1904 office-condo-conversion in downtown Cleveland was completed. She'd be very happy with our friends, and their dogs and goats and big yard to run in, although the day we said goodbye to her she was hiding under a chair – her own special place of time-out away from all the action in her new, temporary home.

We had expunged a lot of our stuff from our lives in preparation to downsize from our five-bedroom, two-and-a-half garage colonial on Wilmington Island and ease into our new life in a three-bedroom condo in downtown Cleveland. We held a garage sale and made more trips than I can count to Goodwill to drop off unsold items and the stuff that had never made it out to the driveway for our big sale. Everything else was packed up and carted off to temporary storage in some unknown mystery location – North Carolina, perhaps? Omaha? Overseas? Who knew? We never did find out where all of our belongings went, but it didn't matter. We were ready to roll. Or so I thought.

From out of nowhere, I was slugged in the gut by a big, globby fist of buyer's remorse. I felt sick. I had one of those panicked, Talking Heads moments of, "My God! What have I done?" Grief lodged itself somewhere between the lump in my throat and lower intestine. Flipping back through the mover's guide in my mind, I didn't recall seeing anything on the checklist about the emotional distress that the move would bring. Was it there? Did I miss it? Did I intentionally overlook it in my joyful expectation about the move?

Apparently, up until that moment, I had just been tricking myself into believing that I was ready to go. "Let Cleveland be the journey, not the destination," I had sung to Beth months earlier when I convinced her that we should pack up and leave behind our eight years in Savannah. A new city, a new church, being just a little bit closer to our Canadian family and friends, and an opportunity to end my strange sense of homelessness by joining with others in the rebirth of a great American city was in order, I rationalized inwardly. It had all sounded as promising as a coastal sunrise on a cool autumn morning or, for Northerners, a blanket of fresh fallen December snow just waiting to be disturbed, snow angels to be brushed in, snow forts to be erected. Unfortunately, the day of our departure, I experienced quite the opposite. Everything we were leaving behind finally made itself known.

• • •

As we motored away from our summer rental on Tybee for the very last time, my heart was a grief-soaked sponge. Every mile brought with it another memory too cherished to be released, yet too large and too tender to be held for longer than a moment: The Sugar Shack and Tradewinds on Tybee Island where my daughter scooped ice cream for beachgoers each summer and, when she was old enough to drive herself, became the unofficial "recycler-in-chief" by hauling all the recyclables – and a family of Brown Widow spiders, to the blue box in our home on Wilmington Island. George's of Tybee, the lovely restaurant where my son earned tips from women smitten by his young Fabio Lanzoni long blonde hair and good looks while he nervously plucked out classical and flamenco guitar music on Thursday and Saturday nights.

As we zipped across the causeway, I inhaled one last, full and cleansing breath of the nutrient rich aroma wafting from the marshes and brackish tidal creeks. I reminisced about the wondrous places where we kayaked and, only my daughter, courageously swam. The mud-packed trails where we hiked and biked. The beach where we swam and got stung by jelly fish, and I unwittingly stood on the back of what quite easily could have been a giant horseshoe crab and shouted, "Look at me. I'm standing on a rock!"

I was awash in a high tide of Savannah memories as we buzzed down the Islands Expressway and through the city toward the Talmadge Memorial Bridge which would lift us up and over Conrad Aiken's Savannah River into South Carolina and north from there. We took one last drive by the wonderful schools that my kids had attended – St. Andrews on Wilmington Island, the Savannah Arts Academy in Ardsley Park, and Sol C. Johnson where my son attended high school. We rolled by the Gryphon - a charming downtown café and tea room housed in the historic and former Scottish Rite building on Madison Square - where I held my CD release party for my third album aptly titled, Destination Unknown, and then passed by the Civic Center and inwardly recalled the pride Beth and I had felt the day our daughter processed into the arena with her fellow graduates wearing her cap and gown and then made her way to the stage to deliver her Valedictorian speech.

The closer we got to the bridge – our final exit from Savannah, the more my heart ached for the truly remarkable and grace-filled people we were leaving behind: the incredible members and friends of the Montgomery Presbyterian Church where I learned to love and be loved by the some of the most authentic, albeit quirky, and endearing bunch of Christians anywhere. My awesome friends and colleagues from the amazing Savannah College of Art and Design where I taught over one thousand undergraduate and graduate students from all fifty states and more than eighty countries – each of them bringing something incredibly personal and unique to my classes.

"Just keep driving!" Beth ordered me. She had to. I had been caught by an incredible force from an invisible electromagnetic pulse binding me to Savannah. In my mind, I was now circling the streets of the city while negotiating the possibility of a last-minute change in plans. My foot was easing off the gas and about to make a dive for the brake. "We've made our decision, our plans are fixed." Beth urged me forward, "Let's keep going!" Like the biblical character, Lot, warning his wife not to look back, Beth held her ground against my haggling lest I turn into a pillar of salt.

"We could tell our congregation we were wrong," I began the negotiations. "We made a mistake. Maybe they would take us back. I could call the college. I'm sure they'd give me my teaching job back." I was panicking, not to mention, whining. "We could rent an apartment in downtown Savannah, take the money from the sale of our house and just live off of it for a while." Grief counsellors would say that I was bargaining. Call it what you want, I would not have cared. With my far flung, last minute, Hail Mary proposals, I was desperate to find a way to undo our decision to move. Cosmos Mariner, be damned. Destination Savannah!

It was too late, though. The mighty Talmadge Bridge from downtown heaved us up and over the Savannah River as greater ocean-going cargo ships than Conrad Aiken could have ever imagined passed beneath us and then dropped us down to the other side where the causeway quickly brought us into South Carolina. For the last time, I caught a glimpse of the Hostess City shrinking in my review mirror.

Through eyes moist with tears, my vision blurred. My stomach sank. A big cotton ball lump formed in my throat. Even if I could speak, there was really nothing left to say. The negotiations had come to a close. The gavel had hammered down a stop to my bidding. For the duration of the two-day drive to Cleveland, Beth and I remained in silence. Two sturdy but grieving souls whisked down the highway at 70 miles an hour, our faces set toward the new place that waited for us, the place that held the promise of home. It was clear to me now: To go and die with our new city, we would first have to die to our old one.

For Savannah, the song had ended, to paraphrase the great composer, Mr. Irving Berlin. How quickly we would learn to cherish the melody that lingered on.

Chapter Three

Hello, Cleveland!

"This just in: Beverly Hills 90210, Cleveland Browns 3."
–Colin Mochrie

———————————

THERE WAS A HORRIFIC TIME in our not so distant past, you may recall from your high school history or social studies classes, that our ancestors used a brutal form of torture and execution sometimes euphemistically called, "pressing." More descriptively accurate, it was also called, "crushing." Crushing was used to exact a confession from the presumed guilty by splaying them out on their backs – arms and legs tied out and away from their sides. A large wooden plank was placed across their torso and then an increasing amount of weight, comprised of heavy stones or pieces of iron, would be incrementally piled on top until death. It was a no-win situation for the accused. Either you were crushed, or you confessed in which case you were executed, presumably, more mercifully. Either way, guilty or not, you were dead.

Historians tell us that sometimes death by pressing could come quickly, as in the case of England's St. Margaret Clitherow, the "pearl of York" who, being accused of harboring priests, was splayed by Jesuits over a sharp rock the size of a man's fist. Her own front door was ripped from its hinges and laid across her body. Within fifteen minutes she was dead, her back broken under the weight of the seven hundred pounds of rock that had been heaped upon her and her front door. More often than not, death would be very slow and painful, taking hours or even days before a person's lungs had collapsed to an unbearable point that not a single breath could be drawn. It has been said that Giles Corey, who was accused of witchcraft, and was the only person in American history to be executed by crushing, choked out his defiant and now, legendary last words: "More weight!"

There was no more of a crushing time in Cleveland's recent history than the year 2008 and the year or two following. I could not have chosen a worse imaginable time than that era to begin life in Cleveland. Like the heavy rocks of some bizarre sixteenth century form of torture, one by one, a sequence of unfortunate events crushed down on the good people of Cleveland. Get out a note pad. Make a check list. It will include everything from humiliating defeats and dismal statistics for Cleveland's losing football team to record unemployment, mass murders and high-profile government corruption. Tally up the hardships confronting the city during this period, the whole was, by far, greater than the sum of the parts. Crisis heaped upon crisis created an almost intolerable weight that choked out a spirit of hope for many and left me, almost from the beginning, second guessing my move to Cleveland.

There were other years that were bad for Cleveland, of course. I could have moved to Cleveland in 1969, the year the Cuyahoga River caught fire. Or 1952, the year the Cuyahoga River caught fire. Wait a minute. In Cleveland, the river used to catch fire a lot. Bad example. How about 1995? I could have moved to Cleveland that year - the year Art Modell broke every Clevelander's heart when he announced that he was moving the beloved Cleveland Browns to Baltimore. Or just about any other year when it was just one or two stones being plunked down on the city. I moved to Cleveland, however, during one of the most dehumanizing, spirit-flattening times in the city's recent history.

Woody Allen once joked, "I'm not afraid of death. I just don't want to be there when it happens." I was there when it happened for Cleveland. Hi honey, I'm home!

• • •

My first few weeks in town, I was eager to discover all the awesome things that Ohio's great city by the lake had to offer yet, every now and then, I caught myself secretly questioning the decision to move north. On the one hand, I was eager to get started with my new ministry, excited to meet new people, and explore all the exciting things about Cleveland that the pamphlets and online research about the city promised. Everything that I had read about Cleveland before the move pointed toward a potential rebirth for the city, too, particularly for its downtown. I was 'geeked' to be a part of the coming resurgence. On the other hand, I was lonely for my kids and still grieving the loss of our quiet community in Savannah - our church, our friends, the faithful can-do attitude of the South. Cleveland didn't seem to be a very friendly city by comparison. I met lots of folks who were just plain disgruntled about their lives. Almost everyone had a story to share with me about how bad things were in Cleveland. Many born-and-raised, but stuck-in-place Clevelanders asked me that first year: "Why would anyone live in Cleveland if they didn't have to?" My doubts were affirmed many times over.

Beth and I had our own concerns, of course, before we even moved to Cleveland. We understood all too well that we were 'coming back' to the industrial heartland, and to a dying city very much like the one where we met, Windsor, Ontario. Naturally, returning to the heartland blessed us with a soupy mix of both excitement and anxiety. Late August of 2008, when Beth and I left the silky-smooth I-77 which had zipped us and our peppy, metallic-blue sports car north from Savannah directly onto Cleveland's pockmarked and pot-holed Ontario Street - bouncing and banging us and our little Japanese car the final half-mile into downtown, we were suddenly overwhelmed by a lugubrious weight of contrition.

There's a wonderfully frightful 2007 movie starring John Cusack which Beth and I had seen at the theater just the year before our move. It's based on one of Stephen King's short stories called 1408. 1408 is a hotel room number. The numbers add up to the unlucky number, thirteen. No one ever goes in that room in New York City's fictitious Dolphin Hotel anymore because, well you know, it is haunted. And it is not so much haunted by a ghost or even a phantom. "It's an evil f---ing room," says co-star Samuel L. Jackson's character, Gerald Olin, the hotel manager. He tries to dissuade Mike Enslin, Cusack's, I-could-care-less character from spending the night in room 1408, the way most of our family and friends tried to dissuade Beth and me from moving to Cleveland. But Enslin, the skeptical, there's-no-such-thing-as-a-ghost writer dares to spend the night in the room so he can embellish his non-experience for his next book.

However, the room seems possessed by a truly dark spirit that will not let Cusack's character go. Enslin is locked-in the room. There is no way out for him. While trapped in the room, he experiences all sorts of bump-in-the-dark, eerie moments that will make you jump out of your seat. There is blood. There is fire. Death is all around him. And, yes, there are lots of ghosts, too. Even Enslin's own personal ghost makes an appearance – his dead daughter cries out to him from the room, "Daddy . . . I'm cold . . . I love you Daddy. Don't you love me anymore?" It's a bone-chilling, hair-raising experiencing for Enslin. And there appears to be no escape. Mwahahaha!

Spoiler alert: near the end of the movie, Cusack's character finally gets sprung-free. He travels all the way back to the West coast to write his new ghostly book about room 1408. In one dramatic scene, he has gone into his local post office to mailout a hardcopy of the final draft of his polished manuscript to his publisher in New York. In a surrealistic Salvador Dali-like moment, however, the walls around him begin to crumble. So does the roof above him, and the floor under his feet. As the California post office around him is shredded, Mike Enslin comes to the realization that he is very much still trapped in room 1408. He has never left the room at all. After a face-clenching, teeth-grinding, hair-pulling, vertigo head-spinning Hitchcockian moment, Enslin cries out a terribly anguished and, to me, memorable line, "I was out! I was out!"

All this is to tell you that at the precise moment that Beth and I maneuvered our way around that potholed obstacle course that was the decrepit streets of downtown Cleveland as we entered the belly of the beast, the heart of the city, this is exactly what my beloved shouted to no one in particular, or perhaps it was at me: "I was out! I was out!"

We had escaped our humble industrial heartland beginnings in Windsor, Ontario, and had been living in sweet, sweet Savannah for almost a decade. Now, however, the ground on which we had been standing, the terra firma beneath our feet was shifting. We had come back to our humble rustbelt beginnings – and at the worst possible time. "Hello, Cleveland!"

Beth's cry reminded me that in Savannah we had begun a new and sunny coastal life far away from the lake effect snowstorms of our youth, and the cracked concrete of the dying industrial cities of the

North – Windsor, Detroit, Toledo, Cleveland, Erie, Buffalo, Rochester. Drive around the Great Lake Erie. These rusty cities are plentiful, and many of them are dying a slow post-industrial death. Now, like being caught in the swirling vortex at the center of North America's waste-water toilet, Cleveland was sucking us down into the familiar hole from whence we had begun.

"We're baaack!" I bantered with my own horror movie quote. Perhaps my movie trivia repartee would let Beth know that she had been both heard and understood, and in a playful enough way to tease out the acute anxiety that was bubbling up within us both. It was a darkly revealing moment when we realized that we had just traded away the sultry coastal breezes of one of the prettiest cities in America for the biting Erie winds and the even more daunting spirit of hangdog hopelessness prevailing in Cleveland, Ohio. "Give it a chance," I reasoned with her. "Trust me. You'll like Cleveland," I promised her in the same sort of way that I had told my big brother when he was twelve that if he blew into the face of our neighbor's Pit Bull, it would make the dog happy. Beth compromised, stopping short of a fang-revealing response. She agreed that we could give Cleveland a try for three years. Little did we know that our north shore adventure would turn into almost a dozen.

Now, I know you may think I'm being hard on ol' Cleveland, taking an enormous hyperbolic swing at a humble city that has been down for the count far too many times to count. And I suppose, at this point, I am. However, as you read on, you will discover that today, I'm one of Cleveland's biggest cheerleaders, a true "Clevangelist." I told a friend recently that "I'll always wear a 'C' for Cleveland on my cap, and more importantly, on my heart." In those early years, though, I was just beginning to learn that C can also stand for "crushing."

• • •

Sunday September 14th, 2008, just three weekends into our great Cleveland adventure, I felt a stone of loss for the city of sorrow heaped upon us. It wasn't a heavy stone. But I did wince just a little.

With unpredictable jabs, wind gusts of up to sixty miles per hour punched through the late summer air. Tree branches crashed down on power lines throughout the inner and outer ring suburbs. Windows rattled in the aging wooden frames of charming downtown apartments and condos – the recent conversions from historic warehouses and offices. The remnants of hurricane Ike were making themselves known throughout Northeast Ohio.

The real slap in the face for Cleveland that day, though, especially for the 73,048 Cleveland Browns fans who jammed into their waterfront stadium – the place comedian, Mike Polk, would later dub "the factory of sadness," and for countless others who huddled around televisions to watch the game from basement rec rooms or neighborhood bars, was hardly from the gale-force winds that dogged the great State of Ohio that weekend, but from the stinging 10-6 defeat from arch rivals, the Pittsburgh Steelers over their hometown favorites, the Cleveland Browns. It was their second home game of the season. And it was their second loss. They were on a streak!

As a newcomer to the city, just a handful of weeks earlier, I had been cautioned by new acquaintances, Cleveland long-timers, to make 'lickety-split' from downtown after church on Browns Sundays. "Things can get, um, out of control," I had been warned.

During the weekly coffee hour following worship, one woman drew close to me and, as if letting me in on a local secret while admonishing me to steer clear of downtown's Warehouse District where fans, she said, would gather for "rambunctious parties" before and after the game. Chuckling, her husband joined in the conversation and encouraged me to watch the game on television from someplace a little further away. Like Akron.

"Win or lose, Browns fans can be extremely rowdy," he said, stretching-out the word, "extremely" as if to emphasize his code-orange level advisory.

Another new friend, sipping coffee with us, chimed-in with his own cautionary tale: Years earlier, he had mistakenly gone to his downtown office to pick-up some papers and got stuck in the post-game, bumper to bumper traffic on the Warehouse District's W 6th Street, a wonderful walking street lined with quaint restaurants, patios and night clubs. This particular Sunday evening, however, the street was teeming with an angry river of disgruntled football fans (another day of loss, who da thunk?) swarming from the stadium back to their cars.

The crowd, he said, included a huge huddle of well-lubricated Browns backers stumbling past him. Seeing him stuck in traffic behind the wheel of his zippy little Miata, they were overcome by a glorious light of inspiration. They were slain in the spirit of victories past and disappointments present. Like wolves moving in for the kill, they encircled my friend and his Mickey Mouse shoe-shaped car.

Bolstered with strength from on-lookers and crowds chanting, "Here we go Brownies, here we go! Woof! Woof!" the small group of well-lubricated men gathered superhuman, Browns' brute and hoisted the tiny roadster into the air like the championship trophy they had been denied every year since 1964, and then gave it one hundred and eighty degree turn before carefully setting it down nose to nose with the car behind. My friend now found himself staring into the face of the driver behind him. He simply shrugged in helpless surrender as if to say, "Oh well. What can you do? It's a Browns Sunday."

Never mind storm warnings or Hurricane Ike advisories, if you happen to be around Browns' stadium on any given Sunday during football season, especially when the hometown team is losing, which is often, take good care.

Sadly, the heavy winds of defeat dealt Cleveland another staggering blow almost simultaneously that fourteenth day of September. Just a mile or so away from the Browns' stadium, 29,530[7] Cleveland Indians fans watched their team thrashed by the Kansas City Royals for a third time that weekend. This time by a whopping score of 13-3.

I felt a weight of sadness pressing down on me. It was entirely unexpected this early in my move to Cleveland. My Cleveland honeymoon was just getting started and already I was wondering if I had made a pledge to the wrong girl. A win by the Browns, or the Indians, or heck, even a local middle school volleyball team would have helped.

• • •

If someone was writing a novel or movie script about Cleveland and included everything that was going badly in 2008 or 2009, readers would protest, "Oh, come on! Nowhere can be that bad!" And yet, for Cleveland, it was. This esteemed city was once home to powerhouses like John D. Rockefeller, founder of Standard Oil, and Charles Brush,

---

[7] ESPN. http://www.espn.com/mlb/game?gameId=280914105. Accessed May 31, 2018.

inventor of the arc light, Langston Hughes, poet, writer, and social activist who would later lead the Harlem Renaissance in New York City, and Frances Payne Bolton, who helped establish the U.S. Army Corp of Nursing in WWI and who would, in 1940, be elected the first woman congressperson from Ohio, and a celebrated list of so many famous sports and entertainment icons throughout the twentieth century that you would need at least ten hands and ten feet with all their fingers and toes still intact to count them all. Yet, by all accounts, in 2008, Cleveland was dying. Everyone and their mother knew it.

Clevelanders have an exceptional skill, a gift, really, for reciting long lists of the things that once made Cleveland great. They can captivate you with the number of Fortune 500 companies that used to call Cleveland home. They will wax nostalgically about the good old days when everyone used to come downtown to shop in their bustling department stores like the May Company or, during the Christmas season, to visit Mr. Jingaling at Halle's department store and then, after Halle's closed in 1982, at Santaland on the tenth floor of Higbee's department store. They will regale you with dramatic tales from the days when the Cleveland Browns used to be one of the hottest football clubs in the nation. But when I asked them about their hometown in 2008, nary a one had a kind word to offer. That's not an exaggeration, either. Their negativity was consistent, incessant, and insistent, and it was weighing heavily on my recent decision to leave Savannah and move to Cleveland.

In America there are three types of people. Those who love Cleveland. Those who hate Cleveland. And those who love to hate Cleveland, trash talking the city with the energy and imagination of a late-night comic. I was just surprised to find as many of the latter two categories in Cleveland itself as I did in 2008.

Just imagine your sense of gut-wrenching disappointment if, on your wedding night, your newly betrothed, over and over, rehearses stories of what a fabulous person they used to be: they used to earn a great living, they used to have a dream, or they even used to be good in bed, for crying out loud. But now that the vows have been exchanged and you've put a ring on it, your dearly beloved comes out and admits that moving forward, they're going to pretty much stink as a life partner. If you don't mind spending your future days reveling in past triumphs, you're welcome to stay. Keep your expectations low and you'll do just fine.

I tried to shoo-away my growing doubts but they kept landing on me like pesky Lake Erie midges after a June hatching. While the Browns and Indians were losing, clearly, buyer's remorse was scoring big points. Coming to Cleveland was starting to feel like one of the worst trade deals ever.

I found myself second-guessing so many of the things we had left behind when we moved from Savannah: the gracious tree-canopied squares, one of the most walkable cities in America, the strangers who often smiled or even greeted one another as they passed by on Bull Street or Broughton. Not to mention, some of our best friends ever, and the home where our children had come of age. All that in exchange for the cracking concrete and corroding steel of a dying Midwest city, lowly sports teams, and a vague hope, with odds against, of a major comeback for one of America's quintessential rustbelt cities. Unlike Savannah, where a person could drown in gracious pleasantries, during my first month or two in Cleveland, when I smiled at fellow pedestrians in downtown, they responded like it was an open invitation for them to ask me for money, or for something more. One crisp autumn morning, I said "hello" to a woman while we waited for the walk sign at an intersection and she responded as if I was propositioning her. And by responded, I mean she responded positively! She leered at me with lascivious eyes and greeted me with a lusty Joey Tribbiani, "How you doin'?" If I was quicker on my feet, I should have told her, "A little down in the dumps, to be perfectly honest. I'm having some difficulty adjusting to my new hometown." The light gave us the walk and I offered her, instead, a "God bless you," and my most pleasant smile as I stepped forward from the curb.

•   •   •

These days, family and friends are confused by my jump-up-and-down-joy at the seemingly small successes that Cleveland has achieved in more recent years. By comparison to the load-bearing years of 2008-2010, those more contemporary successes are monumental. When the CAVS made it to game seven of the 2016 NBA finals, for example, I made my mother's schnauzer, Vincent, wear a CAVS wine and gold jersey for good luck (I'm sure that's why the CAVS won). And when they defeated the Golden State Warriors in the final minutes of that game to win it all, they had to peel me off the ceiling. And you better believe that Beth and I happily jammed ourselves into a crowd of over a million other jubilant parade goers to celebrate the CAVS victory. Or when Heinen's grocers of Cleveland opened the world's most beautiful grocery store in the restored Cleveland Trust building at the corner of East 9th and Euclid, the first full-service grocery in downtown Cleveland in decades, I couldn't stop talking about it for months. My daughter was living in Paris at the time. I'm sure I was terribly annoying to her: "Sure you guys have Notre Dame and the Louvre," I might concede, "but have you seen our new grocery store?" As a matter of fact, I still rave about it. (Google it! Better yet, visit it in person. You'll be impressed. I guarantee it!). And when the news came through that Cleveland won its bid to be the host city of the 2016 Republican National Convention, beating out seven other almost equally great cities, I'm sure my Canadian family thought I was completely off my rocker. When I announced the good news, I had to choke back tears of elation. They thought I was crying because Donald Trump looked like a potential candidate at the time but mine were tears of joy. Score one for Cleveland!

How bright the light shines after a time of deep darkness. I think people sometimes forget, or cannot imagine - why would you want to, just how dim things were for Cleveland less than a decade ago. Admittedly, Cleveland had seen bad times before but the year 2008 was, statistically, the murky bottom of the rusty barrel as far as recent history was concerned, Browns notwithstanding.

In 2008, the U.S. Census Bureau identified the poorest major cities in the United States. Not only did Ohio have the exclusive honor of having three of its once-gleaming urban centers, all of them now crawling in abject squalor, rank on the top ten list. Toledo and Columbus came in at eighth and seventh respectively, but my new hometown, Cleveland, held the distinction of being the second poorest city in America. Longtime Clevelanders, accustomed to bad news, fluffed off the Bureau's pronouncement with jokes like, "Thank God for Detroit!" or "Awe! No fair! We never get to be Number One!"

That very same year, Forbes Magazine, identified a list of dying cities in America. Yep, you guessed it, Cleveland showed-up on this roll as well. During the first seven years of the new millennium, said Forbes, "painful waves of unemployment and barely growing economies" drove roughly 115,000 people out of the already gasping city toward any place else in the country less desperate than Cleveland. Anywhere at all: Frankenstein, Missouri; Hell, Michigan; Mosquitoville, Vermont, or any other place that might show up on lists of weird towns in America would have been better than Cleveland, with the exception of maybe Flint or Detroit. And even then, while it hadn't died more than those two bastions of Michigan decay, Cleveland was dying more quickly, earning it the title of "fastest dying city in America." Woot! Finally, we were Number One.

Like so many once-great American cities, the core of the city of Cleveland was almost completely decimated by decades of sprawl to the suburbs outside of the city. In many ways, the abandonment stripped Cleveland of vital resources and left it with a series of complex problems to be solved. Urban abandonment was both physically and spiritually crushing for cities like Cleveland. It deflated the spirits of those who were left behind just as surely as the stones heaped on the plank across Giles Corey's chest wrung the last breaths from his diaphragm. And, as in the case of Giles Corey, urban decline in America's rust belt cities and everywhere else, brought a slow death of increased crime, unemployment, decreased tax revenue and resources for schools, safety, roads and other infrastructure that contribute to the overall common good and sense of well-being for the community.

In 2008, at 5:00 P.M., like someone pulled the plug at the bottom of the tub, tens of thousands of workers who decades earlier had called the city home and who once contributed to the life and vitality of the city, now drained it as they poured out to the suburbs. When the whistle blew, workers punched out and then raced down a complex web of interstate highways and expressways that, when built, scored fatal cuts through the hearts of longstanding neighborhoods. At quitting time, office workers and factory laborers could simply abandon the city, rolling-up the streets behind them.

Our first two years living in downtown Cleveland were lonely years, especially after normal business hours when commuters flurried to the suburbs like gusts of lake effect snow every night at 5:00 P.M. and downtown shops and services locked themselves up tight for the evening. We believed things could change, and would change, but those first few years convincing the majority of Clevelanders that downtown was going to make a comeback, was a hard sell. I had to work hard at staying positive for them, and for myself.

•   •   •

As affluence and engagement in the city rolled down the highway, crime had come to take its place. Like a boil ready to burst, Cleveland's crime index had swollen to almost triple the national average. Boarded-up shops made Cleveland's once bustling main drag, Euclid Avenue, look like a scene from a post-apocalyptic horror flick. People in our new congregation wondered why on earth we would want to live downtown, "the armpit of the city" as a friend - a retired police officer, called it.

It discouraged me to hear people describe their own city, their hometown, with such overt disdain, as if they had nothing to do with its current state and no ability, nor desire, to improve it. The deprecation of place signaled a lack of hope born from decades of disappointment, present unhappiness, and a lack of faith in their own ability, or the abilities of their leaders, to manifest a brighter future for all. Most disheartening, for me, was that the derision, particularly toward downtown, unwittingly served to demonize the city. To keep it down. The late Yale scholar, Letty Russell once compared the American city to a battered woman. We take what we want from her - jobs, resources, sports and culture. At 5:00 P.M., we abandon her for the suburbs leaving her isolated, weary, and with insufficient resources to sustain herself. Then, when she fails us, we blame her as if she somehow did this to herself. How easy it is for us to take what we want from our cities while disavowing any responsibility for them.

The love-hate relationship people had with Cleveland was overt. Cleveland had been "tore up and tore down" one of my new friends, a longtime Clevelander, lamented.

My Canadian parents came for a visit during our first couple of weeks in Cleveland. These good-guy, always apologizing Canucks are friendly folks and great walkers. They couldn't understand why, in the dusk of the September evening, I resisted letting them walk the twelve blocks from the church on Public Square to their hotel at East 12th. Never mind the fact that the entire street was ripped-up with construction for the forthcoming Health Line Bus Rapid Transit system. It was a bubbling mud hole that looked, in my mind, like the aftermath of a Beirut bombing. Even more, no matter how much charm my parents could exude, I knew that in 2008 their kind of Canadian Kum-Bah-Yah sweetness could get you killed in downtown Cleveland!

Outside of downtown, other Cleveland neighborhoods were in peril, too. Those new highways of the 1950s and 60s had sliced through old neighborhoods dividing neighbors from one another, and from their churches, schools and other community anchors. Folks were faced with the hard choice of staying behind to administer life support to dying communities or to follow neighbors to the suburban promised land. Those who could afford it, more often than not, chose the latter.

Abandoned homes in the city were left to rot or become new homes for illegal drug trade and human trafficking throughout the 80s and 90s and into the early 2000s. The mortality rate in some neighborhoods during the first decade of the new millennium was a full twenty-five years less than in contiguous outer ring suburbs just a mile or two away. City councilman, Joe Cimperman - an eloquent and passionate public speaker and spiritually thoughtful student of the Jesuits at John Carroll University, delivered a speech one day where it appeared that, overwhelmed by the disparity in our city, he just lost control. "How can people in one neighborhood be dying at such young ages, and people who live just a mile or two away get to live well into their seventies. What the hell is wrong with us?" Joe simply posed the question we had all been asking or, for some, denying.

2007-2009 were also the years that serial killer, Anthony Sowell was making himself busy by raping close to a dozen or more women, murdering at least eleven of them and attempting to conceal their remains in his Imperial Street home. Like a vicious dog burying his bones, Sowell buried the bodies of four women in shallow graves in his basement and, likely, when he ran out of room, or the stench of decaying bodies just got too bad even for this despicable monster, he shoveled three more women into backyard graves. By the time the police showed up to investigate reports of an odorous miasma wafting from the house, the bodies of another two women were found simply rotting on the living room floor. The head of the eleventh woman was found in a bucket, also inside the house.

Concurrently, just six miles away from Sowell's "house of horrors"[8] on Imperial, other horrific crimes were being committed. Kidnapper-rapist, Ariel Castro was holding hostage three young women whom he had abducted and then, for almost a dozen years, continuously raped, impregnated, and repeatedly beat to force miscarriages and to exact power and control. Michelle Knight, Amanda Berry, and Gina DeJesus eventually escaped Castro's MetroWest hell house on Seymour Avenue, but not before one of the girls had given birth to a child and all of them had been profoundly scarred for life.

I would meet Michelle Knight in 2014, just a few months after she broke free from her almost twelve-year nightmare. She was a sweet young woman, pleasant and positive given all that she had been through. She was admirably trying to navigate her way as a celebrity du jour. She made the rounds on all the networks, made appearances on the nightly news and, especially, the morning shows to tell her story of horror and heroism.

---

[8] A term used by Cleveland-based journalist Robert Sberna who wrote an award-winning book entitled *House of Horrors: The Shocking True Story of Anthony Sowell, the Cleveland Strangler* published in 2012 by Kent State University Press.

Michelle had requested the use of the Old Stone Church sanctuary to film part of a music video for her single, Survivor. When she came in for a pre-shoot orientation, I was immediately taken by her resilience and determination to heal, move forward, and then help others by rewriting her narrative. I think, though, she and I both knew that her story of how she survived almost twelve years of abduction and torture would also be a part of Cleveland's larger collective narrative for a long time to come, a brutal entry burned into our public record that would make it all the more challenging for her to move beyond it. I pray that she has found healing. And peace.

As I escorted her throughout our historic sanctuary, Michelle raised her gaze heavenward. I didn't know whether she was searching for God, or whether she was simply marveling at the warmth of the open space of Old Stone's lofty ceiling above her – its height exaggerated in contrast to her elfin stature of a mere four feet and seven inches. Her eyes revealed a kind of innocent, childlike awe belonging to someone much younger than her thirty-three worry-worn years. Mostly she betrayed a grit-teethed tenacious hope that belonged to those who have persevered against great odds, those who have paid a great price for their resolve. But somewhere beneath the surface of her I-will-survive determination, there was still a child, free and full of wonder.

Postscript: Castro pleaded guilty to 937 criminal counts of rape, kidnapping, and aggravated murder. He hung himself in prison with his bedsheets after serving just one month into his sentence of "life plus 1000 years." Sowell spends his remaining days on death row. Mercifully, for neighbors and all Clevelanders, both of their homes have been bulldozed.

The crimes of Sowell and Castro, of course, were the most sensational of Cleveland crimes at the time. Unfortunately, they seemed to serve as a peculiar distraction from the fact that crime rates in general were swelling, almost proportionally to the rate of the city's population hemorrhage. As residents abandoned old neighborhoods for new, crime flooded in to fill the void.

I knew that there was good work to be done in the city – that is, in part, why I came, after all. I hadn't even begun to comprehend the full measure of the situation, however, until my walking shoes hit the Cleveland pavement. While there were just over 434,000 people living in Cleveland in 2008, the number of assaults, burglaries, thefts and car thefts totaled over 35,000. Incidents of rape were up by over ten percent from the previous year. So were homicides. In that year alone, Cleveland witnessed a staggering 102 murders.

Just so you don't think I am exaggerating, here, let's put that number – 102 murders, in national perspective: According to City-Data.com, that same year, New York City's murder rate was 6.3 murders for every 100,000 people. Los Angeles's was 10 per 100,000. Chicago – dangerous Chicago, the city everyone references when they need to haul-out some horrifying statistic about gun violence, had a murder rate of 18 per 100,000 residents. Tragic, yes. All of them. Murder is murder. Now consider, however, Cleveland's murder rate that same year. In 2008, Cleveland had a mindboggling 23 murders for every 100,000 residents! When it came to murder, once again, all we could do was shake our heads and say, "Thank goodness for Detroit!" which ranked impressively that year at 33.8 murders per 100,000 people, though you can hardly call murder impressive.

Having a murder rate less than Detroit's is not something to brag about. I mean, it is not the sort of thing the Chamber of Commerce, or the local convention and visitors bureau, Destination Cleveland is going to put in a tourist ad to promote our fair city: "Come to Cleveland! Home of the Rock & Roll Hall of Fame, the world-renowned Cleveland Orchestra, and a murder rate slightly less than Detroit!" "Cleveland: You'll love it . . . If you survive!" Maybe the Greater Cleveland Film Commission could have built on that idea and proposed a new reality show: Survivor: Cleveland. Michelle Knight could have sung the theme song.

I know, it is shameless to joke about the loss of real lives. As you can see, I developed a bit of the Cleveland edginess along my way. Living in Cleveland for more than a decade will do that to you. If you didn't laugh about your city at least once a day, you would probably cry yourself to sleep every night.

It is not that the good, hardworking folks of Cleveland didn't see it, or as if they didn't have any ideas of how to stop it. Clevelanders are exceptional at getting themselves organized, finding solutions, and then getting down to work.

Following an execution-style shooting of two Cleveland Clinic employees, Jeremy Pechanec and Jory Aebly, near downtown's Perk Park on Chester Avenue in early 2009 that left Pechanec dead, city councilman and all round, good guy, Joe Cimperman and I partnered with local police to host a community forum at the Old Stone Church on the topic of crime in downtown. There was the usual "this is what we are doing" kind of briefings from the police and the mayor's office. And there was a deluge of heated comments from the one-hundred-and-fifty or so concerned citizens who showed-up to voice their opinions. Many of those who gathered expressed outraged that we were hosting the event only because, they argued, the victims were white. Had they been African American, exploded angry participants, we would not have bothered to gather at all. In Cleveland, in America, there is well-founded justification behind that kind of fiery accusation. Even so, a murder is a murder. And if we can use it to bring attention to crime in our cities and create proactive solutions that make our homes safer for all, then I say, "Let the people gather!"

After the usual dignitaries had their moments at the microphone, we broke into table groups for neighbor to neighbor discussions. I floated from table to table to listen. The heaviness of despair was evident in every group. One man, frustrated by failing government programs for teens and young adults in Cleveland, clearly understood the relationship between unemployment and crime. "Pastor," he shook his head, "our kids don't need another program. They need jobs!" Unfortunately for him, and for so many Cleveland kids matriculating to the workforce that year, decent paying jobs were few and far between.

The need for jobs is a recurring conversation in Cleveland, and in 2008 the need for jobs was at a peak with unemployment rates in the double digits. "Give a man a fish, he'll eat for a day. Teach him to fish and he will eat for a lifetime," says the old cliché. However, in Cleveland, I came to understand that teaching a person to fish is pointless if the fish just aren't biting, or if there simply aren't any fish at all. Fishing conditions in Cleveland in 2008 were terrible, and had been terrible for quite a few years. The pond had run dry. Opportunities for the city's many unskilled laborers were in very short supply. The offshoring of many of Cleveland's once great manufacturing opportunities was unprecedented. Many corporations abandoned American cities like Cleveland because of their voracious appetite for cheap labor, low taxes, and opportunities in nations with little to no environmental or ethical labor standards. Even more detrimental to the security of American workers were new automated technologies that simply bumped aside workers here at home and replaced them with robotics and other machines that could do the work at a lower cost and with fewer hassles.

Even the remnant white-collar jobs in Cleveland's core were disappearing at alarming rates. One of the most disappointing blows came in that same year. One of the few remaining Fortune 500 companies in the city, the Eaton Corporation, cut over ten percent of its local work force. Then, in early 2009, Eaton announced that it was moving its head office, along with its 440 employees, twenty miles outside of the city. Incentives from the neighboring town of Beachwood and from the state of Ohio were too much of a draw. Cleveland couldn't compete.

For the record, Eaton Corp was offered fifty-three-million-dollars in state tax breaks and another twenty-four-million-dollars in land acquisition loans if it agreed to remain in Ohio. Eaton's state funded move to the suburbs proved that the great state of Ohio was clueless to the failures of suburbanization. The state paved huge tracts of farmland for new roads to connect suburban commuters to their now sprawling work places. Millions of tax payer dollars front loaded expenditures for new infrastructure – roads, water, sewer, power to serve the far reaches of the city, ignoring the fact that the core itself already had an infrastructure in place, aged as it was, designed to accommodate the needs of a city more than 2.5 times as big as Cleveland's current population. Instead, the county and the state both spent or allowed for the spending of diminishing tax payer dollars to court a company that was already in town. Hello! Did our state legislators miss the U.S. Census? Three of the top ten fastest dying cities were in their state. Even so, lawmakers continued to short change public transportation, housing, public education, and other initiatives necessary to strengthen cites, while offering huge tax breaks to businesses who promised to stay in Ohio. A fellow downtown resident who worked at Eaton's downtown office would now exchange his ten-minute walk to work for a thirty-minute drive. "Well, at least I'll be a 'reverse' commuter," he shrugged, acknowledging that while the heavy morning traffic flowed into the city, he'd be driving out. And then back in again in the evening.

•　　•　　•

The declining tax base from business and residents within the city of Cleveland meant that the existing infrastructure had less and less funding necessary for updates and repairs (a drop in the proverbial bucket compared to the cost of building new infrastructure twenty miles beyond the city). City streets gouged with potholes took their toll on people's spirits as well as their cars. Perhaps the City just found it cheaper to set up a special fund in the Law Department's Moral Claims Division to replace flattened tires and bent rims for those who could prove legitimate claims than to finance the fixing of potholes. With every jarring slam to vehicles, with every burst tire, we were reminded of the Cleveland's dire straits.

Diminished tax revenue also meant less money for schools that were now saddled with maintaining buildings, structures and programs that had been put in place in an earlier day when the city was twice its current size. An aging water treatment system often overflowed, sending raw sewage into Lake Erie. Parks and beaches were regularly closed due to the high levels of fecal matter in public swimming areas.

To add more weight to the crushing board, in November 2008 all commercial truck traffic had been restricted from traversing the failing inner belt bridge, the main artery connecting the I-90 and its thousands of daily commuters with downtown Cleveland. Commuters who crossed the bridge each day on their way in and out of the city held their breath, white-knuckled the steering wheel, and uttered silent prayers that the bridge would hold until they made it across to safety.

One civil engineer discretely confessed to me that he had found an alternate route into downtown since he wouldn't dare drive even his car over the bridge until it was repaired or replaced.

The conflation of issues confronting Cleveland in 2008 was compounded by the fact that Clevelanders were suffering the abuses of a number of corrupt politicians who had their hands so deep inside the cookie jar of county government that citizens who longed and worked for a healthy, vibrant city hardly stood a chance. Scandalous rumors of racketeering among some of the region's most prominent leaders had been shared over open lunchboxes in the plants and whispered around office watercoolers for years. In 2008, however, official news hit the proverbial fan and smeared the city in political dung and disgrace. What was once sealed in the shadowy backrooms of the Cuyahoga County offices was brought out into the dull light of day.

On July 28, 2008, 150 federal investigators executed successful raids on the homes and offices of County Commissioner Jimmy Dimora and County Auditor Frank Russo. Yep, those are real names, not characters from a Mario Puzo novel. Comments online and in the newspaper were not kind to Italians in general during those days. Contributors often remarked, "What do you expect? The guy's last name ends in a vowel." The Feds also rounded-up a full chain gang worth of private contractors who also had been under investigation.

In a story that played out in the daily paper like a trashy crime novel, the two biggest fish, Dimora and Russo would eventually be charged, tried and, after plea bargaining deals, sentenced to a total of fifty-two years in federal prison. Twenty-two years for Russo[9]. Thirty for Dimora.

---

[9] In May 2020, at the age of 70, Frank Russo received an early release from the Butner Federal Correction Institution on the grounds of COVID19 risks at the North Carolina institution. With four years of his sentence remaining, Russo lives in the Cleveland area.

•   •   •

The bitter icing on the cake for the year was the market crash of 2008, which impacted every American, as well as personal and national economies around the world. On September 29, 2008, just one month into our fresh start in Cleveland, the Dow Jones Industrial Average panicked everyone by dropping a staggering 777.68 points in a single day, and then continued to plummet for the next seventeen and a half months from the October 2007 high of 14,164.43 to just 6,594.44 – a more than fifty percent drop in value in just a year and a half. Economists, politicians, and the like, will tell us exactly why we crashed: deregulation in the financial industry and the erasing of consumer protections, which led to wild hedge fund trading, and demanded subprime lending and predatory loans to sustain the insatiable appetites of bankers and other traders. In the end, President Obama's administration followed through on a similar President Bush plan of bailouts to banks and some manufacturing companies such as General Motors and others.

For many Clevelanders, the crash had less impact. They were far ahead of the curve having experienced major slowdowns in their Northeast Ohio economy, a devaluing of real estate and an increase in home foreclosures when many major and even some smaller manufacturing companies replaced workers with new automated technologies or moved factories outside of the United States.

Others were hit much harder. Particularly those who lost retirement investments and/or were forced out of longtime professional positions when banks such as Cleveland National City Bank closed or were forced to merge, consolidate, and downsize. Every day, just as we did after the terrorist attacks of September 11, 2001, we remained glued to our television sets, trying to understand the graphs and charts, squinting at them in search of signs of hope, if not recovery. We listened to the analysts and commentators who pointed fingers of blame at banks and mortgage companies, or at politicians and those to whom they chose to give bailouts. Only incidentally did we face ourselves in the mirror to explore our own greed, our lust for more, though every day we asked the question of one another, "Do you think we'll ever recover?" until we just got tired of asking.

·   ·   ·

As if to heap even more weight on to the good folks of Cleveland in what was already one of Cleveland's most crushing years, not only did the Browns lose their home opener to the Steelers, they concluded their 2008-09 season with a dismal 4-12 record and earned the distinction of having gone twenty-four straight quarters without a single touchdown. In the end, Romeo Crennel, then head coach, took the hit and was sacked.

"What a lucky guy," I groaned. "Take me, instead!"

Chapter Four

In the Heart of the City: The Old Stone Church

"Possibly Cleveland's best-known religious building, Old Stone Church is a symbol of the city's birth and development. The church is the oldest standing structure on Public Square and is home to the second oldest religious organization in Cleveland. Origins of the church's congregation date back to meetings of the Union Sunday School held on the second-floor of Cleveland's first log cabin courthouse in 1819. The church was officially established the following year by approximately fifteen residents of the village. Out of these early prayer services, which were often interrupted by the gunshots of hunters in nearby thickets, First Presbyterian Church would grow into one of Cleveland's most prominent and influential religious institutions."

–Richard Raponi, Cleveland Historical

YOU MAY BE ASKING yourself an obvious question at this point: If Cleveland was as bad as it was in 2008, why did I leave Savannah and come to Cleveland in the first place? I would be completely remiss and altogether deceiving you if I left unstated the most important reason for choosing Cleveland in my quest for home: The Old Stone Church on Public Square. I might have been grieving the loss of my church and community down in Savannah, but I was eager to serve a great church like this historic one in downtown Cleveland.

Officially known as the First Presbyterian Church in Cleveland, Old Stone was Cleveland's biggest draw for me. Old Stone is the city center church that often shows up on city-view postcards or in the grand photos and paintings of the city's artists because of its architectural beauty, its prominence in the greater Cleveland narrative, or simply as one of the most recognizable structures in the city. Last time I was in the Cleveland Hopkins International Airport, I noticed that there hangs, among other iconic Cleveland landmarks, a rendition of the Old Stone Church drawn in fonts by a Cleveland Institute of Art student.

There was a desire to live closer to our Canadian family, for sure. Living in Cleveland would put us within a seven hour drive north to my parent's home in Owen Sound, Ontario. We would be even closer to Beth's parents and some dear friends who were living in the nearby Windsor area of Southwestern Ontario. From Cleveland, Windsor was just a three-hour drive and one international border crossing at Detroit.

I also had an eagerness to live in a city that was ready to reinvent itself, and to serve a downtown church that was committed to the city. Cleveland and Old Stone easily fit that bill for me, even if at that point in its recent history, reinvention was more out of necessity than desire. Savannah's recent awakening had already happened twenty or more years earlier under the leadership of the Historic Savannah Foundation and the generative impact of the Savannah College of Art and Design. I had missed it. Cleveland's revival, however, was primed and ready to go. There was plenty of room for a newcomer like me to be involved.

The lure of the Old Stone Church tugged at a deep longing - a calling within me, to pastor a church in the city. A church that might bring a faithful voice to a city that was short on resources but long on possibility. A church that could speak to the needs of the city, to work faithfully alongside politicians, planners, and other civic leaders as they attempted to do the seemingly impossible – help the city re-emerge from the long, dark winter of car-dependent suburbanization, sprawl, and a very real subservience to the automobile. "Work and pray for the wellbeing of the city, for in its wellbeing you will find your own" urged the prophet Jeremiah (29:7). I wanted to be a part of a church that would give prophetic witness to the possibility of vitality for all – safe, walkable communities, meaningful education, economic growth, sustainability, the restoration and re-purposing of some the greatest architecture the world has ever known, and creative opportunities that would help the city thrive again. A church that was not just in the heart of the city but, also, had a heart for the city.

Long before God had shaken my bed in the middle of the night and called me into ministry, I had spent a great deal of my undergraduate education studying subjects like human geography and urban planning, collective behavior, and the patterns and movements of people within their cities. I was fascinated by life in the city even before I was aware of the New Urbanist design movement and how the church might participate in shaping walkable/bike-able, eco-just and sustainable places that are friendly to real flesh and blood human beings.

From a very young age, in fact, I was curious about cities, particularly the city of Toronto where I spent a great deal of my youth. Like a kid trying to understand the mystery of how the interconnected parts that are squeezed into the back of a watch function almost seamlessly as one to keep perfect time – its gears and pivot wheels, set screws, ratchets and levers rhythmically turning and spinning, clicking and ticking, I was fascinated by how the complexity of cities blended together to function as a whole. I pondered for hours, the ironic ease of mobility by which thousands of people streamed like rivers along concrete sidewalks in and around dense clusters of polished stone and gleaming glass and steel towers that touched the sky. Who were these people flowing without resistance through the city? To me, the diversity of skin color which was the warmth of chestnut and the mysteriousness of ebony, creamy or golden, and hair styles – straight or braided, and even curly like mine, and the brightly colored fashions and tongue-twisting languages that people spoke as they coursed along their labyrinthine pathways made them appear to have come from exotic places in the farthest reaches of the planet. They were my windows to the world. And here, in the city, these people formed a beautiful, textured mosaic that called out of me a sense of wonder and awe. There was something holy in the people of the city, and in the city itself.

I loved, too, feeling the powerful rumble of a street car clacking down a roadway or avenue as I walked along the sidewalk, or the earth trembling beneath my feet as a dozen subway cars thundered under the very ground on which I stood, rocketing hundreds of people through sable subterranean tunnels toward hundreds of destinations unknown.

The city was a place of independence for me. Public transportation was my liberation. In the suburbs, I depended on lifts from parents or older siblings which demanded negotiation and the adherence to tight schedules and places – "Be here at this place and at this time and we'll pick you up. Don't be late!" In the city, however, if I knew the routes and had a few coins in my pocket, I was free to come and go when and wherever I wanted. The international transit consultant, Jarrett Walker, likes to say, "show me a map of your city's transit system, and I will show you a map of your freedom." Even as a kid, at an intuitive level, I think I understood that public mobility meant individual freedom. Even more so as an adult, I take great delight in those cities with exceptional public transportation that allow a person to leave the car at home, or to be liberated from the responsibility of automobile ownership altogether.

For the first decade and a half following my 1990 ordination to ministry, I had not so secretly longed to pastor an urban church like Old Stone. I wanted to be in the heart of it all. I wanted to be a pastor in and for the city. I imagined myself one day becoming a high-pulpit preacher in a high-steeple church, one who would speak a prophetic word from God within and from the congregation of a historically prominent church like Old Stone, and from the heart of a great American city like Cleveland. Call it fantasy or fulfillment of self-expectation. Call it whatever you want. For a very long time, I had a spiritual itch. A vocational calling. At first glance, the Old Stone Church, Northeast Ohio's prominent institution - "in the heart of the city and with a heart for the city" for almost two full centuries seemed to be a place where and a people among whom that itch might get scratched.

•　　•　　•

Admittedly, when I saw the advertisement announcing that the Old Stone Church was seeking its next Senior Pastor, I had little knowledge of the Old Stone Church or of Cleveland. I had braved the Corkscrew rollercoaster as a teenager during my one and only visit to Cedar Point in nearby Sandusky, Ohio. As a kid in high school, I loved the Ian Hunter song, "Cleveland Rocks." Although living in Windsor at the time and attending lots of concerts at Detroit's Joe Louis Arena and older, Cobo Hall, I was defensive. I couldn't understand why the song wasn't called, "Detroit Rocks!" After all, Detroit was the "home of rock and roll, baby!" as Detroit radio man, Arthur Penthallow ingrained in us teenagers every afternoon on WRIF radio, and the rock band KISS had blasted with their own city-themed rock anthem, "Detroit Rock City!"

I visited Cleveland only twice as an adult, both times to make my pilgrimage to the Rock & Roll Hall of Fame. I ventured there once as a solo pilgrim and then, a second time, with my family when I eagerly pointed out all the exciting artifacts of my youth. "Yes, kids! That's the lurex leotard that Freddie Mercury wore the first time I saw him play in Detroit!" "Did you know that before he fronted the rock band, Queen, he was known by a different stage name – Larry Lurex? Isn't that ironic?" "Look it's John Bonham's bass drum!" "Hey, let's check out the Jimi Hendrix theater!" My children were awesome in their willingness to feign interest while I reveled with youthful rock and roll exuberance, bouncing like a steel ball in a pinball machine from one flashing exhibit to the next.

Down in the dank file room of my mind, I had stored blurry annals of Cleveland, musty manila-colored folders containing fuzzy notions and free-floating attitudes about the city. I'm not sure how or when or even why those records were filed in my subconscious. Maybe it has something to do with the public jabs that the rest of America so often takes at the city. Cleveland gets used often for malignant one-liners in sitcoms, or as the butt of a joke for a late-night comic's opening monologue: "In Cleveland there is legislation moving forward to ban people from wearing pants that fit too low. However, there is lots of opposition from the plumber's union," Conan O'Brien joked. "A gloomy day in New York City is still better than a sunny day in Cleveland," the City of New York recently tweeted.

Maybe the foggy images of Cleveland in my mind were formed by all those reruns of the Drew Carey Show which took place in Cleveland. Or maybe by all those big screen movies that have been set in Cleveland such as Major League which opens with Sister Mary Assumpta - the onetime nun and diehard Indians fan - wearing her habit and Cleveland baseball jacket while feeding pigeons on the lawn of Public Square in front of the Old Stone Church, or Raging Bull, or the dry-witted mocumentary, This is Spinal Tap, which gave the world one of the most hokey Cleveland lines ever: "Hello, Cleveland!"

Is it possible that Cleveland gets mentioned a lot or becomes the setting for stories and films because, like old Tennessee Williams may or may not have said, while it's not New York, San Francisco, or New Orleans, it is everywhere else? Perhaps, Cleveland is a place with which the rest of America identifies.

Then again, maybe people make fun of Cleveland simply because of the name itself, like cucumber or cockroach, Cleveland just sounds funny. Consider the speech about 'words that sound funny' as delivered by the character, Willy, to his nephew in Neil Simon's Sunshine Boys: "Fifty-seven years in this business, you learn a few things. You know what words are funny and which words are not funny. Alka Seltzer is funny. You say 'Alka Seltzer' you get a laugh ... Words with 'k' in them are funny. Casey Stengel, that's a funny name. Robert Taylor is not funny. Cupcake is funny. Tomato is not funny. Cookie is funny. Cucumber is funny. Car keys. Cleveland ... Cleveland is funny. Maryland is not funny. Then, there's chicken. Chicken is funny. Pickle is funny. Cab is funny. Cockroach is funny – not if you get 'em, only if you say 'em."[10]

Mostly what I knew of Cleveland in the year 2007 – the year I wrestled with my call to the city, was that it was a big urban center. An American city. A city that, for that one reason or another, most Americans tended to think of as a rough-edged, mawkish place. It wasn't until the Old Stone Church posted its "pastor wanted" ad in a church magazine that Cleveland would come into focus for me as a

---

[10] Found in Franzini, Louis R. (2012). *Just Kidding: Using Humor Effectively*. Rowman & Littlefield. p. 138.

potential place to make my home. It was only then that I truly started to explore the city and the historic church at its heart.

•   •   •

My research had begun by MapQuesting a map of Cleveland (yep, I was still using MapQuest. You'll find some still do … if you Google it!). As the digital map opened on my screen, I could not help but notice that the star that marked the heart of the city was located over Public Square, directly in front of the church. Actually, the star hovered right about the same spot where Sister Mary Assumpta fed her pigeons in the opening shots of Major League making Old Stone appear vaguely like a Roman Catholic Church.

The fact that the Old Stone Church was situated on Public Square in the very center of the city was good news for me. So good, in fact, that my heart quickened as the page loaded-up and confirmed what I had suspected. The church was physically planted in the center of the city, at the edge of the Northwest quadrant of Ontario Street and Public Square. Old Stone was the place where the city's east met its west, Cleveland's ground zero. The fact that the Old Stone Church was occupying, and had occupied for one hundred and ninety years, a rather significant piece of real estate in the city, meant to me that it had the potential of being in direct civic and theological conversation with the city, its leaders, and its citizens, if it wasn't already.

I discovered, as my research continued, the larger than life historic impact the Old Stone Church and its illustrious story had on the city of Cleveland. Not only had the Old Stone Church been at the geographic heart of the city for almost two full centuries, it had been at its spiritual heart, too. The congregation has gathered for worship on Public Square since 1820, 1819 if you count its start as a Sunday school in the upstairs of the old log courthouse.

Technically speaking, Old Stone is the second oldest church in the city. The oldest, Trinity Episcopal Church is older by just four years. Playfully, however, I like to remind folks that whereas Trinity moved to various locations throughout the city over the years, Old Stone has been worshipping on Public Square without a move since 1820. It is the oldest building on the Square and it is the oldest continuously worshipping congregation in one place, in situ, in the heart of Cleveland.

It amazed me. It humbled me. I was called to be the senior pastor of a church with venerable acclaim. And I would be only the twelfth senior pastor in its long and storied history. To put it into historical perspective, when fifteen folks, some of Cleveland's charter citizens - almost ten percent of Cleveland's population in 1820, founded the Old Stone Church, old George III, King of Great Britain had just died. Napoleon Bonaparte was still living out his final days in exile at Longwood House on St. Helena Island off the south west coast of Africa. Antarctica had just been discovered!

Closer to home, when Old Stone was founded, there were only twenty-three stars on the old stars and stripes American flag. In fact, it would be another seventy-six years before John Philip Sousa would compose his most famous march, Stars and Stripes Forever. The U.S. Census reported that in 1820 there were just under ten million (9,638,453) people living in America, of which more than ten percent (1,538,022) were slaves. William Tecumseh Sherman and Susan B. Anthony were wet-behind-the-ears infants. Abraham Lincoln was just a boy of eleven. And Daniel Boone, the original rugged Marlboro man, died just days after Old Stone got its start. No correlation, I am sure.

On occasion, I was completely annoying to family and friends by pointing out just how old a thing was not by comparing it to how old the Old Stone Church was. In Ottawa, Canada, I might lift my head from the guide book and point to the Parliament Building saying something like, "Wow! Canada's capitol building is really old. It's just thirty-nine years younger than Old Stone!" Or if we were in D.C., I might point out that construction on the Washington Monument didn't even start until twenty-eight years after Old Stone was founded, or that the Lincoln Monument wasn't even completed until over a full one hundred years after Old Stone got its start on Public Square. "Remember, kids, Lincoln was just a boy of eleven when we were founded," I might add.

My wife and I visited our daughter, Daryl, in Paris a few years ago. We caught ourselves, naturally, 'oohing' and 'aweing' over the splendor of the Basilica Sacre Coeur in Montmarte. I turned to my wife and daughter and exclaimed, "Impressive! It's really old; built only ninety-seven years after the Old Stone Church was founded, and only fifty-nine years after our current building was constructed!"

More recently, we were in London for my daughter Daryl's master's recital from the Royal Academy of Music. Daryl is a cellist. Actually, I consider Daryl to be the Jimi Hendrix of cello ever since she rocked, by memory, a very intense performance of all three movements of Kodaly's Sonata for Cello in Atlanta a few years ago. For thirty minutes she assertively plucked the strings with confidence and passion, shredded bow hairs, and stopped just short of picking-up the cello to play it with her teeth or behind her head. While at the Royal Academy we took a tour of the closet-sized on-campus museum. I was impressed by some of the names on the list of alumni which included contemporary greats like Sir Elton John and Annie Lennox. I know that one day Daryl's name will appear there as well. The timeline mural depicting the historic chronology of this prestigious school didn't escape me either. Founded in 1822, the Royal Academy of Music is the oldest conservatory in the United Kingdom. This means, ahem, the Royal Academy of Music got its start a full two years after the Old Stone Church was founded. Pish posh. The Academy had not even received its Royal Charter until 1830.

I know. I'm a historical pain in the neck. I'm getting concerned that no one will want to travel with me anymore. Just a few years back, though, I met my match when Beth and I traveled to Italy with our adult children for a family vacation. We stayed just a block or two from the Anfiteatro Flavio, a.k.a. the Colosseum. My family was quick to ask me how the age of Old Stone compared. Well played, family. Well played.

• • •

While not the subject of this book, one can hardly talk about the Old Stone Church without commenting on its incredible art and architecture. The shell of its current building, a Romanesque Revival style building designed by Heard and Porter architects was dedicated on August 12, 1855. Following disastrous fires in 1857 and 1884, its exterior was twice restored and, ultimately, a new interior was constructed under the design and direction of architect, Charles F. Schweinfurth and built by the very new Cleveland Shipbuilding company, now the American Ship Building Company. Look up at the ceiling. Look way up. It clearly resembles the hull of a massive wooden ship. The sanctuary in its current state was dedicated on October 19, 1884. Its mast - the massive steeple which once sat atop the taller of the church's two towers, however, would not be replaced until 1999, over one hundred years after the original one came crashing down onto Ontario Street in an explosion of flames.

When it comes to stained glass, Old Stone is famous for its four Louis Comfort Tiffany windows - two of which are hand-signed by Tiffany himself, dating from 1885 to 1930. These glorious windows draw hundreds of individual viewers and group-tours every year. Old Stone also houses what may be the only stained-glass window in America with the image of a football stadium included in it. The Stouffer Memorial Window (1976) designed by Noblis Studios includes iconic Cleveland institutions of the era including Severance Hall, the Stouffer Hotel on Public Square, and even the old Cleveland Stadium - affectionately referred to as the Muni Stadium or just the Muni, former home to both Cleveland's baseball and football teams.

Other windows of note include the "Christ Blessing Little Children" window (1920) by J. and R. Lamb and, my particular favorite, the outstanding tri-windowed John La Farge installation (1885) titled "Benevolence" which overlooks Public Square. The three windows were dedicated to the memory of Amasa Stone[11] by his daughters, Clara Stone Hay and Flora Stone Mather. Many people over the decades have come to believe that the image of the standing woman in La Farge's large center window to be of Mary, the mother

[11] Sometimes people wonder if the church was named after Amasa Stone. It was not. The official name of the church is the First Presbyterian Church in Cleveland. It was the first stone building in the city and so was colloquially referred to as the "stone church." After enough years, people called it the "old stone church."

of Jesus. She certainly looks like classical images of Mary – robed in blue satin, her hand gently resting on the shoulder of someone kneeling before her, and her head held tilted in compassionate gaze. Old Stone history books have described the window as 'Elizabeth visiting Mary.' A researcher from the Smithsonian Institution studied the window's original drawings from 2008 to 2009, however, and identified the character as the personification of benevolence from which the piece gets its name.

In La Farge's original drawing, the character depicted on his knees is Amasa Stone. Stone, though remarkably benevolent to the Old Stone Church and other institutions throughout Northeast Ohio, was personally in need of a great deal of benevolent mercy after he had been responsible for one of the worst train disasters in American history - the bridge collapse in Ashtabula, Ohio.

Stone, the hugely powerful and successful railway baron, was president of the Lake Shore and Michigan Southern Railway company. Whether Stone ignored warnings from the railroad's Engineer in Charge, Charles Collins, or Collins was silent in his concerns about the safety of the bridge design – an older wood design being applied to a newer iron bridge, is unclear. Either way, on December 29, 1876 the bridge collapsed underneath the weight of the train just one thousand feet from the Ashtabula station sending one of its two locomotives, all eleven rail cars, and one hundred and fifty-nine passengers plummeting seven stories down into the frigid snow and ice of the Ashtabula River. Heating stoves and lamps set the wreckage ablaze. Ninety-two passengers died. Another sixty-four were injured. Stone never recovered.

For the next six years Amasa Stone suffered personal health issues and a series of major financial setbacks before ending his own life. Sometime between 2:00 P.M. and 4:00 P.M. on May 11, 1883, Stone locked himself in the bathroom of his Euclid Avenue mansion - the street, at the time was dubbed Millionaires Row, and shot himself in the head. When he was found, his body was slumped forward, his head and shoulders leaned into the bathtub. The gun was lying at his side.

I mention the manner in which Amasa Stone's body was discovered not to be morbid, but to draw a connection with how Stone and his family's continued benevolence to the congregation and its ministry impacted the church and the city as a whole for centuries to come. On the occasion of the Old Stone Church's seventy-fifth anniversary in 1895, twelve years after Stone's death, and just ten years after Clara and Flora had dedicated the La Farge window to their father's memory, his kindness and generosity, Dr. Hiram C. Haydn closed his morning sermon with words that hint of Stone's death by suicide while pointing toward his spirit of benevolence.

The fathers have fallen asleep, but they fell in their tracks, they fell face forward; some of them put into our hands treasure to be used for them right here, and said, "By this would I live on and work with you and them that come after you."

A full one hundred and twenty-five years have passed; we are left only to wonder if Dr. Haydn's words about those who "fell in their tracks" are a not so subtle play on words, a double entendre that references at least two things: the train tracks that fell at Ashtabula, and the fall from economic power that Stone experienced following the tragedy. We wonder, too, if the reference to those same ones who "fell face forward" might also be a play on words suggestive of the way that everyone understood Stone's body to have been found, face forward in the bathtub?

Dr. Haydn went on to mention the stained-glass windows in the church, the only two at the time – one a Tiffany, and the other, the glorious La Farge - the three enormous windows overlooking Public Square that Amasa Stone's daughters had dedicated to their father's memory:

These speaking windows . . . let us have more of such things remembering how they who sow and they who reap are to rejoice together – builders all, the work of all gathered up and carried along in the unbroken line of this historic church.

• • •

Early in January of 2008, Beth and I made the long drive up to Cleveland to meet discretely with members of the Pastoral Nominating Committee of the Old Stone Church. We motored off the I-77 onto Ontario Street into the heart of downtown Cleveland. The road was rough, the streets and the buildings that lined it were unattended. And then marvelous urban vista opened before our eyes. We caught our first glimpse of Cleveland's New England styled Public Square and the historic Old Stone Church that sat proudly on its northside. The historic church greeted us as we pierced thc heart of the city. Cleveland's First Presbyterian Church, its steeple stretching close to twenty stories heavenward, watched over what appeared to be, at one time, a well-intentioned square, but now had streets slicing through it, making the city-center park look more like a four-piece puzzle of disparate traffic islands than a gathering place for city residents. Towering skyscrapers looked down on the church and Square, and an impressive Beaux Arts style court house a couple blocks further north helped frame the image for us. I was smitten.

I met with the capable pastoral search team representing the Old Stone Church at a sandwich shop in the Tower City Mall located on the lower levels of the fifty-two story Terminal Tower on the opposite side of the Square from the church. The nominating committee had reviewed the applications of over one hundred and fifty candidates. I was impressed by how very seriously they took their task of researching and recommending a candidate for the congregation to elect as its next pastor, especially how carefully they honored the demands of discretion and confidentiality on behalf of both the congregation and the long list of candidates vying for the position. The committee members appeared to be mostly middle class and professional, which is not entirely surprising for a Presbyterian Church.

One member worried aloud, "Dr. Giuliano, do you think our committee is diverse enough?" I had to chuckle. The group of seven or eight, representative of the congregation on the whole, was wonderfully diverse in age, gender, ethnicity, and in intellectual and emotional temperament. I bantered, "You're diverse enough to be your own sitcom."

After our official meeting had concluded, one of the members of the search team walked Beth and me across the Square and then snuck us through the church and up to the second-floor office to meet the Interim Pastor, the Rev. Dr. David Horn. On our way, we passed through the church's seven hundred seat sanctuary. It was then that we caught our first in-person glimpse of the interior of this magnificent historic church – its radiant stained glass windows, towering pipe organ, and rich wooden buttresses. We were like many Old Stone first-timers - completely overwhelmed by the beauty of the space which seemed to hum with the very presence of God. There was an immediate sense that we were in a holy place, standing on sacred ground. Remarkably, even after a decade of preaching in the Old Stone Church, I was still overwhelmed by a sense of the sacred within its sanctuary.

I had been taken not only by the magnitude of the sanctuary that first visit, but by how well the church had been cared for. Glassy-eyed with astonishment, I turned to Beth and, with a rare tone of wonder in my voice, remarked, "Clearly, this is a church that has been loved!"

It is also a church that has been well financed, making it a just a little easier to care for than had the foremothers and forefathers not endowed the church. The comfortably financed church was another part of the story that I would only come to understand in more detail later on. During my first visit, I was simply informed that if I was elected to be the Senior Pastor of the Old Stone Church, the church had enough in financial reserves that I would never have to preach the "sermon on the amount." Ironically, as the years unfolded, I came to learn that the large amounts of money the church has at its disposal have been both a blessing and, in some ways, a curse for this too often conflicted congregation. God's good people on Public Square, I would come to discover, were suffering from an acute case of what psychologists to theologians have called affluenza – a social disorder suffered by people who are consumed with worry about not having enough or losing what they have already.

• • •

After that first meeting in January 2008, I explored in further detail the Old Stone Church as a prospective call. I was most impressed by both its geographic and civic prominence in the city since its early days. Old Stone is the place where Clevelanders have gathered for two centuries, whether to ring out the end of the Civil War with a service of thanksgiving or to pray as the body of President Abraham Lincoln was held in state on the Square just off the steps of its grand edifice. It was the place where people came for spiritual comfort and support during times of war. And it was the place where the city gathered to grieve and to find strength in times of tragedy and loss such as they did after the assassination of the Rev. Dr. Martin Luther King Jr. or following the terrorist attacks of September 11, 2001. Both of these services were attended by thousands, more than the church could hold, and were viewed by thousands more as they were broadcast live on television throughout Northeast Ohio.

Many impressive figures have spoken at the Old Stone Church, too, including Senator Bobby Kennedy who gave an impromptu speech from the steps of the church to the thousands who had poured into to the Square on April 5th, 1968 for the MLK memorial service at Old Stone before making his way down the street to address members of the City Club. The Rev. Billy Graham used the sanctuary as a place of prayer for himself and his leadership team before he preached to a crowd of more than seventy thousand worshippers and seekers alike at the old Muni stadium down by the lake.

Every mayor since 1820 has spoken at the Old Stone Church. My first year in Cleveland Mayor Frank Jackson responded positively to my invitation to be a speaker for the first of what has now become an annual spring symposium called, Hope for the City, when I reminded him that he was the first mayor who hadn't spoken at the church. My second year, then Congressman Dennis Kucinich, as well as the congregation's Clerk of Session and myself released doves from the steps of the church as part of Old Stone's one-hundred-and-ninetieth anniversary celebrations. Many of us who knew that a family of peregrine falcons lived across the Square atop the Terminal Tower were silently praying that those doves would not become lunch in a public feeding that would have been sure to make news for the media which were often present for Old Stone events and significant services, as they were that day.

Many of Cleveland's most important civic leaders were members of the church, including Mayor Ralph Locher. History has not judged Mayor Locher kindly, though. His poor handling of the Hough riots of the 1960s is still well known. Not surprisingly, following his second term in office, Locher was defeated by Carl B. Stokes in the Democratic primary. Stokes went on to become the first African American mayor of a major U.S. city. Even so, Locher remains a prominent figure in both Cleveland and Old Stone history. I later performed the memorial service for the former first lady, Eleanor Worthington Locher, before interring her ashes next to her husband's in the church's indoor columbarium.

At one time, Old Stone's membership rolls read like a book of 'Who's Who in Cleveland.' Prominent members, to name drop just a few, have included: industrialist and co-founder of Standard Oil, Henry Morrison Flagler who served as Elder on the church's Session in the 1870s; Louis Severance, founder of Standard Oil Trust and first Treasurer of Standard Oil; John Hay, personal assistant to President Abraham Lincoln and Secretary of State under Presidents William McKinley and Theodore Roosevelt and who also married Amasa Stone's daughter Clara; renowned philanthropists Flora Stone Mather and Clara Stone Hay who helped support and even establish many of Cleveland's institutions including the College for Women at Western Reserve College (later renamed, Flora Stone Mather College for Women); Sunday School Superintendent, Sereno Fenn, a founding partner at Sherwin-Williams Company; William R. Hopkins, Cleveland's first City Manager who helped pave the way for the construction of the Terminal Tower and the first municipal airport - now called Hopkins International Airport; and Maggie Kuhn who would go on to form the Gray Panthers, one of the largest advocacy groups for senior citizens in America, after she suffered a forced retirement from the former national office of the Presbyterian Church in Pittsburgh.

I was watching an old episode of NBC's Saturday Night Live online during my first year in Cleveland. Candice Bergen was interviewing Maggie Kuhn on the stage of Studio 8H at NBC's headquarters at 30 Rockefeller Plaza. I about jumped out of my seat and pointed at the television screen. "Maggie Kuhn was a member of Old Stone!" I cheered to no one in particular. Keep your Tiffany windows. Apparently, I'm just as impressed with a member of the church who had made an appearance on one of my favorite nighttime comedy shows.

Kuhn was in her early seventies at the time. Bergan asked her what advice she had for the SNL audience, particularly older Americans. Kuhn, with a sweet-sounding voice spoke softly but with a big stick: "Get off your asses and do something!" Words to live by. It appeared to me that Maggie Kuhn had been influenced by many of her brave foremothers and forefathers of the Old Stone Church.

Old Stone's history has paralleled Cleveland's history in many ways since the time that ol' General Moses Cleaveland (correct original spelling), the Connecticut surveyor ascended the banks of Lake Erie at the mouth of the Cuyahoga River looking for a tract of land on which a new town could be planned and exclaimed, "This'll do!" Cleaveland saw great potential for a new settlement which would have both river and lake access.[12] With a "keep the car running, mates" kind of spirit, Cleaveland worked quickly. On July 22, 1796, Cleaveland "named it and claimed it" - surveying the land until October of that same year and then left the area never to return. He never did step into the city to which he had endowed his name. For that, he now has a statue to his honor in Public Square.

The Seneca were also impressed by the same area of land. In fact, they were so impressed that they had already been using the area for occasional hunting grounds for over one hundred years before Cleaveland popped his head up like a gopher to survey the land beyond the banks of the great lake and call it his own, as did the people of the Ojibway settlement just south of the area in what is today known as Brecksville, a suburb of Cleveland. According to the National Parks

---

[12] See Encyclopedia of Cleveland History's cursory summary of Cleaveland's visit. https://case.edu/ech/articles/c/cleaveland-moses (accessed April 7, 2021).

Service, however, few American Indians remained in the Cuyahoga Valley by 1805. Treaties had previously stripped them of their lands and sent them to reservations in western Ohio."[13] To this day, neither the Seneca nor the Ojibway have a statue in Public Square. Personally, and for many reasons, I think a statue to their honor would be an exceptional way of remembering the important people on whose land our European ancestors once settled.

One of those first settlers was Rebecca Carter, a founding member of the Old Stone Church. Rebecca and her husband Lorenzo Carter were the first white settlers to the area not more than a year after Moses Cleaveland had mapped out a plan for the town. A 1976 replica of Lorenzo and Rebecca's cabin sits down by the east bank of the Cuyahoga River in downtown Cleveland. Lorenzo and Rebecca lived out their days hunting, trapping, trading, and spreading the gospel from their home along the banks of the now famous river. Lorenzo died in 1814. A short time later, Rebecca joined the Plan of Union 1801 Sunday school, a national ecumenical partnership between the New England Congregational Churches and the Presbyterian Church in the United States of America. In 1819, the local group began meeting on the second floor of the log cabin courthouse on Public Square. A year later, in 1820, Rebecca, along with fourteen others established the church on Public Square. Ever since, women have continuously played strong leadership roles in and through the church, although, to date, the church has never called a woman to serve as its senior pastor.

Many of Cleveland's great institutions were founded by Old Stone and Old Stone members, including the YMCA of Greater Cleveland, Cleveland State University, Case Western Reserve University, and the first hospital in the city, what is now University Hospitals.

The Old Stone Church also took it upon itself, as part of its great mission to the world, to sponsor many new immigrant communities in Cleveland. The church hosted Sunday school classes for new Americans such as the Ukrainian and Chinese communities that allowed participants to learn how to read and write in the English language by studying the Bible. From its beginnings, the Old Stone

---

[13] National Park Service, Cuyahoga Valley. https://www.nps.gov/cuva/learn/kidsyouth/american-indians.htm. Accessed May 26, 2018.

Church had a great commitment to the care for "the least of these" (Matthew 25:40-45).

Of particular note were the lengths that Old Stone members went to help Cleveland's Chinese community establish itself in the late 1800s and early 1900s, particularly the women's mission group – the "Sisters in Charge." When white Cleveland refused to lease property to the Chinese so that they could set-up laundries for the mill and other factory workers, the Sisters in Charge leased the property themselves and then sublet it back to Chinese businessmen. When the same white establishment refused to sell or lease laundry equipment to Cleveland's Chinese immigrants, the Sisters in Charge purchased it on their behalf. So committed to the Chinese community were the Sisters in Charge, so the story goes, that when two Chinese men were falsely accused of murder, the Sisters in Charge gave them sanctuary inside the church until they could receive a fair and proper trial. The men were eventually acquitted and went on to integrate into the Cleveland community. Cleveland's Asia town and its popular night market are still located just fifteen blocks or so east of the Old Stone Church.

As the city expanded, like spokes jetting out from the hub of a wheel, it spun roads outward from Public Square: East Superior, West Superior, Euclid and Ontario. Public Square – its towering banks, corporate offices, a few new residential office-condo and apartment conversions, a city-center park, and the oldest in situ church in the city remain at the center. It is the very intersection of community and commerce, arts and spirituality - past, present and future.

As I considered a call to become the pastor of Cleveland's historic church, it was abundantly clear to me that this grand dame church in the heart of the city, and with the city at its heart, continued to hold the potential for meaningful leadership in the city's rebirth. As much as I wanted to be a part of a city on the rise, I longed to be a part of the Old Stone Church and its illustrious story. I wondered if I could become a part of that story. To find my home within its on-going narrative.

•   •   •

In the Presbyterian Church, once a candidate has been named and is ready to be presented to the congregation for election, there is often one more step before the vote is taken called, "preaching for the call."

The congregation wants to hear a person preach before they vote. It is sort of like taking a new car out for a test drive before you sign the sales contract. The church wants to give you a test run in their pulpit to hear how your motor sounds in a real-life scenario. I had many more conversations with the search committee since our first meeting in January 2008, and a more formal interview or two, and then returned that spring, Father's Day 2008 to "preach for the call." My sermon was entitled, "A Bright and Blustery Future" – a title that unintentionally would foreshadow my ministry at Old Stone and my time in the city. Following the service, I was escorted to the conference room where I would wait while the congregation debated my worthiness and then voted. All in attendance were in favor of my being called with the exception of one who voted against. I never knew who voted against my coming to Old Stone or why, but I could live with that kind of majority. The leadership plugged me into a receiving line following the vote where each member filed by to shake my hand and congratulate me. With good humor, I made sure to congratulate them, too. After all they had just elected one heck of a new senior pastor! One gentleman, a straight shooting, blue blood business type who would later become one of my lifelong friends, grasped my hand firmly, offered congratulations, and then leaned in to whisper in my ear, "Now, don't screw it up!" Although things would get messy down the road, I pray that I didn't.

• • •

In September 2008, the first day back to the city since being elected to my new position, I circled the Square in my little blue sports car. I kept my eye on the church while also absorbing the fullness of the entire life-sized Public Square diorama. I slipped down an alley beside the church and tucked my car into the little parking spot reserved for the senior pastor. I switched off the ignition and sat for a moment to consider what this new ministry and my new life in Cleveland would hold. I inhaled a few deep centering breaths and prepared myself to enter the building for the first time as the next leader in a succession of great leaders. I was the Twelfth Senior Pastor of the Old Stone Church.

Only after I got my feet firmly planted on the ground and myself fully immersed in my new ministry would I come to understand that the Old Stone Church, like the city it had served since 1820, appeared to be overwhelmed by the conviction that its best days were firmly located in its past. Old Stone, like Cleveland, struggled to find its new self, to carve out a fresh identity for a new millennium, to discover a contemporary spirit within its historic narrative. The grand history of the Old Stone Church, I would only later discover, would be one of the congregation's greatest obstacles. The Spanish philosopher, George Santayana famously stated that, "Those who cannot remember the past are condemned to repeat it." I would propose, however, another axiom: "Those who cannot live beyond their past are doomed to fade with it."

2008-2012: DENIAL

"It's not denial. I'm just selective about the reality I accept."
- Bill Watterson

Chapter Five

Sweating the Small Stuff?

*"It's a hard thing to imagine how somebody copes with grief
and at the same time has to build a new life."*
Caitriona Balfe

——————————

A PASTOR FRIEND of mine once told me about the time that his daughter's rabbit, Bun Bun, died. As you can imagine, it was a terribly sad affair, particularly for his daughter who was just ten-years-old at the time and had never experienced a loss like this before. The family conducted a backyard funeral for Bun Bun. Gathered around a small hole in the earth and a shoebox containing Bun Bun's remains, they offered kind words of remembrance, lifted a prayer of thanks for Bun Bun's life, brief as it was, and then buried Bun-Bun near his favorite patch of grass. The memorial for Bun Bun, the family had hoped, would help ease the burden of the ten-year old's grief.

The next day, after school had let out, my colleague's daughter and her friend charged up to the house to find her dad who was working in the garage. Almost out of breath from excitement, his daughter panted, "Dad, can I get a cat?"

Her father crouched down beside her so he could speak to her face to face. He took her hands in his and offered the wise counsel of a father to a daughter.

"But, Sweetheart," he said, "Bun Bun just died. You need time to grieve."

His doe-eyed daughter was perplexed. "Dad, I'm just a kid," she reasoned. "I grieve quickly!"

While my colleague's daughter may have believed that she could heal quickly following the death of her rabbit, grief for adults tends to inch forward at a much slower pace. My grief over the loss of our life in Savannah and the stress of adapting to the coarser edges of Cleveland would take just a little longer to process. I was learning to take the small, seemingly insignificant things in stride. To not sweat the small stuff, as the late Richard Carlson urged us to do many years ago.

I could handle the big stuff – the rising rates of unemployment, poverty, and crime, the crumbling infrastructure and corruption in our local government. Those were things happening to others. In part, those kinds of challenges were what drew me to Cleveland in the first place. I wanted to be the senior pastor of a great city church, one with a proud history of being a regional beacon of light in a dark time such that it was. I had come to be a pastor to others who were hurting, others who needed to hear some good news in the midst of bad. I just didn't expect to be one of them.

It's rarely the major life events that break us, though, or cause us to wave our white flag of emotional surrender. More often than not, it's the accumulative effect of successive small occurrences that give us the most trouble. The sour milk we unwittingly poured into our morning coffee. Our lost keys that refused to be found on the day we were running late for work. Our phone that we forgot to charge overnight and discovered only as we were dialing in to our important conference call. The lack of sleep from the night before. Like the interest on an unpaid debt, the small things compound. They add up.

From 2008 to 2010, it was the small challenges, the unanticipated surprises that came with my new life in this old city that challenged me.

For starters, I didn't expect to get sucker-punched within the first few months of my arrival in Cleveland. I wasn't expecting to get sucker punched at all. By the time you are in your forties you assume your days of getting entangled in physical altercations are mostly behind you altogether. But still, this is Cleveland.

Striding through Cleveland's Public Square on my way to work one chilly autumn morning, my focus was on the new-to-me erratic winds of Northeast Ohio, and the sandblast of cold autumn rain they brought with them. Bracing myself against the tornadic force as it whipped its way through the concrete towers in the heart of the city, I angled my trusty umbrella sideways into the wind to sturdy myself against the elements with my wire and nylon targe shield of defense. I joked to Beth, who walked alongside me behind the protective shield of my umbrella, that I felt like Batman and Robin with the Bat Shield out in front blocking them from potential oncoming harm. It didn't really work for me like it did for Batman, though.

Without warning, I simultaneously felt and heard a thud crunching into my face. My whole head snapped back as if I had just been clotheslined by a tree branch. With my hand, I reached for my mouth to make sure that my teeth were still there. I stared dumbfounded at the twisted metal shaft of my umbrella and for a very brief moment, wondered if I had inadvertently collided with a pole or the side of a car or, what felt like the front end of a Mack Truck.

As it turned out, I hadn't experienced an unexpected collision with any obstacle whatsoever, unless you count the heel of a three-hundred-pound man's hand jamming an umbrella down your throat an unexpected collision with an obstacle, which I suppose you can since when I turned to face him he looked to me about the size of a city bus. Unlike one of our fine city buses, however, the man staring me down from just mere feet away was not in motion. He was just standing there in the middle of our shared crosswalk with a stare of indifference as if to say, "That's right, I just mashed the stem of your umbrella into your face. So what are you going to do about it?"

My office is one short half-block from the Cleveland Justice Center. I could easily imagine that this elephantine monster who now locked me in his sights, grunting and growling in my direction, pawing the ground readying himself to trample me, may have just been released from lock-up. Maybe he had been celled-up all night in the drunk tank and was cranky and sore and, upon his release, had a primordial need to punch wimpy Cleveland newcomer in the mouth. Or, perhaps, this Goliath had just left the jail following a miserable, plexiglass-visit with a guy who owed him money – gooey telephone handset pressed to the side of his pudgy potato-shaped ears as he mumbled something to his debtor about getting his money or else needing to break the kneecaps of a loved one. Or, maybe he had just gone to pay the bail for his older, hairier, and much bigger, soon-to-be-released brother.

Heck, I didn't know what this guy's problem was. Maybe he just didn't like the look of me and my umbrella.

The only thing I was certain of was that I wasn't interested in losing any more teeth or even mussing-up my freshly pressed Men's Warehouse suit and tie. Call me a wimp. Call me a daisy. Call me whatever the heck you like, just make sure you do it while we are speeding down the street in retreat from any teeth-exacting Cleveland crushers on Public Square because that's where I will be.

It took almost my whole first year in Cleveland for the dental surgeon and dentist to get me fixed-up. It was a drawn out period of dental surgery, which included the extraction of the remaining stump of my front tooth by way of some double-edged, medieval auger-type torture implement (if I said that the surgeon's equipment was rusty, you might say I was exaggerating, so I'll leave that part out). The surgeon then bone-grafted a titanium implant up into my maxilla – the front part of my upper jaw where my late lateral incisor once lived. For the six months the bone graft would take to anchor itself permanently in my mouth, I was fitted with a temporary plastic roof-of-my-mouth insert and single fake tooth called a 'flapper' that made me sound drunk when I tried to talk or, worse, preach with it in my mouth. When I dared to eat with it, the dummy tooth and flapper made me look like a dog trying to chew gum. This wasn't a good look for the new pastor who had many lunch meetings and events to attend. I opted, instead, to simply apologize, turn and remove the offending mouth piece with my cloth napkin, turn back to my table mates with my toothless grin, and apologize again. Finally, a brand new, bright and shiny lateral incisor was manually screwed into the two-thousand-dollar metal socket in my jaw. When all was said and done, my biggest disappointment was that my new fake tooth didn't match its neighbors well, not in color or the direction it was angled. Still, I would learn to live with it. I tried to slough-off the embarrassment of getting my front tooth punched out by joking that it just seemed ironic that I had lived in Georgia for almost ten years, but came north - all the way to Cleveland, to lose a tooth in the first three months. Weird.

•   •   •

Life in a Northern town ("Heya ma ma ma") can be hard, especially when that town is Cleveland, Ohio. Cleveland isn't just rough at the edges, it's tough everywhere. It was far scrappier than I had imagined when I first visited for my various interviews and conversations with the search team months earlier. Clearly, during those times I must have been in denial, choosing to see only what I wanted to see – a renown historic church, a great American city ready to rise, and a search committee generous of spirit who, in spite of their incredulous attitude about my desire to leave Savannah and come to Cleveland, welcomed us into their lives and into their hearts. But still, when I arrived, the street life in Cleveland caught me off guard.

I didn't have any misplaced notions that Clevelanders would exhibit the gracious civility or walking gentility of Savannah, of course, but Cleveland could have done with a little less pedestrian vulgarity for my liking. I had never lived in a place where so many people laid down so much of their nasally body fluid – aka "snot" on the very concrete where they and others walked.

Do you remember that disgusting scene in Steve Spielberg's 1990s monster blockbuster, Jurassic Park, when Nerdy, played by Wayne Knight (aka Seinfeld's "Newman"), gets splattered in the face by a great big gob of greasy grimy Dilophosaurus spit? That's what I saw in Cleveland. Bipeds moving through the streets of downtown while hawking up loogies, expectorating wads of phlegm and smearing the sidewalk with glistening gobs of goo.

Were these sputum sprayers going for distance or accuracy? It was hard to tell. Maybe both. It certainly seemed like a skillfully crafted art, one passed down, perhaps, not from father to son since I also saw some, albeit fewer, women spitting, but from generation to generation the way cultures preserve their unique and special talents. For centuries, for example, the Italians of the Venetian island of Murano have been known for their exceptionally crafted and beautiful artistic glass. The Manganeses de la Polvorosa people of Spain are famous for their, now banned, goat throwing. Jamaicans are the best barefoot runners in the world. There are no barefoot runners in Cleveland, though. They wouldn't want to step in spit!

Sometimes I took the spitting personally. As I approached on the sidewalk, I often heard people – mostly men, but sometimes women, too, gravel-up a wad of rattling catarrh from somewhere deep within the back of their throats and then, just as I passed, turn their heads and fire-off their globular projectile to some particular target on the concrete not too far from my right foot or my left.

It was almost exclusively men who spat when Beth and I walked together. Beth turned to me one afternoon after a man had just sprayed saliva in front of us and asked, "Is he marking territory?"

Yes, it's disgusting. I know. Please don't shoot the messenger. I'm just issuing a word of caution. Early one evening, Beth and I were walking on Cleveland's main drag, Euclid Avenue, when we saw our neighbor approaching in a 'boot,' one of those Velcro, strap on casts wrapped around her leg.

"What happened?" we asked in unison while looking down at her foot with compassionate concern.

"Ugh" she groaned. "I slipped in some sidewalk spit and twisted my ankle!"

Spend some time on the sticky streets of Cleveland. Just do it at your own risk. They can bring you down in more ways than one!

•   •   •

It wasn't just the spitting that made the streets of downtown Cleveland uninviting those early days in Cleveland, it was also the male-on-female glaring. Is that how a Cleveland man tells a woman he is interested in a relationship? Just stare at her with come-hither eyes and drooling smile (maybe excess drool is why they spit so much) until somehow, by the powerful strength of his Svengali-concentration, the woman of interest will be drawn toward him? There is no attempt at subtlety or discretion, not even a tip of the hat or a how do you do. On Cleveland streets, somedays it is a free-for-all id-gone-wild experience. Just hardcore staring, maybe a suggestive eyeing up and down just so the woman really gets the point.

Beth calls it 'tracking.' Some Cleveland men are trackers. They will lock a woman in their sites and track her as she approaches, and then leer at her until she has fully passed by. It's not just his eyes that track her, either. Cleveland men track with the whole face, the head spinning like the tip of a needle on a compass aiming for true north until she moves by fully, or until the next woman moves into view. Heaven help the woman who accidentally makes eye contact with a tracker. She will most certainly be propositioned. Numerous times Beth received proposals from men on the street – whether I was there with her or not, and often from such eligible bachelors as the panhandler at East 9th, or the homeless guy on Public Square. At least these guys have good taste in women.

Some days, Cleveland's streets and sidewalks were disappointingly far removed from the grace, the etiquette, and the sophistication of what Jane Jacobs, in her book The Death and Life of Great American Cities, described as the "ballet of the good city sidewalk." I would say that there were times when Cleveland streets resembled something more akin to Wrestlemania weekend on the WWE network than a ballet but I'm afraid that might be a put-down to wrestlers everywhere.

• • •

Riding public transit wasn't any more inviting than walking, though Cleveland does have an exceptional transit system, the Greater Regional Rapid Transit Authority - affectionally referred to as the RTA. The RTA does a remarkable job providing decent public transportation in spite of the fact that it is woefully underfunded by the state. Cleveland was one of the first cities in America to connect its airport to downtown via rail. More recently its newer award-winning, eco-friendly Health Line has connected downtown with uptown, University Circle - the cultural epicenter of Northeast Ohio. Since it started operation in late 2008, the Health Line has spawned a great deal of economic development along the roughly five-mile, twenty-five-minute route from Circle to Square, as well.

When Beth and I first came to Cleveland, we sublet a little apartment "up the hill" on Lennox Avenue in Cleveland Heights. I was excited to be able to walk down to the University Circle stop on the transit rail's Red Line - a one or two car train that would take me directly to Public Square in the morning, and then return me at night. "I'll have time to clear my head or read a book," I mused about my new car-free life as a public transit user.

Riding the rails, however, didn't turn out to be the joy I had hoped it would be. My attention each morning was devoted to survival! I often encountered public drunkenness, drug deals waiting to go bad, and volatile conflicts between riders. It was an affront to my soft-spoken Canadian politeness and Savannahian civility.

During one particular autumn morning commute, I found myself caught in the DMZ between two embattled riders unabashedly shouting at one another from one end of the car to the other. Lobbing a barrage of F-bombs and other explosive expletives back and forth over the heads of the other riders on the train, a spray of accusations whistled like bullets from a gun over top of our heads. A gun, of course, was my real concern, as it was for every other commuter on the train that morning. I quickly scrolled through my mental files searching for a "Lord, don't let us get killed today!" prayer.

The young woman at the front of the car, perhaps an older teenager, seemed to be on the defensive but was stomping her feet like a raging bull and screaming at the top of her lungs something about someone who slept with someone else's boyfriend, or girlfriend, or cousin, or all of the above. I couldn't follow it if I had a roadmap.

The person at the back of the car was of a similar age. He was a young male rider, roughly seventeen or eighteen years of age, wearing a baggy green quilted nylon coat. I tried to memorize his appearance in the way that I assumed I would be making an eye-witness report for the police sometime before my morning commute had come to a full and complete stop. That was if I survived. This guy called her every name in the big book of profanities. I recognized most of his terms, but admittedly, not all of them. He didn't appear to be gardener but he used the word "hoe" a lot.

Amidst the flurry of hate-filled comments, we heard him use a phrase that we all recognized: "I'm gonna shoot your f---ing head off, bitch." This was the moment at which we all dove down in our seats and began praying in earnest.

Something remarkable, actually quite honest and beautiful happened, though. A humbly dressed, thirty-something year-old man sitting with what appeared to be his six-year old son turned in his seat and, face to face, addressed the man at the back of the train. "Hey! There are kids present here. Why don't you ease up a bit?" Concerned that he was just provoking the couple, stoking a fire that was already flaming out of control, I considered shushing, Dad: "Hey, buddy, there's a cowering pastor present here. Why don't you ease up a bit!" There was no need. With that one comment about not scaring a child, the situation had been deescalated.

Clevelanders are decent people. They handle confrontation directly, I was learning, and with an appeal to an altruism, particularly when kids were present. If you can't not shoot your woman down because, well, that's murder, then please do it for the kids.

By the time we got to the Tower City terminal, the young woman was standing at the front door to our train and ready to dash-off into the protective arms of the RTA police. Truth be told, so was I!

A friend of mine wasn't so lucky. His head was mule kicked by a handful of hooligans, his jaw broken in numerous ways and places, while simply standing by the track waiting for his train. It took major surgery and months following for him to physically recover. His tragic experience was hardly small stuff. I wonder if his emotional scars will ever heal. However, his story increased my anxieties about using public transportation. My daily commutes were far more stressful than, perhaps, they needed to be. "Show me a map of your public transit system, and I will show you a map of your freedom," Jarrett Walker has wisely stated. I'm just not sure that same image would have shown Clevelanders a map of their safety fifteen years ago. Walker argues, that our "transit agency's vehicles and staff may fail to meet the most basic standards for civility, safety, and comfort"[14] which ultimately discourages ridership as it did for me in Cleveland in 2008.

• • •

Underneath those early distractions and disappointments in Cleveland I savored the adventure. I was energized by the liminal world I was inhabiting. The yet but not yet. I was nowhere. No longer a Savannahian. Not yet a Clevelander. I was transitioning from a former self and discovering my new self. In fact, I was homeless. I was Mark Giuliano of 'no permanent address' – a humble sub-leaser of a furnished one-bedroom apartment. "Please forward all my mail to my office," I often instructed family and friends, "I'm only in this apartment until mid-October." I shrugged off my sense of dislocation and added, "I'm not sure where I'll be after that." My time of my final destination was still unknown.

No sooner than we had arrived in Cleveland than Beth and I were informed by our condo developer that the completion of our unit needed to be pushed back by a couple of extra months. The build out of the old 1904 office conversion in downtown was just going a little more slowly than he had anticipated, he said, as he asked for our patience.

The delay didn't seem like that big of a deal at the time so we rolled with it. Sure, all our belongings – the bulk of our wardrobe, all of our furniture, family photo albums, CDs, DVDs, stereo, and all those other personal life artifacts that bless a person with a familiar sense of homey comfort, were still in storage in some mystery location and had been for months. We had come this far, half a year of carting our lives around in the back seat of our little hatchback. What difference would another nomadic month or two make? We chose to see the delay as a nothing more than a bump on the uneven road of our great Cleveland adventure, a glitch on the itinerary though we were eager to make it

---

[14] Jarrett Walker, *Human Transit: How Clearer Thinking about Public Transit Can Enrich Our Communities and Our Lives*, Island Press, 2012, https://humantransit.org/book, accessed May 28, 2021.

home to our not-yet-ready condo in downtown – whenever that time would come.

Little did we know that our contractor's delay was only the first of many blips to come in the sordid story of our dream home. In time, we would find ourselves living a nightmare that would move us to the brink of personal bankruptcy, rob us of our life's meager savings, and drive me almost hair-pulling, teeth-grinding mad over the next ten years.

For the time being our things could remain in storage – wherever that was - for a couple of more months. It really wasn't that big of a deal. When the owner of our Cleveland Heights apartment returned and our sublet expired, we could find another furnished apartment – maybe closer to downtown. We just kept rolling forward while quietly praying that we might be in our new home by Christmas.

If you have ever had a house or condo completely built from shell to finish, you have learned – likely the hard way, that closing dates are really just arbitrary numbers on an extremely fluid timeline. They are designed to get you to offer-up an earnest check and a sizeable down payment to put the developer in motion. In reality, your move-in date is a free-floating number that gets blown about by the winds of any number of seen and unforeseen variables. When a contractor offers you a move-in date, that date is a lot like one of those little squiggly specks, floaters, in your eye that you see swimming around at the edge of your peripheral vision. You can see it vaguely hiding there at the corner of your eye, but every time you try to lock in on to it, the speck glides from your sight. Your move in date is always moving. In time you start to believe, less and less, of anything that comes out of your builder's mouth.

For the first time in twenty years, Beth and I were learning to live as empty-nesters. Our kids were off to other places in the world, starting exciting new lives of their own, and Beth and I found ourselves confronted with the invigorating reality of trying to figure out who we were going to be on our own.

We had a lot of great times that sustained us, too. "For everything there is a season," says the Book of Ecclesiastes. This was the season of Mark and Beth – sans les enfants! We missed the kids but there were also certain joys about being honeymooners again. For the first time in over twenty years we were savoring the freedom to do what we wanted and when we wanted without the daily demands of our two busy children, the first of whom had arrived in our lives just two years into our marriage. Our cool little Cleveland Heights apartment was perfect for two new empty-nesters, too, albeit temporary. With no Wifi or even a television to distract us, we spent many evenings drinking Italian wine, listening to jazz on a shoebox-sized boom box and dreaming aloud together about our new life in Cleveland as fresh September breezes whispered to us through open windows. Other evenings we held hands and walked the block over from our Lennox Avenue apartment to the popular Heights night club, Nighttown, for dinner and live music. Some evenings, after work, we opted to stay downtown to try out one of Cleveland's amazing new eateries in the Warehouse District on East 4th before heading-off by foot to cheer our way through the last period or two of a hockey game.

Fridays were our sabbath days to rest, play, and discover. We eased our way into those mornings with fresh brewed coffee and bagels at our local Bruegger's and then set out for a day's adventure to explore Cleveland. Our trips led us to such delights as the remarkable Westside Market, Ohio City's historic indoor/outdoor market and oldest in the city of Cleveland. Sometimes we topped a visit to the market with lunch just down the street at the popular Nates Deli on West 25th - a favorite for locals – for some of the tastiest fattoosh, hommus, falafels and baba ganooj anywhere. Other Fridays we strolled, hand in hand, along the lake, or took a hike in one of Cleveland's spectacular metro parks, and then squeezed our way into Parma's Little Polish Diner for, in my newcomer's opinion, some of the best potato and onion pierogis in the city, unless you're buying them fresh at the market.

These were the pleasant distractions, gifts from our new hometown. They helped heal me from my small bout of empty-nest syndrome. Like the guy who, after all those years of knowing better, walks out into the street without looking both ways, I never saw it coming. I needed that time of curious discovery, a Cleveland honeymoon, to help me transition to my new life in Cleveland. Call it denial, if you like. But for the bad rap it takes, all the negativity associated with it, even denial has a way of blessings us. Elisabeth Kübler-Ross said that "Denial helps us to pace our feelings of grief. There is a grace in denial. It is nature's way of letting in only as much as we can handle."[15] Those charming days of novelty and discovery were like a shoehorn that eased my Savannah-shaped feet into my new Cleveland-sized shoes, while preparing me for the hard work ahead.

Even my son, Dylan, who lives in Toronto came to enjoy the newness of Cleveland and our enthusiasm for it. Dylan called me on the phone one afternoon with a proposal: "Hey, Dad, I see that Alice Cooper is playing in Cleveland in a couple weeks. Why don't we get tickets and go together?" The Cooper concert in Lakewood, a nearby suburb of Cleveland, was great fun, although I lost my hearing for a few days after forgetting to bring my earplugs to the show. More importantly, though, Dylan's visit proved to be just what I needed to jump start my new life as an empty nester. He came for the weekend. We were so happy to see him that Beth and I kidnapped him for three full weeks.

•　　•　　•

We were a half a year into our Cleveland experiment when our sublet expired. It was time for us to find a new place and move again. We squeezed all our things into suitcases and handy plastic travel bins, lugged them down the three flights of stairs we had just months earlier hauled them up, stuffed them into the trunk and backseat of our hatchback again, carefully laying my suits and some of Beth's things on hangers across our luggage, and then drove our way into downtown and to our new temporary home. Eager to live closer to work and to be in the city-center vibe, we found a furnished two-bedroom unit in an old loft-style warehouse conversion called the Bingham that made life feel a lot like we were living in a college dorm. The halls reeked of soggy pizza boxes and other takeout containers.

---

15 Found on Elizabeth Kübler-Ross Foundation, https://www.ekrfoundation.org/elisabeth-kubler-ross/quotes/ (accessed April 27, 2021).

There was lots of loud music and late-night parties, and in the wee hours, fire alarms often blared because some drunk inexperienced partier yanked the red switch on the wall. The first time or two, Beth and I even got up and left the building on the off chance that there was a real fire smoldering in that charming old building. Most other times we just poked our heads into the hallway to ask neighbors what the fuss was all about before closing the door and going back to bed.

We weren't in our permanent home yet, but it was good to finally be living downtown. There was an energy about life in the city. We were beginning to connect with other new downtown residents for happy hours and dinners, trading stories of the joys and challenges of living in a city that wasn't quite used to having many people living in its core.

In spite of still being transient, I was excited about the coming of Christmas, too. It would be our first Cleveland Christmas, and we would celebrate with the good folks of the Old Stone Church for the very first time. Beth and I tried to make our generic loft as homey as possible to reflect our good cheer. We assembled our Charlie Brown Christmas tree - the three-foot artificial tree we had borrowed from the church. We bumped it up a bit, giving it a little extra height by setting it up on top of one of our gray plastic car trunk travel bins and warmed it by wrapping the base with a small red table cloth. We adorned the tree with decorations that family and friends had sent to us in the mail, or ones we picked-up on the cheap at a department store in the nearby Steelyard Commons shopping plaza. It was a pretty humble Christmas tree, as was the entire Christmas season that year. Even so, our kids traveled to Cleveland to be with us for the holidays. We gathered together with our new church family to celebrate the birth of Jesus in the spectacular sanctuary of the Old Stone Church on Christmas Eve – pine boughs and red velvet bows adorning the rich woods of the balcony and choir loft, oversized wreathes impressively hung behind the pulpit, and then walked out into the crisp night air to enjoy the bright lights of the season on Public Square. On Christmas morning, we huddled together under blankets in our drafty little loft. We didn't have much that first Christmas in Cleveland but we did have each other and that was all that truly mattered. Their visit was the greatest gift our kids could have ever given us. Cleveland was beginning to feel like home.

• • •

In Cleveland, even around the holidays, joy can be fleeting. Like Christmas and New Year's celebrations, our kids had come and gone. The week after New Year's, I was at a restaurant having lunch with some men from the church. I bit down on a piece of crusty bread and heard a crack at the back of my mouth. I had split a molar. Yes, on a piece of bread! Like a huge chunk of ice breaking away from an arctic glacier, my tooth had fissured from the surface all the way down to some dark, throbbing place of pain beneath my gum line. For the rest of the lunch, I grimaced a forced smile while attempting to engage in polite conversation. I didn't want to disclose to the others my inner panic about another lost tooth. As soon as lunch was over, I drove directly to my dentist's office. He took one look in my mouth and groaned, "Mark, I am so sorry to tell you this but that whole tooth will have to be surgically removed, and now!" Later that evening, in the living room of our downtown rental, as I stuffed cotton balls into my mouth and tried not to spit blood so that the cavernous hole in the back of my jaw could heal, our developer called with more bad news. Our condo still had work to be done on it. He needed to push back our move-in date again.

"How much more time do you think you'll need?" I mumbled through the cotton balls.

"At least another two months."

I tried not to cry. Or swear.

I whispered to myself, "Mark, don't sweat the small stuff . . . Soon. Soon, we will be home."

Chapter Six

Home?

"No house should ever be on a hill or on anything. It should be of the hill. Belonging to it. Hill and house should live together each the happier for the other."

Frank Lloyd Wright

_____

IT HAD BEEN more than eight full months since we wrapped up the "stuff" of our lives, carefully snugging it into the small crates and purchased packing boxes from the container store on Wilmington Island, sealing it all up with the gummy packing tape that always seemed to run out and send us back to the store for more. Like well-preserved time capsules containing trinkets and treasures for some future generation - or at least our future selves in Cleveland, we had judiciously entombed all of our belongings, everything we assumed that we could live without for a few months while we were in transition.

You never realize how much stuff you have accumulated until you make a move. We held our garage sale, hauled our leftovers out onto the driveway expecting some passerby to pick it up – one person's treasure is another person's clutter, and we made countless trips to the Goodwill, feeling just a little embarrassed every time we returned to unload another car-full of odds and ends. Still, we were left with a mountain of boxes and furniture to move and store and then move again before finally landing in our new condo in downtown Cleveland. Such was the stuff of our lives.

It had been seven months and ten days, but who's counting, since July 4th - the day we had waved goodbye to the moving van and driver that would transport our belongings to storage in some unknown location on this continent, or perhaps another, while we waited for our condo in Cleveland to be constructed. When the mover told us that he wasn't sure where our stuff would be stored, that he would take our things only so far before they would be transferred into a storage container by another crew, we joked that maybe our stuff would be shipped offshore by one of the many ocean-going freighters we often saw leaving the port of Savannah. Who knows? Maybe it was. We told family and friends that our things would be stored in Omaha, just so that we could hear them shout, "Omaha?!" with incredulity. Which they did. It helped make the in-between time of our move seem more like an adventure than the annoyance it had become. For the better part of a year, we were nomads moving from summer rental to extended stays with family and friends, and then back to another summer rental, before moving to Cleveland Heights apartment to downtown apartment, and finally, to condo. Home.

Our Cleveland developer was still telling us that, to really finish things up with our condo, he needed another month or so. It was the "or so" that troubled me the most. He was a well-intentioned guy and I could see how dedicated he was to the overall project. This was his baby. Some of the work he was doing in our unit and in a couple of the others was beginning to take shape, too. High end finishes, custom cabinetry, and the preservation of original maple floors and other hardwoods throughout were impressive. The fact that our developer was restoring all the original oak doors and window frames and not simply ripping them out and substituting them with cheaper ones lacking in historic and skillful craft, or tearing-up the original floors and replacing them with veneers or, worse, eco-hostile carpets was one of the reasons we invested in the Park Building project rather than buying a home in a more modern building, or one where developers used more cost efficient but mass produced and generic-looking finishes.

Even so, we were just plain old tired of waiting. Tired of living out of our suitcases. Tired of negotiating sublets and temporary leases for furnished apartments. Tired of always feeling like we were sleeping in someone else's bed. Tired of notifying family, friends, and the US Postal Service of new forwarding addresses. Tired of calling the moving company and being stuck on hold to talk with a real, living, breathing human being in customer service to extend our storage agreement. Mostly, we were tired of being ready to set down roots but not having any soil yet in which we could plant ourselves.

"You're ready enough," I growled at our developer one afternoon. I was scheduling the movers to haul our stuff out of storage and deliver it to our new place whether it was fully ready or not. The fact was, we were done with waiting.

Without a certificate of occupancy, which I'm not sure is entirely legal, and without the closing papers in hand, we took up squatter's rights in our new, almost completed condo on Public Square in downtown Cleveland on February 14th, 2009. It was Valentine's Day but for Beth and me it felt more like Christmas.

We were giddy with excitement. Like kids tearing through gifts found under the tree on Christmas morning, we ripped open our dusty moving boxes.

With each item unboxed, there was another surprise.

"Oh, I totally forgot about this!" I shouted to Beth from the study.

"Oh, did we keep that?" Beth laughed with surprise.

"Oh, my goodness, where will we put these?" we stood in the living room and wondered aloud while holding some oversized object from another place and time.

When they were just grade schoolers, my kids played a game one afternoon where they wrapped up their own toys in brightly colored Christmas paper and then exchanged them with one another as gifts which, ultimately, they were. After all, isn't everything we own a gift? They loved the joy of giving and receiving, and the delightful surprise, real or feigned, of opening their gifts to one another. In a way, that's what Beth and I had done when we packed and stored our stuff only to receive it later in the year.

It's odd how important the material things of our lives can seem at any given moment along our journey. Us and our stuff. We're interconnected. I'm defined by what I own and, more poignantly, by what owns me. My identity is shaped by the things in my life, and the life in my things – the memories, stories, and activities connected to those things. Change the context, however, or move a few more steps down the road, and those things can seem dramatically out of place. Foreign. As if they belong to somebody else's life.

In our unpacking, there were many moments when our present selves wondered about the contents that had been shipped to us from our past selves. So many things from our Savannah life just didn't align with our unfolding lives in downtown Cleveland. Where would we hang the wispy water colors of the pastoral scenes of Savannah's Sabal and Pindo palms in our hardscaped urban condo that was more window than wall? Or the soft-focused Bryan Stovall photographs of Lowcountry marsh grass and tidal creeks? For that matter, where would we place our bulky nine-foot sofa and complementing patterned chair from Rooms2Go - the Garanimals of late twentieth century American home-design meant to fill out the cavernous spaces and gluttonous square footage of our suburban home? It worked so well in our Wilmington Island 'McMansion.' The visual space in our new condo was overwhelmed by the large wooden entertainment unit, billowy brown couches and oversized burgundy chairs. Our new home looked like a used furniture store, a bargain barn jammed full of second-hand furnishings that belonged to a different family - strangers from a bygone time and place.

Still, packing paper flew and fluttered through the air, falling like beige wrapping paper on Christmas morning. Bubble wrap was unwrapped, snapped and popped filling our new apartment with cheerful sounds reminiscent of the colorful Christmas crackers that adorned our family table, and even New Year's fireworks.

• • •

From the beginning there was some question as to whether our Public Square condo could be a home for us. We certainly wanted it to be. Throughout the years to come, we experimented with a lot of different things to try and make it homey if not a home, decorating and arranging furniture in certain ways, gathering lots of people for dinners and parties to help us fill the place with love and friendships. One by one, we connected with new neighbors as they moved into the building throughout those first couple of years. We got ourselves engaged in the life and work of the broader community just beyond our doors, too. Are these not, after all, the things that make a house a home?

Physically speaking, though, our condo just didn't look like any home we had ever lived in before. In his 1953 poem, The Things, Conrad Aiken wrote of his move North from Savannah:

"No longer the chinaberry tree nor the dark mockingbird to sing his glee nor prawns nor catfish; icicles instead and Indian-pipes, and cider in the shed"

For me, my move from Savannah to Cleveland meant that there was no longer the sweeping front porch, nor back screened-in lanai, nor woven seagrass chairs to rest on while Beth and I, and sometime even the kids, visited from sunset to long past dusk; no longer centipede grass or wisteria and wildflower gardens exploding with color to gaze meditatively upon as hissing sprinklers quenched them in the early morning, rainbows forming above misted green petals and blades of grass. No longer were there flowering winter camellias or springtime azaleas, nor palms or live oak trees, home to singing cicadas, crickets, and draperies of Spanish moss - which really isn't moss, that blessed us with cool shade on hot afternoons and always with beauty.

Our condo, on the other hand, had a temporary feel to it. It looked like an apartment. It was an apartment.

Admittedly, our place was dramatic. And inviting. A path of rich mocha-colored slate tiles welcomed all who entered through the double-wide vestibule which opened on to a warm, contemporary great room. The soft honey-colored walls made a perfect backdrop for the contrasting full-sized black marble mantle and gas fireplace, the dark wood frames of our many expansive windows, and the restored original maple floors. Ours was one of the largest units in the building. With sixteen hundred square feet – huge for the price and unique location overlooking the Square, especially compared to a New York or Toronto apartment, we enjoyed three full bedrooms including our primary bedroom with oversized walk-in closet and fully-complimented en suite bath. Ours was a corner unit as well, which meant that we were often flooded with natural light in the daytime, and enjoyed the dramatic lights of the city at night.

One of the things we missed, however, was personal outdoor space. We'd been spoiled in Savannah where we sipped coffee in the mornings on our lanai, wrapped in our housecoats, while listening to the morning birds sing their awakening songs to us, or enjoying the simple pleasure of a glass of wine in the cooling of evening as hummingbird moths sipped nectar from the deep purple Mexican petunias in our gardens. Our condo offered no place for flowers or gardens, no soil in which we could dig, plant and grow living things, things of beauty. With the noise of the city surrounding us, we opened our windows only on rare occasions, a warm and quiet Sunday afternoon or Saturday morning when a fresh breeze was blowing, perhaps.

Our building lacked a rooftop deck, too. Instead, innovative owners made do with unofficial access to the rooftop of the neighboring building. We were overjoyed when we discovered a way to access the rooftop of the adjacent six-story Southworth Building - the gutted warehouse building that almost connected to our building.

With the exception of two other couples who had moved in the same weekend as Beth and me, our nine-story, twenty-one-unit building was almost entirely unfinished and vacant for months. At night we often had the run of the place and so did a great deal of exploring. At the end of our hallway there was a door that led nowhere. Well, actually, it led four stories straight down. Workers had planked a few long boards in a makeshift bridge between our building and the Southworth next door. When we were feeling particularly daring, Beth and I would edge out across those fifteen-foot long, open-air planks and alley four stories beneath us. Once across the precarious bridge, by flashlight, or phone-light, we could navigate the various rooms of the old warehouse – some dusty, others musty – until we reached the shadowy stairwell that would lead to the roof.

Our particular unit in the Park Building did have a miniscule space directly outside the back window of our den - the room we use to affectionately refer to as the urinal room since, before being converted to a condo, it once served as a men's bathroom for the old Park Building offices. During the tear-down, we saw three perfectly aligned pipe holes in the concrete floor – the tell-tale giveaway of the location for the three porcelain urinals belonging to the one-time bathroom. The narrow deck beyond the window was the rooftop of what would eventually become our neighbor's study beneath it. On the design plans for our unit, our builder euphemistically labeled it as "Mark and Beth's terrace" – an overstatement if ever there was one. To access the terrace required climbing a ladder and crawling out the window.

To fully imagine this unique outdoor space, picture the bottom of a twenty-foot deep concrete pool. The floor is dry and surfaced with a layer of sandy grit. An empty potato chip bag and an old crumpled beer can have blown down into the hole from the roof of the neighboring building, or have been tossed there by a rooftop construction worker. Imprinted into the stretched membrane surface of our terrace are the crusty remains of a dead bird. Now imagine the walls squeezed together. The terrace is just fifteen-feet long and six-feet wide. You can almost reach out and touch both dingy grey walls at the very same time. Inhale deeply through your nose. Do you smell that occasional whiff of sewer gas that wafts up through the drain pipe at one end? If you do, then you have a pretty good idea of what Beth and I mean when we referred to our condo's terrace.

We made an admirable attempt to dress up the cramped concrete space with a jade-colored indoor-outdoor carpet, some woven nylon deck furniture that we picked up from the year 1965, and some shade-hardy plants that made every effort to survive by nursing the one hour of direct sunlight that the deck received on those rare days when the sun shone. Still, construction workers, not knowing anyone might be down there, continued to flick cigarette butts and toss trash down on our humble terrace.

Later, I reinforced a stair-stepped Ikea bookcase and installed it under the window. It was my inventive, do-it-yourself staircase solution to make accessing the deck easier and appear more intentional though you still had to crawl through the window. I stopped calling it the terrace and simply referred to it as our "Friends" balcony, though that is being generous since Rachel and Monica's cool Lower Manhattan digs on the television show Friends actually had a view, albeit of "ugly naked guy" who lived in the building next to them. Ours didn't have a view at all. It was just brick walls going up five stories on one side, and two stories on the other.

I understand that private outdoor space in any urban context, particularly in larger cities, is a truly desirous amenity. I am sure New Yorkers reading this right now are shaking their heads and shouting, "You have a six by fifteen-foot outdoor space attached to your condo? Quit your belly-aching! There's so many creative things you could do to make that space work!" which, in fact, I did – with a little help from a very talented friend.

In early 2014, I invited Diana Balmori, the renowned urban landscape architect, to speak at Old Stone's annual Hope for the City symposium. Architectural Digest (AD) had just named Diana as a top ten innovator of 2013. She was a perfect fit with our program. While in town, Beth and I invited Diana to our home for a light lunch overlooking the Square. I was both honored and humbled to have someone of her caliber in my home and breaking bread at our table. After lunch, I sheepishly reminded her that AD had stated that no job was too big or small for Diana or her Manhattan based architectural firm. I even brought out the article and showed her where Fred Bernstein, the author of the article, had said that she would even "tackle a backyard if it gives her a chance to experiment. She worked with architect Joel Sanders on a Bedford, New York, property whose stone deck twists like a Möbius strip into a retaining wall."[16]

Diana was an exceptional person who had just won a bid to design a huge, multi-billion-dollar project in Korea. She and her company had also recently designed an ingenious water diversion projects for a major city here in America. Why on earth I ever imagined that she might help us with our pocket-sized urban terrace, I didn't know.

The set-up was obvious. Diana smiled knowingly and played along anyway. I led her into our den, the AD article still in my hand, to show her our Friends balcony and asked if she thought it was

---

[16] Fred A. Bernstein, Architectural Digest, "AD Innovator: Diana Balmori," September 30, 2013. Accessed June 20, 2018.
https://www.architecturaldigest.com/story/diana-balmori-ad-innovators-2013-article.

beyond hope. Amazingly, she didn't laugh at me, although she did chuckle with me as it was the smallest project she had ever been asked to work on.

Diana graciously agreed to create something from nothing for our tiny urban space. She assigned one of her interns to take the lead on our project and Balmori and Associates came up with a spectacular urban oasis for us, something so seamless and integrated into the urban environment that it truly felt as if it should have been there from the beginning. The little deck and the buildings surrounding it could "live together each the happier for the other."[17]

Unfortunately, as the years tumbled by, the terrace continuously leaked into our neighbors' home below us, a problem our condo association struggled to resolve with the developer for years. It left me reluctant to initiate the Balmori design. Much more heartbreaking, though, is the fact that Diana died in 2016. As an architect and as an individual, she was a person of extreme talent, skill, and vision. I will remember her always as a person of good-humor, grace and humility. She blessed our little home and our table by the windows overlooking Public Square with her shining presence. She opened our imagination so that we could see beauty even in one of the smallest, most hardscaped places in our city – our special urban oasis. It would have given me great satisfaction to complete it, if for no other reason than to pay a small Cleveland tribute to the generous spirit of Diana Balmori. It would have also given me some bragging rights for having the smallest Balmori-designed project anywhere in the world.

• • •

Lack of personal outdoor space was only one condo challenge among many. Parking was an adventure in creativity and innovation. In fact, there wasn't any parking at all. At least not for the first two years.

When we brought home groceries, or luggage, or plants that we were preparing to torture by lack of sunlight up on our Friends balcony, we employed a two-person delivery system sometimes called

---

[17] Frank Lloyd Wright: An Autobiography, (1932) p.168.

the 'drop and roll'. Other times, if it was extra busy, we called it the 'switch and hustle.' One of us rolled the car up in front of our building, blocking a long line of honking car and bus traffic on one of the busiest streets in downtown Cleveland, while the other would hustle groceries and other purchases from the trunk or backseat to the front door. "Oh, if only the city planners and road designers had thought to give us a little cut-in for loading and unloading in front of the building," we grumbled. The broad bricked-sidewalk between the car and the entrance to our building was always teaming with curious onlookers - peddlers, panhandlers, and other pedestrians who stopped and stared at the odd folks living in downtown Cleveland. We were a novelty in those days. Just two of the six thousand people who lived in the downtown core in 2008.

The runner stacked our purchases inside the lobby, making sure the sticky front door got closed, and then hurried back to the car to grab another load. Whoever was driving ('drop and roll'), or if we happened to switch out drivers ('switch and hustle'), would then motor around to the other side of the Square, park the car down the alley in the pastor's spot at the church, and then hoof it back through the Square to help with the unpacking – navigating an obstacle course of happy weed smokers, angry street preachers, and aggressive folks pacing you while working you for spare change. We performed the move for almost two years before attached underground parking in our building was completed. It would be another year or so after that until we had an elevator that would take us directly from the parking garage up to our floor.

Over and over, we found ourselves adapting to our new life in the city - sometimes in big ways, sometimes in small. In those early days, we still enjoyed an abundance of the kind of energy and imagination that life in a fixer-up city demanded. At the time, I was only vaguely aware of how these adjustments, along with a myriad of other issues belonging to our condo, or to the city as a whole, were adding up to an overall urban fatigue. I chose to savor the blessings rather than dwell with the burdens. Those were minor inconveniences, really, in the early going of life on the Square. Only later would those challenges come close to breaking me.

•   •   •

From the outset, we reminded ourselves that it was all part of the adventure. The move to one of the most intense districts in the city, downtown, was part of our midlife experiment in downsizing so that we could live in a more walkable and sustainable community. We were eager to "live more simply so others could simply live," as the bumper sticker slogans and social media memes preached, or at least to live more simply so that we could live. Like so many folks of our generation, the suburbs had been wearing on us.

How much of our time in the suburbs had we spent each week mowing our one third of an acre lawn, edging the walks and driveway, repairing the lawnmower and edger, fixing the sprinkler system, spreading our natural fertilizers, weed killers, and grub poison while cursing the moles that came in search of a chewy feast of grubs and that left so many tunnels and open holes in the grass that we could have opened our own putt-putt golf course? How many hours had been consumed by our raking and power-blowing leaves, sweeping out the garage, replacing the roof, installing a new central air conditioning system – one for the downstairs and one for the upstairs of our five-bedroom house in the burbs? I loved our Wilmington Island house. It was one of the prettiest on the street, and it holds some of our sweetest family memories. It also required, however, an inordinate amount of time and energy to maintain.

How many hours did we shave off our lives each week in the car driving to and from work, and the kid's schools, evening performances, music lessons, and other extracurricular activities? How many hours did we spend in the car driving to grocery stores, drug stores, and shopping malls? We waved at our neighbors as we passed by each other at twenty-five miles an hour yet rarely stopped to spend time with them.

For one period in our suburban life, we had only two drivers in our house yet, for some strange reason, we owned three cars and a motorcycle. There was insurance to pay for, too - an umbrella policy, of course, since no one can drive all those vehicles at the same time.

There were general maintenance and repairs, fuel costs, not to mention, weekly trips to the gas station even after we got environmentally righteous and purchased a hybrid.

It's not surprising to me that, after a childhood spent in the back seat of our little cars, or being double-buckled together in the one front passenger seat in the days when I drove two seaters, both of my adult children are now happy to live in cities where they do not need to drive at all. Like many young people of their generation, neither of them even has a valid driver's license.

A voice within kept telling me that the suburbs just were not sustainable anymore, if they ever were. It was a voice as blaring as the screaming leaf blower that my neighbor used every Saturday morning to dry off his SUV after washing it. As Christians who wanted to practice a stewardship of the earth, heck, as human beings who knew very well that they needed to share the planet with the almost seven billion other inhabitants on the earth at that time, we felt less and less at home in the suburbs of Savannah, and more and more a call to do something about it.

"I need to get my butt out of the car and my feet on the ground," I confessed to Beth one morning over coffee. For my health. For the environment. For a greater sense of community, I argued. I wanted to live in a place where we could walk to work or to shop. I longed for the freedom to step out of our front door to go see a movie without ever having to pull a car out of the garage. I wanted to enjoy the liberation of not owning a car at all. I wanted to live someplace where we did more than just wave at neighbors as we motored down the street and out of our subdivision. I wanted a place where we might stop and visit with them or, perhaps, even allow impromptu encounters to change the course of our day. I imagined that a chance encounter with friend and neighbors in the city would lead us to go share a morning coffee or an evening drink with them simply because our paths just happened to cross while sharing the same sidewalk. City living held the potential to bless us with these kind of pedestrian interruptions. With the kids moving out, there was nothing holding us back. I was ready and eager to make the move from sleepy suburb to downtown living.

Cleveland didn't offer everything I was looking for in a walkable, sustainable urban neighborhood. Not when I first moved to the city, anyway. Downtown Cleveland wasn't even considered a neighborhood at the time. However, it certainly showed promising signs that it could become one, and it afforded me an incredible opportunity to participate in what it was becoming, to be a citizen who could help shape an inner-city neighborhood simply by living it. I was anxious to make a change and, in some ways, be the change. Our hip new condo in downtown Cleveland, I believed, could be the place the transition would begin.

• • •

Our new city home was an extraordinary place. Even more remarkable than owning a three-bedroom corner unit with a Friends balcony, was the awe-inspiring panorama from our ten enormous knee-to-ceiling windows.

From almost every window in our condo, we marveled at a spectacular view of Cleveland's eleven-acre Public Square, and surrounding it, three of the four highest skyscrapers in the entire state, not to mention the historic Old Stone Church - the oldest building on the Square. When we signed our purchase agreement, I joked with our developer that he should offer Beth and me a discount on our place since the magnificent view of the historic Old Stone Church on the other side of the Square was one of the main selling features of the Park Building.

I couldn't help but notice that a remarkable view of the city was always with us as Beth and I pushed, pulled, and dragged around our bulky suburban furniture from room to room, trying to make everything fit with in our new chic downtown digs. The towering presence of the city watched over us. Like one of those kooky paintings of Jesus where his eyes seem to be looking at you no matter where you stand, the soaring buildings outside our windows were always peeking in on us. Beth said that our windows were like living canvases that blessed us with ever-changing scenes of the living, breathing city just beyond them. Our views were alive with the moment-to-moment drama of the Square, and the lives of the thousands of people that intersected with it, almost non-stop, day and night. Just a bit further away, there were views of the lakefront - the top of the Browns Stadium which glowed with white light on game nights, the Great Lakes Science Center and its high-tech spinning windmill, and the six-story glass I.M. Pei pyramid that housed the Rock & Roll Hall of Fame. Each morning, when we opened our blinds to greet the new day, there would be no mistaking the city in which we lived. So many of Cleveland's iconic buildings and spaces, the Great Lake and its ever-changing moods, were all visible from our new home on the Square.

We were blessed, too, to have the ability to welcome people into our home, to make room at our table for others. It was only when we filled our condo with family and friends that our apartment truly felt like home.

It was one of our greatest joys to host church members and newcomers, family, and friends for dinners, pre-theater drinks and hors d'oeuvres, meetings, and parties, and especially for concerts or other events happening in downtown. For over a decade, our condo offered us front row seats to every major public event that happened on the Square, such as the famous Cleveland Orchestra's annual Fourth of July Star Spangled Spectacular concert and fireworks grand finale, or the annual Winterfest pop-music concerts, and lighting of the Square and, uhm, fireworks grand finale. The city-center park is brilliantly illuminated with colored lights and sparkling decorations from Thanksgiving Weekend through New Year's. Until the Square was revamped in 2015 and 2016 and the lighting scheme changed along with it, Beth used to tease that the Square looked "like Christmas threw-up on it." Even so, we were happy to share that glowing season with friends and family, too.

Through it all, visitors never ceased to be captivated by the world they beheld through our windows. For first time visitors, the view often brought a jaw-dropping, awe-inspiring moment, especially in contrast to the warren of unfinished entrance ways, aging and now decommissioned elevators, and the dimly lit hallways of our dusty old building that visitors had to gerbil their way through to find our particular unit. As they made their way to our floor, like participants in some "escape room" challenge making directional decisions to go right or left, or hallway and stairwell door choices - this one or that one, I'm certain they wondered why the heck Mark and Beth would live in such a dreary looking place. Crossing the threshold into our home, however, through the restored double Bordeaux doors, frosted-white glass framed in a deep oak, and into the light drenched space of our condo, the response was often a gasp of amazement: "What a fabulous place! And check out the view!" More often than not, we didn't even get an opportunity to hang up coats before visitors were drawn to the view.

In 2018, I took the Canadian philosopher and cultural critic, Mark Kingwell, up to our place for a vantage point from which we could talk about recent developments in the city. His immediate reaction was, "Wow! It looks like American pastors do a lot better than their Canadian counterparts." I tried not to feel judged. Coming to know Mark as I did, I'm sure that I wasn't. Besides, it is possible that American pastors do enjoy a slightly better standard of living. More likely, I explained, was that for its many drawbacks, Cleveland offers more affordable urban living than does his hometown of Toronto with its over-the-moon housing prices. The low cost of living in a city that offers as many, and at times, better amenities than cities three and four times its size, is one of the things that make living in Cleveland very attractive.

For many, our home on Public Square would become something of a welcomed fascination in the city, which was just fine with us. We were happy to share our new home with others. One of our goals in moving to downtown Cleveland was to help convert Clevelanders – both the naysayers who questioned our sanity when we told them we were going to live in downtown, and the city's leaders who needed encouragement and inspiration as they worked tirelessly to breathe new life to their aging downtown. Sure, to a certain degree we sacrificed a private life, but how many pastors enjoy much of a private life anyway?

After a vegan lunch at the Flaming Ice Cube - a daring little vegan café that didn't last long – near the bank on the main floor of our building, we were pleased to bring Cleveland's former Mayor and current Congressman Dennis Kucinich and his beloved, Elizabeth, up to our condo. Dennis was delightful to watch. As is typical of Dennis, his response was playful, unreserved, and genuine. Like a kid racing up to the glass of an exotic aquarium for a closer look as rare species of sea life swim by, Dennis dashed to our front windows and pressed himself up to the view of the city he loves. His wide eyes lit up with an expressive "Wow!" of wonderment.

Clevelanders have a love-hate relationship with Dennis. There are those who love him unconditionally for standing up for the little guy and against corporate powers, and his unceasing commitment to bring peace and justice for all into the world.

In 2001, as a U.S. Congressman, Dennis introduced a brilliant bill to congress to create a U.S. Department of Peace, a department which, as Founding Father, Benjamin Rush had proposed in his 1793 essay entitled, "A Plan for a Peace-Office for the United States" would be on equal footing with the U.S. Department of War. Dennis explained his logic to me saying that if you have a hammer, everything looks like a nail. Currently, America's hammer is in the shape of a war department. Every conflict in the world looks like a war-shaped nail. Why not make a peace-shaped hammer? Conflict might appear very different, as would outcomes. As a peace-making Presbyterian with Quaker roots, I was immediately impressed. Apparently, so were others. In 2007, the bill was cosponsored by seventy-six members of congress and by 2008, the first Republican - Representative Wayne Gilchrest of Maryland, signed on as well. More recently, Democratic Representative Barbara Lee of California has introduced a similar bill, H.R. 1111, which calls for a Department of Peacemaking.

At the same time, there are also those who cannot stand the guy. They blame him for bankrupting the City of Cleveland back in 1978 when he refused to sell off the city's publicly owned electric utility, for being pie-in-the-sky unrealistic about his social goals, and for never, ever going away. At the time of this writing, Dennis, the never-say-die leader is running for mayor once again. He once had a contract hit placed on his life by the Cleveland mafia. Love. Hate. When it comes to opinions about Dennis, there are few who stand in between.

Dennis's feelings about Cleveland, though, are unquestionable. He loves his hometown, Cleveland, and the good people who call it home. He loves their good hearts. Their values. That day in the living room of our condo, Dennis was moved by the way the city was growing. With Elizabeth by his side, Dennis, always eager to share more of his life with her, and now with Beth and me - the newcomers in the room, pointed out various buildings and streets and regaled us with memories of the people and stories that truly make Cleveland a great city. Later that afternoon, we went to the Greek Fest together. The four of us spent the afternoon walking the streets of Tremont, the neighborhood where Dennis spent much of his childhood. Dennis told me that as a kid he had moved over twenty times. His father was a truck driver. His mother, a stay at home mom. She had seven kids to raise. Dennis was the eldest and was often charged with finding affordable housing for the family. I'm sure that personal history, in part, is what makes Dennis as grounded as he is a hard-nosed, a tough-as-nails-fighter for the least among us. His stories, like his kind and supportive spirit, made me feel just a little more at home that day.

•   •   •

The first few years in our condo, the downtown outside our window grew only by spurts and sputters. A new café, like the Flaming Ice Cube, or a retail store like Dredger's Union on East 4th, might open to everyone's great excitement and celebration, only to close a short while later. In the meantime, one of the greatest novelties were all the adventurers taking-up residence in the urban core. As a pastor, and as the pastor of the second oldest and one of the most renown churches in the city, I seemed to be one of the biggest points of interest among them. If a pastor and his wife would live downtown, so people thought, surely things in downtown were getting better.

Longtime Clevelanders and, particularly, church members burdened by the memory of more dangerous times - days in the eighties, nineties, and even into the early two-thousands when pedestrians were mugged on Public Square with Swiss-clock regularity, called us "pioneers" as if we were homesteaders in the last untamed wilderness of Northeast Ohio: downtown. Some folks worried for us, encouraging us not to go out after dark. Others were curious and tried to figure out what life might be like for us in the city by always, always, always asking where we shopped for groceries, as if living downtown was akin to being stranded on an island. It was difficult for them to imagine that we might do the very same thing that they did: we got in the car and drove to the grocery store. Still, others were proud of their trend-setting urban pastor and his wife, even though their pastor, at times, may have expressed a little too much zeal for Cleveland's burgeoning new urbanist opportunities and successes.

Occasionally, on days when we ran home for lunch, we'd look out our front windows at the church on the opposite side of the Square and spot an Old Stone Church docent or open-door greeter standing on the front steps with visitors. With pointed finger they'd count up the floors until their fingertip landed on our unit. "That's where our pastor lives!" they'd boast. We felt like the kids who had to perform a trick or recite the pledge of allegiance or periodic table whenever newcomers came for a visit. We were very much on display.

Media saw our new home on the Square as something as a novelty, too, and viewed Beth and me as expert witnesses in the story of Cleveland's growing downtown. To radio, television, and print media, we were boots-on-the-ground reporters embedded behind enemy lines. Interviews, some of which took place in our living room, often felt like dispatch pieces from the frontlines.

In 2014, I was asked to contribute a regular essay to a new column for the Plain Dealer and its online companion, Cleveland.com, about the challenges of living in downtown called, "From the Trenches." By that time, however, the idea was already outdated.

In the inaugural essay, I began by asking the question: "Can we really call downtown Cleveland 'the trenches' anymore?" Maybe we could have during my first year in the city - 2008, however, I wrote,

"Five years later, the trenches are being backfilled with the rich soil of economic development. Major streets have been repaved. Cranes are in the air. Movies are being shot around town. We're reveling in a $4 billion economic boom which has brought new energy and hope to downtown Cleveland. Downtown has become a 24-hour-a-day party where locals not only work, but come to eat in some of the finest restaurants anywhere, play in the casino, dance in the clubs or listen to live jazz at the new Take 5 on West Superior. Constantino's has expanded its upscale grocery store. Even Heinen's is exploring an urban location in the old Rotunda at East 9th and Euclid. Not to mention, with the opening of the new Convention Center, downtown is enjoying an influx of visitors from around the world. Downtown Cleveland is coming of age."[18]

I guess I wrote myself out of a writing opportunity. The Plain Dealer immediately cancelled the feature. So be it. I was happy that my life and my home on the Square were part of the positive transformation happening downtown. Changing minds and attitudes about the livability of our cities was why I had chosen to make my home in downtown in the first place.

That's not to say that there weren't still challenges. There were. Many. Especially in those early years. Some, though, we chose to embrace as charming eccentricities that blessed our cool condo with character.

During the first couple of months, for example, we discovered that we had a haunted elevator. It had a mind of its own and chose to start and stop whenever it felt like it, which was most often in the middle of the night. There were only six of us living in the entire nine story building at the time. It was mostly a shell of a building which made it downright creepy to hear the elevator clattering up and down the shaft at 3:00 A.M. and echoing throughout the darkened hallways of our mostly uninhabited building.

The elevator began its nightly rounds downstairs in the first-floor lobby. Lacking the smooth operational grace of newer, modern lifts, the elevator would angrily slam its brass doors shut, chug its way up to the ninth floor and then clunk its way back down again. However, on its return trip the elevator always stopped on one floor. Our floor. It rattled open its doors, and then a second or two later, clapped them closed again before continuing its journey back down to the lobby.

---

[18] "From the Trenches: R. Mark Giuliano," Cleveland.com, September 4, 2013. Accessed June 25, 2018. https://www.cleveland.com/from-the-trenches/index.ssf/2013/09/from_the_trenches_r_mark_giula.html

Stopping on our floor, and on our floor only, seemed intentional. Non-coincidental. It seemed like the elevator was aware of our presence in the building and on our particular floor. Was it looking for us? Taunting us? Beckoning us, nay, daring us to go for a middle-of-the-night ride?

In the daytime, if we were not careful, the elevator would attack my wife and my daughter, Daryl, who was staying with us between her college freshman and sophomore years our first summer in the condo. We could not help but notice that when she or Beth stepped on to the elevator, the doors would crash shut on them prematurely, body-slamming them in the shoulder. It never seemed to do that to a male rider. We wondered if the elevator might have had issues with women.

One morning during a visit from Toronto, my son awakened and came into the living room from the guestroom which shared a wall close to the elevator shaft, and asked who was riding the elevator all night. When we told him about the elevator's peculiar behavior, he said with a low, ominous voice, "Perhaps you have a 'hellavator!'"

Only months later did we start hearing stories about an elevator repair person named John who, years earlier, had either been killed, or had a fatal heart attack while working on the elevator housing up on the roof of the building. From that point on, when the hellavator was misbehaving, we would just say, "Oh, there goes John again!"

We were less good-humored, though, when it came to the constant work being done on our building. For the first four or five years, the building was under constant construction as each unit was built-out only after it had been sold. For the first year or two alone, the unit directly beneath ours was used as a shop for builders who came from their day jobs elsewhere in the city to run their grinding power tools under our feet long into the evening. Thankfully, we were eventually able to negotiate a 10:00 P.M. shut down that was honored - most of the time.

Historically, very few Clevelanders lived in downtown. Why would they want to? To many, the city was dirty, dangerous, and, if you could afford it, there were so many better places to live than in the core. It was difficult, therefore, to get workers to understand that there were now people actually living in the very building that they were pounding away at with their power hammers, drills and saws. For Beth and me, our condo was the place we ended our work day. For them, it was where they began. We thought of it as our home. They thought of it as an active construction site. We were often left to mop up the floor of our unit after contractors had tromped through to finish up long overdue punch list items in their cruddy work boots and paint-soaked overalls, sometimes without invitation or even knocking first. On more than one early morning occasion, we opened the front door of our unit in our housecoats and politely asked plumbers, woodworkers, and electricians to quit shouting up and down our hallway to partners on other floors. "Oh, and by the way, can you please turn down your radio?" There was always a look of incredulity on their faces when they saw us. Comprehending that there were other people in the building, let alone living there was a constant stumbling block for them.

About the time work on the units in our building was coming to completion, another developer started construction on the Southworth Building next to ours. Both our den and our study shared a wall with the Southworth. I was forced to wear earplugs when sitting at my desk to muffle the banging, grinding, buzzing noise just on the other side of the wall. The earplugs were no match for the vibrations shaking my desk, or rumbling the floor beneath my feet, or rattling the book shelf or now crooked pictures on the wall. Mercifully, that project wrapped-up in about sixteen months. But then it was time for the demolition and rebuild of the entire Public Square which brought bright lights and the sweet sounds of jackhammering and backhoeing at two in the morning. Across the street at the church where we worked, there was hardly any relief for our rattled nerves, either. The interior of the twenty-one-story Standard Building that shared a wall with our church offices was being demolished and converted from offices to apartments at that time, as well.

I joked to Beth that if someone was ever to write and perform a play about our lives in Cleveland, they would have to have construction noise constantly blasting from the wings of the stage throughout every act. Actors would have to project even more than usual to be heard over the endless noise filling the stage and theater. If by the end of the play actors and audience weren't truly frazzled, stressed to the point of feeling an imaginary impulse to kill someone, then the play would have failed for its lack of urban realism. Beth laughed but pointed out that it would hardly be a hit play, "No one would come to see it." There were days, and nights, that I wondered why we had come to live in it.

The problem with the bright lights of the big city that pierced our bedroom through the chinks in our louvered shaded windows each night was easily resolved when we hung some basic blackout curtains in the bedroom. The discordant symphony of noises emanating from the sidewalk a number of stories beneath our windows was a much greater challenge.

Our nights were filled with frenetic pandemonium, a cacophony of noises. Drunks fighting, arguing, vomiting, glass shattering on the concrete below, sirens screeching, buses with their vehicle motion alarms continuously beeping as they idled at our corner waiting to turn and then blasting their horns as they made their turn - an RTA requirement, it was rumored, following an incident where a distracted bus driver hit and killed a pedestrian on the other side of the Square. A wobbly manhole cover jarred us with its percussive clanking and clunking when cars at the busy intersection drove over it – first the front tires, then the back. I invested a great deal of energy into my belief that drivers were purposefully aiming for the iron disk in the concrete. We were sometimes jolted from our sleep by blasts of gunshots that made it difficult for us to rest with any of the peace we were accustomed to in Savannah where we left our windows open and night owls and tree frogs serenaded us as we slept. No longer "the dark mocking bird to sing his glee!" Now, just the sound of the shouting man having a pee.

Even in the daytime, noise wore us thin. In front of our building, we had our own special street vendor, let's call her Agnes, who sold the homeless newspaper, the Cleveland Street Chronicle for donations. Agnes wasn't homeless but found the Chronicle a great way to supplement her meager social security check each month. Agnes had a piercing voice that could not be missed. The blaring car traffic, the roar of accelerating buses, or even bulldozers dozing, were no match for the voice of Agnes.

Beneath our window, ad nauseam, with the coarseness of sandpaper, relentlessly Agnes bleated, "Hi! Wanna help the homeless?" It was her sales pitch. And it worked. Not surprisingly, then, she shouted it a lot. And by a lot I mean hour after hour, day after day, year after brain-frying year! "Hi! Wanna help the homeless?" Never mind closing your windows. Even with them sealed-tight and bolted shut, her scratchy voice had the effect of some sort of haunting aural torture.

If you just happened to be walking by our building you could choose to ignore Agnes, block her out for a minute or two as you moved on. Or you could purchase one of her papers if you liked. If you were a resident of the building, however, you were stuck. You couldn't run. You couldn't hide. Her grating pitch found you anywhere and everywhere throughout the building, particularly the Northwest corner where I was upstairs burying my head under pillows, or stuffing my ears with the highly rated sponge earplugs that I'd purchased from the online earplug store – yes, I discovered in desperation, one really exists: "Hi! Wanna help the homeless!" Her voice felt like a drill bit gorging its way deep into my ear canal and piercing my tympanic membrane. It drove me so absolutely buzzy-brained-crazy that at times I fantasized about dropping something imaginary from my window to get her to cease and desist. Something imaginary but heavy.

I even considered offering Agnes fifty or a hundred dollars to go down the street to sell her papers somewhere else but I am positive that she would never take it. She had a prime location right there on the corner of Public Square and Ontario Street. It is one of the main intersections in the city and it is less than fifty feet from the casino, banks, and office towers. "Fifty dollars? Ha!" I imagine Agnes would have laughed in my face and then shouted, "Hi! Wanna help the homeless?"

At year five, I broke down and spent thousands of dollars to install sound-proof windows. They were a big expense, for sure, but worth every penny. Beth went so far as to call me a "genius" many times over for having our amazing windows custom designed and installed. We could not believe we waited five years to do it! Almost immediately the windows lowered our stress level to outpatient status and restored our sanity against the teeth-grinding din of blaring cars, accelerating buses and delivery trucks, rumbling Harley Davidsons and ruckus rock concerts on the Square, and even the haunting voice that could be heard above it all: "Hi! Wanna help the homeless?"

Those early years in our Public Square condo asked me to move beyond my preconceived notions of what a home was. To release them. They also taught me how to adapt. To accommodate. To innovate. I learned to be more patient, tolerant, and even welcoming of the challenges that life in the city, and in our not quite finished condo brought with them. Our new being – who we are becoming and what we will offer, after all, is forged in the flames of adversity.

I came to understand that a lot of things to which I had clung so tightly – lush lawns and colorful gardens, my own private peace and quiet, would have to be compromised or even traded away completely for life in the city. Those former notions of what home was were torn down; something new was being built up. I was figuring out urbanist workarounds such as soundproof windows, or converting an extra-large window well into a makeshift terrace, or discovering a snaking path across a wooden beam and through an old warehouse next door that led to an abandoned rooftop where Beth and I could enjoy a glass of wine in the evening. Like the condo itself, my life was under construction. Better yet, reconstruction. My new home in the city, if I was ever going to find it, would not be about children and pets, shade trees or Spanish moss. I believed that home would emerge only after I made peace with the absence of these things belonging to another place and time, and fostered friendships with both the challenges and charms of the city – our own ghost elevator, a never-ending parade of construction workers who were busy making old things new, panhandlers and peddlers I would come to know by name and story. Then, and only then, I imagined, could I learn to love where I lived. Finally, I was making it home.

Chapter Seven

Visual Impairment

Piglet: Good afternoon, Eeyore.
Eeyore: Good afternoon, Piglet, if it is a good afternoon, which I doubt.

———————

AT EIGHT YEARS of age, my son, Dylan, asked me what the world looked like through my eyes. We were in the car, driving, when he asked. It may seem like an odd question for some people but not at all for a blind kid.

Doctors call Dylan's visual impairment, retinitis pigmentosa (RP). In practical terms, RP means that Dylan has very little peripheral vision – up or down or side to side. His field of vision was less than five degrees back then. It is much less now. Having RP means that the world comes at Dylan through a very narrow pinhole of sight. Some people call it tunnel vision. At night, he can't see a thing.

That particular day in the car, I was attempting to help Dylan understand what peripheral meant. The street was busy with activity in front of us and all around us, too.

"What do you see?" he asked, trying to understand what he might be missing. No doubt, he was also looking for a little reassurance that his dad knew how to maneuver the one-and-a-half-ton vehicle they were riding in as, together, they motored down the busy city street at thirty miles per hour. His life was in my hands.

"Hmm," I had to think about it for a moment. I wanted to give a thoughtful response to his thoughtful question. "I see everything around us, I guess." I made a list of all the things I could see from the car windows so he might know in more detail what I meant. "I see the traffic right in front of us and even the ones seven or eight blocks down the road. I see the cars in the lanes beside us, and people walking on the sidewalks on both sides of the street. I see the trees beside us and the branches and leaves hanging over the roadway. I see stores and businesses as we pass by them, too."

"All of that? At the same time?!" Dylan was flabbergasted that sighted people had to take in as much as they do. "How do you know what to look at?" When you stop to consider how much of the visual world we observe at any given moment, directly or indirectly, you realize that Dylan has a very good point. It is quite remarkable.

"Wow!" my son said. "If I had to see everything all at once, I think I'd puke!"

During my first three years in Cleveland, I was struck by a peculiar narrowness of vision from which many in the city seemed to suffer. While others spoke passionately about their incredible city, I also encountered, every single day, Clevelanders who betrayed a kind of myopia – an inability to see possibilities for Cleveland, or the ways that the city might rise above its history of decline to become a thriving twenty-first century city on one of the largest fresh water lakes in the world.

Clevelanders had a difficult time even spotting the profuse beauty that existed all around them – soaring historic and contemporary architecture, public art, an 'emerald necklace' of accessible parks and greenspace that ringed the city, not to mention walkable access from downtown to both a river and a lake. It was especially surprising to me since, having just moved to the area, my spirit was sparked with fresh optimism and curiosity at the splendor of this great American city. I was impressed by the overwhelming number of amenities that the city offered, many of them free. Cleveland offered many of the things that much larger cities boasted. In Cleveland, however, it all came with a much more affordable cost of living.

I was befuddled, though, by the number of folks who walked with their heads down, missing many of the grand city charms as they hurried along city sidewalks while spectacular late-nineteenth, early-twentieth and mid-century edifices towered above them. When they took shortcuts through the magnificent secret places such as the stunning historic Cleveland Arcade - the breathtaking 1890 Victorian interior promenade modeled on the Galleria Vittorio Emanuele II in Milan, Italy, I just couldn't understand why so few people ever stopped to take notice.

Blindness isn't always a physical issue; it can be a spiritual one, too. Sometimes we have difficulty seeing beyond our own experiences – usually negative ones like the pain of loss or disappointment, or beyond our well-rehearsed habits and patterns of behavior. We might find ourselves placating or even resisting when others try to help us see in new ways. "We've always done it this way" or "We've tried it and it won't work" or "You're new; you'll learn after a while" are the litany-like mantras of those who choose to stay where they are rather than trust or even experiment with an updated vision.

Spiritual blindness brings with it a kind of denial or even a poverty of spirit. It has emotionally rewired us to the point where we just cannot see opportunities before us. We experience something akin to a conversion disorder – a psychosomatic or hysterical blindness that is not connected to any physiological or medical abnormality, but an emotional one.

In my work as a pastor, I sometimes see spiritual myopia holding people back from becoming the healthy, hopeful people God would have them be. It is not that people won't see a vision, it is that sometimes they just can't, especially when a particular way of seeing their lives or the world around them has been enculturated, as it was for some in Cleveland.

In 2011, one of the young professionals in the congregation straightened me out on this matter. He saw the resistance to change that I was meeting from the church's two conflicting boards. He recognized my confusion, as well as my growing frustration. I hadn't seen it in myself. I'm truly thankful that he had the perspective to see it for me.

"Mark, I understand what you're doing here. "You're trying to change the culture of the church."

"Right! That's exactly what I'm attempting to do!" I was elated that someone understood.

"Just don't forget," he cautioned me, "the culture you're trying to change is almost 200 years old!" I appreciated his wise words that day and have returned to them often. His wisdom helped me understand the kind of tunnel vision that can creep into any organization over time, even the church.

Like the time I proposed a shuttle to bring people to worship on Sundays since the church didn't have a parking lot. I was told that I just didn't understand. "Cleveland was a car town and always will be," thoughtful members pointed out as if sharing old information with the new pastor would help straighten him out. "Nobody wants to park their car in a lot and then take a shuttle the rest of the way to the church," I was advised.

When I countered that Atlanta is a car town, too, yet many of the largest churches in the city – even the country, used shuttle systems, I was told, "Of course they do. They're really big churches. They need shuttles." When I suggested that maybe they were really big congregations, in part, because they made it easy for people get to church with shuttle vans and buses, folks just rolled their eyes as if I was from another planet. I guess I was, if you consider Georgia another planet.

I often found myself in these kinds of hole-in-my-bucket conversations; new ideas and proposals were met with a series of answers rationalizing why these new ideas just would not work. For a long time, very little forward progress happened. Only in time, would that culture that took almost two hundred years to form, begin to budge.

The award-winning cartoonist, Dennis Fletcher created a one-frame cartoon that pokes playful fun at this very issue. In the scene, members of a pastor search committee are sitting around a boardroom table discussing attributes they hoped to find in a new minister. The chair of the committee says to the rest of the members, "Basically, we're looking for an innovative pastor with a fresh vision who will inspire our church to remain exactly the same." I have saved Fletcher's cartoon to the photo file on my phone for easy reference in times when some of the leaders I work with encounter resistance to change.

It wasn't just the church in the heart of the city that suffered from spiritual myopia, though. That same prevailing spirit often hung like fog over the city as whole city. Many Clevelanders didn't see or didn't care to see how many of the things holding us back were systemically connected to the way we had been conducting business. Behaviors in one place often created problems in other places. For every action there was always an equal and opposite reaction, we learned in our high school physics class but forgot somewhere along the road to adulthood.

On March 23, 2011, for example, Cleveland.com, the electronic version of the print newspaper, the Plain Dealer, posted an article with the headlines: "650 Cleveland teachers could be laid off, seven more schools may close as district struggles to trim costs." When we scrolled down to the very next article, the headlined read: "Cuyahoga County Council approves more spending for Juvenile Justice Center." The dots were not easily connected for many in our community. Even though our most widely read news source stacked the articles, one on top of the another, and squeezed them into our email inboxes, it was almost impossible for some to make the connection that decreased funding for education would necessitate increased spending for the juvenile system. It reminded me of that old Three Stooges gag where one stooge slams closed the top drawer on a filing cabinet and the bottom drawer pops out and hits him the shins. He slams the bottom drawer closed, and the middle one pops open, punching him in his big belly. As kids, we laughed hysterically at the bit. As adults, though, it surprised me how many good folks missed the irony even when it was presented in such an obvious way. There was a vision problem.

You could hardly blame Clevelanders, though. Cleveland came by its myopia honestly. Vision was often clouded by the long shadows of almost a century of losses. 2008-2010 were terrible years for the city, for sure. Those two years, however, were two successively bad years in a century-long succession of disappointments. Far worse than my first two years Cleveland, were the seventy or so years that preceded them. Yesterday's heartaches made it difficult for some to hope in a better tomorrow.

In his 1984 book, The Art of the City, Peter Conrad said that, "The city is a built dream, a vision incarnated. What makes it grow is its image of itself." By 2011, Cleveland's collective self-image, in many ways, was the incarnation of decades of decline.

Regularly, I was approached with incredulous curiosity. "Why on earth would you leave Savannah to live in Cleveland?" Clevelanders grilled me in disbelief, as if I had won the lottery but for some mysterious and inexplicable reason had chosen to decline the prize, or perhaps had broken some sort of cosmic law and had been sentenced to Cleveland to do penance.

"Oh, my wife and I had our fill of warm winters, sunshine, and coastal beaches," I would retort. Here, I should pause to point out what I learned very quickly in Cleveland - quick witted sarcasm, especially if it involves even a whiff of irony, is almost always lost on Midwesterners. Sarcasm can be interpreted as "impolite" or "New York-ish," which, in Cleveland, could be considered interchangeable terms, unless they are posted in the online comments that spew-forth from the daily rag – Cleveland.com, where readers gleefully chuck hateful remarks like mud from one sloppy, early-spring-soaked yard to another from behind the relatively secure anonymity of a computer screen.

More often than not, when Clevelanders described their city to me they would not only ask me about my own senses for having left Savannah for Northeast Ohio, but they would refer to themselves in the past tense. Regularly, I heard phrases like: "We used to be one of the biggest cities in the country," or "There used to be over fifty Fortune 500 companies headquartered here." Eyes would often glaze over with sweet reminiscence as long-timers recalled the glory days for me: "I remember coming downtown when there were department stores, and they were packed with shoppers. Downtown was the place to be!" Clearly, Cleveland was a city whose residents saw their glory days through a rearview mirror.

While Clevelanders had a lot to cheer about ten years ago, they tended to idolize the past while spurning the present. The city had simply lost too much over the years to trust the new and the now. Many struggled to look up or forward or anywhere else with any kind of vision that remotely resembled optimism. Decades of political, social, and environmental failures had earned Cleveland its last national title: Mistake by the Lake. Clevelanders wore that sobriquet like their own weighty scarlet letter. In many ways, they allowed it to define them as rough and resilient losers with their own self-defeating mantra: "There's always next year."

Nowhere has the losing narrative been instilled more clearly, more profoundly, more gut-wrenchingly, and in slow motion instant replay, than in the rehashing of the woes of Cleveland's professional sports teams. Some Americans will always remember December 7, 1941 as the worst day ever – the attack on Pearl Harbor. These days, many of us younger Americans remember September 11, 2001 as an infamous day of national sadness – the terrorist attacks on the World Trade Center, the Pentagon, and the thwarted attack on the White House by the inconceivably courageous passengers of United Airlines Flight 93. Millennials will one day tell their children and grandchildren about the great coronavirus pandemic of 2020 and 2021 that swept the globe at an alarming rate, ground economies into dust, claimed millions of lives – more than half a million dead in the United States alone, and sickened millions more. For most Clevelanders, though, the darkest day remembered in recent history is November 6, 1995. That was the day Art Modell made the official announcement from Camden Yards that he would move the Cleveland Browns to Baltimore the following year.

Modell argued that the city was short-sighted (another example of the city's spiritual myopia?). The city had the resources but refused to build a world class stadium in which the team could play. In an instant, the city's unwillingness to invest in a new stadium and Modell's decision, robbed Clevelanders of their famed Cleveland Browns. It was official: there would be no "next year" for Cleveland football fans to cheer about – at least not until 1999 when a new club was formed under the same name.

The successes and failures of our pro-sports teams influence us greatly. For better or worse, they shape both our identity and our vision. They impact our self-image – how we view ourselves, to paraphrase Peter Conrad. Even if we are not avid fans, big wins can lift a whole city, and big losses can just as easily tear us down. Wins allow us to look up and look forward. Losses leave us looking downward at shoes. For cities like Cleveland where loss is integrated in to the city's operative narrative, loss can truly be defining.

My appreciation for the Cleveland identity during those early years deepened only when I considered the many ways our professional sports function, socially speaking, like religion does. Like our religions, we are highly invested in our sports teams and their ability to give us something around which we might coalesce as a people. They bless us with a sense of self-worth, or not. We are dedicated to our sports teams very much like we are to our religious institutions.

Like the rhythm of the church's liturgical calendar, our pro-sports help set the beat to the rhythm of the seasons. Pre-season football games in August, for example, help prepare our minds and spirits for the end of summer and the coming season of autumn. Whether we attend or even watch the games on television, we see the scores reported online, or on the nightly news and are affected by the return of the football season. The advent of long winter is marked by the beginning of basketball and hockey. And next to Easter, nowhere is springtime more evidently celebrated than the home opener down at the baseball park! And just as the church has its playoff seasons – Advent and Lent, followed by bleacher packing Super Bowl services – Christmas and Easter, pro-sports leagues have their peak seasons, and championship events, too.

Like our religions, sport is filled with game day rituals, too - fellowship in parking lots, soloists, and lots of communal singing of national anthems, seventh inning stretches, hymns of victory. Just as church would not be church without the occasional singing of Amazing Grace or Here I Am, Lord, a game would not be a game without the collective singing and stomping to We Will Rock You, or on those rare times of victory, the singing of We Are the Champions. In Cleveland, "Clevangelicals" stand, throw their arms and hands into the air as they shape-out the letters O-H-I-O during the singing of Sweet Caroline, the Amazing Grace among Ohio sports fans.

Nowhere was the connection of religion and sport more clearly articulated than in the full-page newspaper ad promoting Toronto's Air Canada Centre (now Scotia Bank Arena) in the early years of its operation. The stadium is the home of the National Hockey League's Toronto Maple Leafs. The ad proclaimed: "Hockey is our religion. And this [the ACC] is our temple."

Like our religions, pro-sports help indoctrinate cultural myths about conflict and resolution, what challenges we are able to meet and overcome, what obstacles we are able to defeat, for examples. In his Psychology Today article, "Why Are Sports Important?" Mark Banschick M.D. says that "sports draw us in for many reasons, the elegance, the competition, the history, our identification with great athleticism (we may not be able to do it, but they sure can!), a coming together of community in a shared story . . . The drama of these games mirrors the drama of our lives." [19]

The spiritual impact on the collective vision that sports have, pro-sports in particular, cannot be understated – particularly in cities like Cleveland. When we're winning, our vision is good. We are proud of the place we live. We view our city from an on-top-of-the-world vantage point. However, when we're losing, we share a collective slump. The city as a whole, experiences the loss as one. We see the world through a lens tinted by the agony of defeat. Just imagine how your congregation might feel showing up to church for your annual Christmas Eve Candlelight service to celebrate the birth of Jesus, but the baby never arrives, there are no hymns to be sung, and, horror of horrors, the service does not end with the lighting of candles and congregational singing of Silent Night, Holy Night. It would be a major upset, to say the least. Or imagine arriving at the church on Easter morning to celebrate the resurrection, but the pastor announces that the stone is just too heavy today and Jesus will not be getting up. The congregational response would be almost comical if it were not

---

[19] Why Are Sports So Important?, *Psychology Today*, Feb 5, 2012. https://www.psychologytoday.com/us/blog/the-intelligent-divorce/201202/why-are-sports-important. Accessed June 14, 2018.

for the violence and outright mayhem it might cause. We would turn to one another only to behold stunned looks upon each other's faces. What, no songs of victory today? By the time we all formed ourselves into a mob, our pastor would have her bags packed and have made a dash for the nearest exit.

Even worse, consider that you arrive one Sunday prepared to begin anew and the chair of the board announces that the leadership has decided to move your beloved church to another city – Baltimore, perhaps. All of it, gone: your organist and favorite choir members, the staff and your dear pastor who had celebrated with you and your family during the good times and held you, lifted you during the difficult ones, too. I imagine you might be shocked, or outraged! You might organize a protest, sign a petition or two, cry aloud: "You can't do this!" even though the deal was already done.

I imagine that Cleveland fans felt that way. They certainly reacted with similar passionate protest the day that Art Modell moved the Browns to Baltimore. For Clevelanders, the loss of the Browns was the war on their religion.

To this day, over two decades later, you can still spot the occasional Browns fan wearing a "Muck Fodell" hat or t-shirt just as many of the fans did for the remaining 1995 season. It was the final blow following a flurry of Cleveland sports disappointments through the 1970s and 1980s. The emotional expectation for loss had been sealed for Cleveland sports fans for generations to come when Modell took Cleveland's ball and went to play on another field.

It was quite a turn in the Cleveland sports narrative. Yesterday's parents handed down stories of Browns' greatness - the glory days when Otto Graham and Jim Brown were racking-up records that would eventually make them hall of famers, or of coaches Paul Brown and Blanton Collier who each led Cleveland to numerous national championships during their respective years, including the Brown's last national title in 1964. The next generation, however, would tell its children of a number of embarrassing losses and, especially, the near misses of 1986 and 1987. Mention "the drive, the fumble" today and Clevelanders still groan with disappointment.

With the Browns' move to Baltimore, hope would no longer spring eternal for Ohio's Lake Erie steel town. To add Baltimore insult to Cleveland injury, Modell's Ravens won the Super Bowl just four short years later. Dare to utter the name Modell around Cleveland and be prepared for battle!

When I moved to Cleveland, some people warned me about the low expectations for their teams, particularly, though not exclusively, the new Browns who had to start again from scratch in 1999. Others, in true Cleveland style, made self-deprecating jokes to soften the blow of continued loss.

"Mark, a terrible thing just happened. I accidentally parked my car in a handicap spot and got a ticket . . . It was for a Browns' game!"

"A scalper on West 6th was shouting, 'Browns' tickets, $10.00!' I told him that he'd have to pay me more."

On the twentieth anniversary of Modell's announcement, the new but not improved Cleveland Browns came to Baltimore to stand-off against the Ravens. In a pre-game blog titled, "20 years later, Art Modell still did the Browns wrong" Boston sports writer, Alex Reimer wrote that, "it would be a welcome change of pace for Browns fans, who have had to watch their new team sputter over the last 16 years while the club that never should've left wins at a high level."[20] The Browns beat the Ravens 33-30 that day with a three-point field goal scored in overtime, proving that every religion has its own miracle stories.

•   •   •

It is not just football that shapes the corporate identity in Cleveland, though. Cleveland baseball fans have suffered their own misery with only two World Series wins in over a century of club history, the last being in 1948. They got close in 1997 but blew a 2-1 lead over the Mariners going into the ninth inning only to lose in the eleventh. And recently, in 2016, they came close again by evening the score in the eighth inning after lagging most of game seven, only to have their late

---

[20] Alex Reimer, "20 years later; Art Modell still did the Browns wrong," *SBNation.com*, October 11, 2015, accessed June 14, 2018. https://www.sbnation.com/nfl/2015/10/11/9474367/cleveland-browns-baltimore-ravens-relocation-history-art-modell

game inertia robbed with a rain delay, and then a heartbreaking loss in the tenth inning against an even more losing team, the Chicago Cubs. Oh, the humanity!

While the CAVS, Cleveland's pro basketball team, redeemed themselves in 2016, hometown Akron kid and CAV's superstar, 'King' LeBron, first, would utterly crush the heart of CAVS owner, Dan Gilbert, and practically every other Northeast Ohioan on July 8, 2010. It wasn't only the biggest break-up announcement since Art Modell gave notice that he was moving the Browns, it was the most humiliatingly public one, especially for the slighted fans from Cleveland.

LeBron James sat face to face with sportscaster, Jim Gray, in a live, seventy-five-minute, nationally broadcast ESPN television program aptly called The Decision. According to Neilson Ratings, the show was watched by almost ten million viewers, making it the highest rated cable show of the night. After thirty grueling minutes into the broadcast, an additional three million viewers tuned-in just in time to hear LeBron drop the bomb with his decision to move to Florida.

"I'm going to take my talents to South Beach and join the Miami Heat," James said, seeming only slightly sheepish about his announcement in the now famous interview. He was more expressive about his desire to a be a part of a team that he felt was up to his abilities. "I feel like it's going to give me the best opportunity to win and to win for multiple years, and not only just to win in the regular season or just to win five games in a row or three games in a row, I want to be able to win championships. And I feel like I can compete down there."

In front of a total of thirteen million viewers from across the country, James had just dumped Cleveland for an opportunity to be a winner among other winners. It would take Clevelanders six full years and a national championship before they could or would entirely forgive him.

•   •   •

Clevelanders have embraced losing the way Buffalo has embraced its lousy winter weather. It's just a fact. The way the of the world. Losing is in Cleveland's DNA. It is enculturated from one generation to the next. Miserable tales of heartbreak are told as a bonding ritual, or to impress upon the kids just how bad it was in their parent's generation, or simply to prepare them for the harsh realities of growing-up "Cleveland" as was the case one night at the hockey game.

Those first few years in Cleveland, Beth and I were season ticket holders for home games to our American Hockey League team, the Lake Erie Monsters – now called the Cleveland Monsters. The city used to have a bigtime NHL team, the Cleveland Barons from 1976–1978 until they also left town to merge with the Minnesota North Stars in June 1978. Yup. More loss for Cleveland.

CAV's owner and downtown business mogul from Detroit, Dan Gilbert, also owns the Monsters. For an AHL franchise, the team has a beautiful stadium to play in and a small but faithful crowd of adults and kids who come out to cheer them on. Some come for the "dollar dog" hotdog night and tons for the give-away nights. In January 2010, for example, the year that Shaquille O'Neal played for the CAVS, the team broke an AHL attendance record when the stadium drew 19,626 fans by giving away 10,000 Shaq bobbleheads donning Lake Erie Monsters jerseys. Others come to Monsters games to watch the Zamboni clean the ice and the Mullet Brothers – Cleveland's answer to the movie Slap Shot's Hanson Brothers, do their "shtick-handling" between periods, goading fans from the opposing team, mocking the refs, or doing honorary body slams into the glass to work up the hometown regulars. Some come to the games hungry for a fight or two.

I am sure there were other downtowners, like Beth and me, who went to the games - an easy walk from our place to the stadium, because compared to the price of Indians, Browns and CAVS tickets, Monsters hockey games are downright more affordably fun. Cleveland's hockey fans are likely to see a lot fast skating, hard hitting, goal scoring action and, I suspect, compared to the other teams, a lot more wins!

Even so, low expectation among Clevelanders is ingrained the city's psyche. It is the inheritance that one generation passes along to the next.

Beth and I were at a game in early 2010. Our Monsters were winning – up by two goals, going into the third period (that's the last twenty minutes of regulation play for non-hockey folks). The crowd was raucously gleeful. Although, I'm not sure you can safely use words like "raucously" or "gleeful," about hockey fans, especially in the same sentence, unless, of course, you are willing to risk life and limb, which I am not. So, let's just say the Q was rockin' that night. The roar of the crowd was deafening. Like hungry dogs looking for meat, the fans were salivating for a win.

Within the first ten minutes of the third period, however, the opposing team had rifled two quick goals past our goalie to tie the game at three. With those two quick goals against us, the stadium was drilled into a stupefying silence. It was so quiet, you could have heard a puck drop. It was quiet enough, in fact, for me to overhear the father sitting behind us offer this little life lesson to his ten-year-old, "Well son, it looks like we've lost now. You might as well get used to it. We always lose; we're Clevelanders." It seemed as if Dad had voiced his pronouncement loudly enough to draw acclamation from others sitting in our section, perhaps an "Amen" from the congregation seated nearby.

Now I am a smart enough man to know that you don't interfere with other parents and the way they choose to raise their children, at least not in front of the kids. But, clearly, this guy was screwing-up his kid. I mean, couldn't he have at least offered some sort of glib cliché like, "Hang in there, kid! There's still ten minutes left in this game" or "Don't worry, little buddy. It ain't over until the fat lady sings!" Or how about a little inspirational paraphrase from Winston Churchill like, "Never give up. Never, ever give up!" Or maybe he could have encouraged the kid with a personal and inspirational anecdote about the time it looked like his favorite team had been beaten, only to come back and win it in overtime. He could have told his kid anything to encourage hope or faith or optimism or whatever the heck you want to call it that helps normal folks get through tough times.

Instead, dad had just indoctrinated his kid into Cleveland's First Church of Perpetual Loss and introduced him to the doctrine of divine providence: it is providential that Cleveland always loses. It seemed abusive.

Beth heard him, too. We glanced one another as if to say, "Yes, it's wrong, but it's not our place to intervene." I imagined Beth pressing her hand down on my thigh to prevent me from standing up to turn and challenge the man. I would have done it with a smile on my face, of course. I may have created common ground by identifying with the Cleveland plight, but I also would have reminded him that maybe, just maybe, this could be the one, the big win for which we have all been longing. Maybe we could win it for his kid!

As it happened, I said nothing. The game went into overtime. And in the first two minutes the opposing team scored. We lost. Dad was right. What a bunch of losers we are.

I have often wondered what happened to that kid. That was 2010. He would be finished high school by now, already graduated, I imagine. That is, if he had vision enough to see what winning a decent education could mean for his life. Did he stay motivated long enough to graduate? Was he able to envision a brighter future than the one his dad promised him that night? Or did he grow into a true Clevelander, suffering from a generationally perpetuating expectation of defeat.

A representative of Destination Cleveland, Cleveland's cutting-edge answer to a visitor's bureau, spoke at the church's noontime program one year. She gave us a name for the dispiritedness that Clevelanders sometimes suffer from when she called it an "Eeyore complex." Eeyore, as you will recall is Winnie the Pooh's jackass friend who suffers from a head-down expectation of impending loss:

"Have you ever had one of those days when you just can't win, Eeyore?" asks Pooh.

We all chuckle because we know how the donkey is going to respond.

"Yup, I know how that feels," Eeyore brays. And then we laugh. Why? Because that's how Eeyore feels every day. And we laugh because we can see what Eeyore can't. Our vision is still good. We live with hope. We haven't had the spirit of optimism snuffed out of us at hockey games by our parent's dispirited pronouncements, or had our collective narrative shaped down at our pro-sports temples where coaches and players, owners, and even providence repeatedly fail us.

• • •

It wasn't just losses from their professional sports teams that made Clevelanders hang their heads and mumble like Eeyore, though. Seemingly-insurmountable economic and political challenges kept Cleveland awash in a river of toxic disappointment throughout the latter half of the twentieth century, as well. Beginning with, well, the river.

Cleveland's own masked superhero and sidewalk strumming street performer, Guitar Man, once told me that he knows the real truth of how the Cuyahoga River caught fire. Guitar Man is referring to the June 1969 fire, the last and most famous time the river went up in flames taking with it Cleveland's reputation as the "best location in the nation." Not the, uhm, other times the river caught fire.

There had been earlier and more severe river fires prior to that time. It was the 1969 burn, however, that garnered all the negative press and, in turn, ignited an environmental movement across the United States. Among the Woodsy Owl "give a hoot, don't pollute" set, Cleveland quickly became the poster-child city of reckless treatment of the natural environment. Television watchers in 1971 will likely recall old Iron Eyes Cody, the Italian-American who played the teary-eyed Native American in the Keep America Beautiful ad campaign. Cody is seen paddling his birch bark canoe through the waters of a river that looks very much like Cleveland's Cuyahoga River, edged with its cranes and mills pumping toxins into the air and water.

Ironically, by 1969, Cleveland had already started cleaning-up the Cuyahoga. Time magazine had treated the city unfairly when it shifted focus away from the city's shiny new environmental policies and toward coverage of the fire. To accompany its article, the magazine chose for its cover, a dramatic 1952 archival photo of a ship engulfed in a cloud of black smoke, flames snaking across the water and licking at its hull. The photo had been snapped more than a decade and a half before the accompanying article had been written. In his contribution, "Cuyahoga River Fire," posted by the online source, Cleveland Historical, Michael Rotman says that, "no picture of the '69 river fire is known to exist." Fake news or very late news, it didn't matter; the photo brought an inordinate amount of negative attention to the city and left Clevelanders feeling as if Time magazine had just kicked their great city in the mouth of their river.

Sleight of hand journalism aside, Cleveland's earlier identity as the best location in the nation had been cooked by the Time magazine article. The nation now saw Cleveland as the poster-child for bad environmental policy, and worse, Clevelanders lived into the role. Many began to believe that they were truly the mistake on the lake that everyone else told them that they were: "You might as well get used to it. We always lose," said father to son, "We're Clevelanders."

One summer night in 2016, while having dinner on the patio of an East 4th Street restaurant, I spent about an hour talking with Guitar Man. His trusty guitar, strapped over his shoulders, his shiny blue cape, like his long silvery hair, blew gently in the warm evening breeze. After playing us a song or two, he leaned in close and told me and my dinner companions the secret story of the person who accidentally set the Cuyahoga afire that fateful night in 1969. Guitar Man is not permitted to share with me the true identity of the fire starter, of course, because then he might have to strum me to death.

The accidental arsonist, said Guitar Man, was no more than a youth in his late middle school years. The young man – a boy really, built a plastic model of some World War II ship, a PT 109 or a Trumpeter HMS Hood Battleship. Guitar Man wasn't entirely sure about this part of the story. Guitar Man did know, however, that the kid sent his model ship down the river in flames, you know, as kids are apt to do. He hadn't planned on setting the river ablaze or firing-up environmentalists across the nation or torching Cleveland's reputation for a generation or two. He just wanted to see how long his little ship would stay afloat while sailing down the river in flames.

Don't be so quick to judge! What coming-of-age pre-pubescent boy has not burned a GI Joe, a model airplane, or his sister's Barbie doll, and then accidentally ignited a national controversy.

Apocryphal as Guitar Man's story may be, it is, perhaps, as believable as the bogus 1952 photo that Time slapped on the cover of its magazine back in 1969. Besides, underlying Guitar Man's story is a wonderful and healthy attempt to reclaim the city's identity: it's not that Cleveland had an oil-oozing river, bubbling with flammable and life-threatening toxins that gave Cleveland its sorry reputation, but a kid – a little Opie Taylor from The Andy Griffith Show with a model boat playing by the river. Saving the city is Guitar Man's honorable mission. He is out on the street chasing down crooked politicians and diabolical development policies. He is there to bring down the big man and lift up the little guy. He wants to up-end the false narratives that too often end up keeping Cleveland down. If you ask me, we could use a few more just like him - people willing to change the narrative, to transform the old doctrine of loss by preaching a new gospel of hope. We are what we behold, not what we are told. Guitar Man, and other Clevelanders like him, invite us to behold an alternate possibility for the city. Next time you see him in downtown Cleveland, go give him a few bucks, get your photo taken with him and ask him to tell you a few Cleveland stories. Guitar Man has more than a cape full!

Guitar Man has his work cut out for him, though. Throughout the mid to last part of the twentieth century Clevelanders lost most things that gave them a secure sense of pride-filled identity. They lost companies. They lost jobs. They lost adult children who moved to sunnier destinations in quest of rosier opportunities.

In 1920, Clevelanders are happy to remind you, Cleveland was the fifth largest city in America with 796,841 residents. In 1950, just a handful of years before Guitar Man was born, I am guessing, Cleveland was still the seventh largest city in the nation when its population peaked at 914,808 - just under one million residents. Over the last seventy years, however, Cleveland has seen a steady stream of residents abandoning the city for the apparent safety of the sprawling suburbs or for opportunities well beyond Northeast Ohio. From 2000 to 2016 alone, Cleveland lost nineteen percent of its population leaving it now ranked as the fifty-first largest city in the U.S. with a mere 385,809 citizens and counting down.

With an ever-shrinking tax base matched only by over-grown spending under the leadership of Mayor Ralph J. Perk, who increased spending by thirty percent from 1971-1977, not even America's youngest boy-wonder of a mayor, Dennis Kucinich, could save the city from bankruptcy. On December 15, 1978 the City of Cleveland became the first major city since the Great Depression to default on its financial obligations. It would take seven full years, under the leadership of Mayor George Voinovich, and loans from eight local banks for the city to finally get its affairs under control.

As if things couldn't get worse, restless for opportunity, particularly among the African American community, Cleveland's east side combusted in all out civil war. Most renowned among Cleveland's conflicts of the mid-twentieth century were the Hough Riots of July 1966. According to Case Western Reserve University's Encyclopedia of Cleveland[21], it is uncertain whether outside agitators ignited the conflict or simply "exploited" it. Either way, from July 18-24, 1966, almost a full three years before the Cuyahoga River famously caught fire, Cleveland's east side neighborhood went up in flames of its own.

During the six days of unrest, there were hundreds of fires reported. Almost three hundred people were arrested. Thirty were injured and four were killed. Mayor Ralph Locher who, earlier, had been slow to respond to the growing needs of the predominantly African American community[22], where the unemployment rate was almost double that of anywhere else in the city, called in a couple of thousand soldiers from Army National Guard to help quell the riots. It would be decades before the Hough neighborhood would recover and become the emerging neighborhood it is today of new homes and even a popular vineyard and winery – Château Hough Vineyards.

Hough wasn't the only place of racial unrest in Cleveland during the mid-twentieth century, though. The Glennville Shootout of 1968 is, perhaps, less known than the Hough Riots, but its one-hour stand-off between police and residents of Cleveland's Glenville neighborhood, almost two years to the day of the Hough Riots, left more people dead

---

[21] http://www.ohiohistorycentral.org/w/Cleveland_Civil_Disorders_(1966_-_1968), accessed November 15, 2017.
[22] Moore, Leonard N. (2002). *Carl B. Stokes and the Rise of Black Political Power.* Urbana, Ill.: University of Illinois Press, p.82.

including four east side residents and three police officers and set-off another two days of fires, looting and violence.

Longtime members of the Old Stone Church tell me that it was during this time that the Black Panther Party marched on their congregation in the heart of the city where Rev. Dr. Lewis Raymond, an outspoken civic leader was the senior pastor at the time, and Mayor Ralph Locher and his wife, among other influential Clevelanders were church members. I'm told that it was during Dr. Raymond's Sunday morning sermon that a large group of Black Panthers entered the building, lined the sanctuary walls and surrounded the worshippers. The activists announced that they were "taking the church."

Dr. Raymond, confident in the pulpit, responded by saying "Like anyone else, you're welcome to join us this morning if you're here to worship God" and continued with his sermon. I sometimes joke that it must not have been a particularly riveting message that day as the group, after making an impression, stayed only a few minutes and then left.

·　　·　　·

To be sure, there were flickers of hope along the way, a succession of "almost" and "maybe this time" moments in more recent history when it looked like Cleveland might capture something of a comeback. Cleveland had a few wins in the 1990s with new baseball park, lakefront football stadium, the new Great Lakes Science Center and, perhaps, most notably, the victory of being selected as the host city for the Rock & Roll Hall of Fame in 1986, and the opening in 1995. The Rock Hall – a glimmering pyramid-shaped, I. M. Pei point of pride for Clevelanders continues to be one of Ohio's most visited tourist attraction. Wisely, all of these amenities were located downtown and each would play an important part of the core's revival that was still to come.

Even so, the so-called Cleveland "renaissance" of the nineties was short lived or, better still underdeveloped. It lacked full commitment and follow through. Late in that decade, while doing research for her 2003 book, Stiff: The Curious Lives of Human Cadavers, Mary Roach traveled to Cleveland to meet with and interview neurosurgeon Dr. Robert White. Dr. White had become famous in Cleveland for successfully transplanting monkey brains. The good doctor removed living brains from donor monkeys and kept them alive, first, by implanting them into other living organisms such as the abdomens of other animals. "While the inside of someone else's abdomen is of moderate interest in a sort of curiosity-seeking, Surgery Channel, sort of way," said Roach, "it's not the sort of place you want to settle down and live out the remainder of your years." As seemingly mad-scientist-like as was Dr. White's work in Cleveland, it impelled Roach to visit and then, in an oh-by-the-way comment, offer a cutting, albeit humorous, jab about Cleveland's so-called rust belt renaissance of the late nineties:

"I was an hour early, and spent the time driving up and down Metro Health Care Drive, looking for a place to sit and have some coffee and review White's papers. There was nothing. I ended up back at the hospital on a patch of grass outside the parking garage. I had heard Cleveland had undergone some sort of renaissance, but apparently it underwent it in some other part of town. Let's just say it wasn't the sort of place I'd want to live out the rest of my years, though it beats a monkey abdomen, and you can't say that about some neighborhoods."[23]

Comments such as Roach's have nurtured doubt and even self-loathing among residents of Northeast Ohio's city by the lake and have provided good cause for longtime Clevelanders to question whether or not the more recent renaissance of 2010-2020 would actually hold.

It's been almost a century of decline for the-best-location-in-the-nation. The experience of loss has woven itself into the fabric of the Cleveland psyche. Like a security blanket, Cleveland often wraps itself in its own story-quilt of losses-past, as if bracing itself for more heartache – better to get used to it, kid, and be prepared for more losses to come than hope for something better and get hurt in the end.

In other ways, though, Cleveland often wears its losses less like a comfortable blanket and more like a blindfold that limits the city and

---

[23] Mary Roach, Stiff: The Curious Lives of Human Cadavers, London: W. W. Norton & Company, Ltd., Castle House, 2003, p. 210.

her children's ability to see a future better than its past. We may wonder, from time to time, what the world looks like from the winning side of the scoreboard. Mostly, though, that kind of wonder is short-lived in poor rustbelt cities like Cleveland.

In May 2011, I performed the memorial service for former mayoral First Lady, Eleanor (Worthington) Locher and then interred her ashes next to her beloved in the Old Stone Church columbarium, the sacred place for the remains of loved ones. There lie the ashes of many of Cleveland's great women and men of the late twentieth century. There is a padded bench in the center of the small, cave-like room where, occasionally, I was able to sit and be still with God, and with the Old Stone saints who have gone before me. Here, on days when I remembered to pause from the busyness of the day-to-day ministries that keep me on the run most of the time, I meditated. I prayed, which meant that I mostly listened.

Dietrich Bonhoeffer, the famous twentieth century German theologian who was executed as a Nazi dissident and for his participation in a failed assassination attempt on the life of Adolph Hitler, encouraged preachers to walk through cemeteries and preach to the souls who "lie in wait." I found it more helpful to ask questions of the dead rather than preach. I posed my questions to Mayor Locher, and to some of the other giants from that era, whose ashes are contained in polished marble urns or velvet bags sealed behind smooth granite plaques that are engraved with their names and the particular days they had on this good earth. I question these movers and shakers of yesteryear about those days when Cleveland was just starting to slip from glory. Did the city and its leaders see it? Did they sense, in any way, the decay that was beginning to happen around them. Rivers were burning. Neighborhoods were flaming-out in fiery riots. The younger generation and even longtime residents, along with the Barons and the beloved Browns, were streaming out of this once great city, leaving behind a grand history and a stubborn belief in loss, one that some have clung to religiously. Cleveland as they had known it, loved it, and served it, was dying.

I asked. Only every now and then, however, did they answer.

It was my passionate hope that Cleveland would be shaped less by the incarnation of its historic losses, and more by the flickers of hope that were beginning to flash here and there: the burgeoning downtown and near downtown communities, a network of downtown residents who were getting organized and bringing new energy and imagination to the heart of the city, redevelopment projects, and even a little new construction. Still, many Clevelanders found themselves struggling to see with new vision, or to live into an emerging and more optimistic narrative for the city. Promise was just beginning to break through the historic cloud of gloom, though few could see it and even fewer were ready to embrace it. Even us Clevangelicals were sometimes written off as shortsighted fanatics. For too many decades, too many good folks had let the gospel according to Eeyore define faith for their city. They continued to worship down at Cleveland's "First Church of Perpetual Loss."

Chapter Eight

My City, Right or Wrong!

"Cleveland: You've got to be tough!"
Daffy Dan T-Shirt, 1970s

I'M A LITTLE EMBARRASSED to admit that even as a teenager my mom still made my lunch for me to take to school. It didn't matter whether I grunted "good morning" to her not, or how much we may have struggled with, and then fought over, my inability to understand my math homework the night before. Every morning, when I stumbled into the kitchen, bleary-eyed and half awake, there was a little brown paper sack with a cheese sandwich stuffed into it. Tuna if I was lucky. She would have packed a few celery and carrot sticks to accompany the sandwich, too. On really exceptional days, for dessert, Mom may have included a cookie or even a chocolate Wagon Wheel, that flattened Mallomar-type treat coveted by drooling kids from Canadian coast to coast to coast.

Even more difficult for me to admit is the fact that I had the adolescent audacity to complain to my friends about my mother's homemade lunches, though there was absolutely nothing wrong with them (my lunches, that is, my friends were another story). What an insolent little brat I was!

Mom wasn't a stay-at-home mom. She had three almost grown sons to make lunches for, not to mention breakfasts. All this before she headed-out the door to go to work, leaving dinner slow-cooking in the crockpot on the counter behind her. My father wasn't much help in this regard, either. Dad escaped the house early or, more often, hid out in his bedroom listening to the morning news on CBC, afraid to come out of his room until his boys had finished scrapping over the one shower in the house, or who used whose towel, or who left a hair on the soap, and were dressed and out the door. Pick the day. There was usually some sort of kerfuffle. With three teenage boys under one roof and only one shower, odds on conflict were good. I suppose staying out of our regular morning barking and bickering was Dad's small contribution to the morning rush.

It was my mom who did all the heavy lifting here, including packing lunches so that her darling sons would not go hungry throughout the day.

I must have been singing a sad song to my friends about my mom's lunches one too many times, though. One day my best friend joined me on the chorus with a discordant note that just didn't sit well with me.

"A cheese sandwich again! Ugh!" I grumbled across the cafeteria table from him.

"Your mom always makes such crappy lunches!" he grumbled right back without lifting his face from his side of the trough, and clearly not considering that his comments had just triggered World War Three. Historians would look back on the incident one day in the same way they did on the assassination of Archduke Franz Ferdinand of Austria and his wife Sophie, and point to the cafeteria crisis as the pivotal moment when the world once again fell into global conflict, human history irreparably and forever changed.

Maybe my buddy was just trying to sympathize or be in solidarity. Who knows? My response, however, was hardly "thank you for your support!"

There is some debate as to the origin of the phrase, "to see red" – angering a bull with a red cape, on the one hand, or seeing red behind your eyes from increasing blood pressure in times of heightened emotion, on the other. Based on my fiery reaction to my friend's insult, I am going to go with the latter. My head was hot, my face was flushed, and my vision was blurred – a perfect emotional trifecta that called forth an embarrassingly inappropriate response on my part.

Being the more mature of the two of us (ha ha!), I normally would have had the good sense to take a deep breath and just walked away. Be the better man, which I usually was. Take the high road, which I usually did. However, on this particular day, that's not what happened at all.

I slid out of the fold-down bench-seat anchored to our cafeteria table and turned to step away. But in a microsecond a dark spirit of rage grabbed hold of me. My blood boiled. I saw red!

I whirled around and with a World Series pitch, launched my half-full milk cartoon in my best friend's direction. The little cardboard box, a cruise missile with its deadly dairy payload, was now careening directly toward his face. Thankfully for him, and for me, my milky-projectile was intercepted by the edge of the table. Instead of making a direct hit, the carton burst into a serious spray of Sealtest 2%, 8 ounces (or about .23 liters for you Canadian kids) all over my friend and half a dozen or so buddies sitting at our table, not to mention the upper grade monsters feeding one table over and who were now also seeing red.

What became remarkably clear in that moment of culinary critique and emotional outburst, at least to me, was that it was one thing for me to criticize my mother's lunches, but heaven help the poor sap who thinks that he has license to do the same! Best friend or not, that was simply not done. Cross the line of respect, trash talk another guy's mother, or her lunches that had been lovingly made for her son, and there would be a price to be paid. It was a lesson I have carried into adulthood, always trying to be a helpful listener as good folks gripe and grouse about their spouses, their families, their jobs, without throwing fuel on the fire by joining in the grumbling. Even in the worst situations, loyalties run deep.

By 2012, I had become acutely aware that you cannot live in Cleveland very long without spotting that same strong spirit of loyalty at work in the hearts and minds of longtime Clevelanders. In fact, while I have lived in other cities, even a foreign country - if you can really call Canada "foreign" ... or a "country,"[24] I don't think I have ever witnessed a city that goes as far as Clevelanders do when it comes to planting the flag of patriotism to place. It's proudly anchored deep in their diverse cultures - their diverse European and African influenced foods, their fourth quarter fumbling teams, a celebration of their world-famous orchestra (even if they don't attend all that often), their second largest in the nation performing arts district, their historic churches and mid-western stalwart resolve. One only need point to the throngs of people – downtown residents and suburbanites alike, who turned out to sweep up broken glass and haul away debris from the downtown business district after the riots of late May 2020.

"Defend the Land!" Clevelanders shout. Actually, they have incorporated it into their rustbelt-chic fashion, embroidering the imperative to their jackets and hats, tie-dying it on their t-shirts, inking it into their skin almost as a rite of passage that declares one's allegiance to the nation that is Cleveland. It's their city. Win or lose, rich or poor, right or wrong – they 'Cleave to the Land.'

It's one thing for Clevelanders to grumble in anger about their hometown, to gripe about the losing Browns or Indians, the potholes,

---

[24] Okay. I know, as a dual citizen and fellow Canadian that I just ticked-off an entire country. Sorry, Canada. Be honest, though, in so some ways, it's our countrywide mutual love/hate relationship with the United States that helps us eek-out our slightly unique identity in the shadow of the American elephant. Every film we watch we get giddy with excitement when we learn that it was shot somewhere in Canada. Like Americans counting their cash, we count the number of famous Canadian actors and comedians, musicians and athletes who play down here in the American big leagues. When Team Canada wins gold in hockey every single Winter Olympics, in every division (men, women, juniors, little tikes – if they had a fetus league, Canada would win that, too), especially if Canada trounces Team U.S.A., the entire nation gets overwhelmingly verklempt - though, as Canadians, we never use the word verklempt unless we are imitating Mike Myers, that beloved Canadian comedian and onetime cast member on NBC's *Saturday Night Live*, an American show produced by a Canadian, Lorne Michaels. But we knew these facts already, didn't we? Slept with them under our Canadian goose down feather-filled pillows, treasured them in our hearts the way Mary treasured all those kind words about Jesus from the magi and shepherds. All this goes to show that our extreme loyalty means we can identify with "neighbours" (see what I did there) across the lake in Northeast Ohio. Congratulations, Canada! You're Clevelanders, too. And thanks for being so Canadian that you're actually reading the footnotes all the way through. Well done, you!

lake effect snow or awkward three-tower skyline. It's quite another for an "outsider" to do it. Slam the city that rock and roll built and ol' Eeyore is going to kick your ass.

When I first arrived, Clevelanders entertained me with stories of Steelers fans going home with bruised and broken body parts for misplaced comments. Exaggerations? Possibly. But judging by the initial reaction by Clevelanders to LeBron James' 2010 decision to leave their city and take his talents to Miami, I wouldn't want to test the theory.

"Never underestimate the scorn and fury of the Cleveland sports fan" wrote the Plain Dealer's Michael Scott in the wake of LeBron's big decision to move to Miami. "Especially when jilted by a once-loved -- and now lost -- superstar."[25] Some fans shredded their LeBron t-shirts and posters. Others, as if carrying-out some ancient Druid ritual, piled their LeBron artifacts into a pyre and torched them, reducing the Akron wicker man to ashes.

CAVS owner, Dan Gilbert, furious about the decision, saw red and ignited as quickly as I did over my friend's misplaced sandwich comment in the cafeteria years earlier. Gilbert ripped into LeBron by publishing an open letter in the Plain Dealer addressed to Cleveland fans the very next day. Gilbert, a Detroiter by birth, Clevelander by investment, openly attacked LeBron by hurling a long list of insults and accusations: "our former hero" who "deserted" Cleveland fans, "narcissistic, self-promotional," "the self-declared former 'King'" who would be taking the Cleveland "curse" with him down south, which, to Dan Gilbert and most Cleveland fans added-up to a "cowardly betrayal" by LeBron James.

Clevelanders and other rust belters around the Great Lakes whose glory days always feel like the day before yesterday, will sometimes take a critique on the chin, as if they expected it anyway. Other times,

---

[25] Michael Scott, "Cleveland-Akron fans saddened, sickened and angry at LeBron James' decision to leave Cavaliers," *The Plain Dealer*, July 8, 2010, accessed June 27, 2018. http://blog.cleveland.com/metro/2010/07/cleveland-akron_fans_saddened.html

especially if the gibe is coming from a non-Clevelander, they swing back bringing a new, tough-guy meaning to the term rust belt!

The response is not necessarily violent, though. When defending the Land, Clevelanders have an exceptionally refined sense of "f***-you" humor. Having experienced half a century worth of bites and barbs from rival cities and others around the country, Clevelanders have a much higher tolerance for insult than you might imagine. Slam Cleveland and you are likely to get a whole litany of retorts about your hometown in return: Q: What do Peter Pan and Pittsburg have in common? A: Pirates always lose.

In response to a 2010 article I wrote for the Plain Dealer called "Engage in Cleveland to make it vital" (the editor's title, not mine), I was slammed for even my gentle critiques of the city. The essay was intended to be a celebration of some of the great things about Cleveland. "I'm blessed to see, often on a daily basis, good folks who make a huge difference by engaging in the life of our city," I encouraged readers. However, they hardly responded with eager support. Instead, readers went after me for being out of touch or, more aptly, not yet in touch. One reader called "theprovoker" wrote:

"With all due respect Rev. Mark.....you just don't get it. IF the one our sports teams could win a championship (preferably the Indians), the whole city could get rid of its downtrodden image.Try opening up the Bible...page 1...the book of Genesis.... "In the big inninng"..... Well we're still waiting for it from the Indians in both the '97 and '95 World Series. Just tease us again....the devil exists....it's either Mark Shapiro or Larry or Paul Dolan or Mike Hargrove." [sic]

I found the comment from "bena55" remarkably accurate in its ability to call me out on my newcomer naïveté, on the one hand, while exemplifying the Cleveland Eeyore complex, on the other:

"Two old axioms might apply here........
'Looking at the world through rose colored glasses' ......and
'You can't kick a dead horse'

In those first few years, it seemed that with every article I wrote, every city-sermon I preached, every conversation in which I dared to engage, longtime Clevelanders were schooling me on the inappropriateness of my sweet-Savannah innocence or apologetic Canadian niceness. Admittedly, in some ways, they were right! "Cleveland: you have to be tough!" proclaimed a t-shirt. "Cleveland: We'll keep the river on for you" promised another.

Cleveland was, and continues to be a town of loyal defenders who refused to entertain any of my seemingly Johnny-come-lately, pie-in-the-sky visions for a better city. Theprovoker's comment, "you just don't get it" was a phrase I heard often during those first few seasons in Cleveland. I would have to "get it" before I could truly participate in the Cleveland conversation.

I wasn't all that naïve, though. I read articles about the urban blight, and not simply with my tortoise shell glasses professorially perched on the end of my nose while superciliously scrutinizing statistics and meticulously analyzing the philosophical nuances of the Great Lake city in which I was now living. I was aware of the inordinate amount of crime, rising poverty, and the emigrating American economic industrial engine. Jobs were chugging out to sea toward far off lands with little or no environmental standards where underpaid adults and children in deplorable working conditions cranked-out goods to satisfy America's appetite for products at 'low, low prices' while, at the same time, bless them with higher rates of return on their mutual funds and registered retirement savings. I was also aware of the even greater number of hometown jobs that had simply been replaced by less expensive robotics and other new technologies. I knew how rust belt cities had been toughened-up, first in the steel mills and auto plants, and then by the jobs lost from those very same steel mills and auto plants. I had spent a large portion of my formative years in Windsor, Ontario – a heavily industrialized Canadian lunch bucket town nestled along the once toxic Detroit River. I was no stranger to the pugnacious spirit of an American factory town.

It's Cleveland. You've got to be tough.

I was certainly not prepared, however, for the street-fighter toughness of a city that had earned itself the short-lived (thankfully) title, "Bomb City" following the summer of 1976 when over thirty bombs, mostly car but at least two house bombs as well, rocked Cleveland in an all-out war between the one-time union boss of the local chapter of the International Longshoremen's Association and racketeer, Danny Greene, and the Cleveland mafia. Greene blew away, by gun or car bomb, at least eight of his would-be assassins before he himself was killed by a car bomb. The explosion was so powerful that it launched Greene's arm through the air, landing it a hundred feet from the rest of his body[26] in the Brainard Medical building's parking lot in the Cleveland suburb of Lyndhurst. Greene was there for dental work. And you wonder why people hate to go to see their dentist!

Coincidentally, it was the very same building in which I would have the remains of my lateral incisor excised from upper gum and a bone-graft procedure done to permanently anchor a titanium rod in my mouth following my umbrella incident with "Barry the Bruiser" on Public Square my first few months in the city. I knew nothing of Danny Greene at that time, or the Brainard Medical building's sordid past, otherwise, I would have had someone watching the parking lot the whole time I was in inside the building.

That kind of Cleveland toughness revealed itself again just a year or so later when the Cleveland mafia issued a twenty-five thousand dollar hit on Cleveland's young Mayor Dennis Kucinich who, at the time, was waging his own war against the banks and others in the city by refusing to cave to pressure from power brokers to sell-off the city's public utility, Cleveland Public Power.[27] Eventually, the contract was cancelled when the city took the hit after Kucinich's hard-lined tactics, or the bank's, or both, drove the city into receivership.

Cleveland toughness isn't just historical, either. The summer I arrived in Cleveland, City Councilman Joe Cimperman, his wife, Nora, and their one-week old baby, had their home in the near downtown neighborhood of Tremont firebombed. Although no one

---

[26] James Renner, "The Mafia Plot To Kill Dennis Kucinich: A Former Cleveland Police Chief Finally Tells The Whole Story," *FreeTimes*, Volume 15, Issue 9, July 4th, 2007, accessed June 27, 2018.
https://web.archive.org/web/20070708205903/http://www.freetimes.com/storie s/15/9/the-mafia-plot-to-kill-dennis-kucinich
[27] Ibid.

has ever been indicted for the attack, some have speculated that the incident may have been racially motivated. Cimperman had held a rally in support of two African-American families in the transitioning neighborhood who had their homes firebombed the previous summer. Thankfully, no one was hurt in the attacks. The incident just seemed to toughen Cimperman's resolve as a leader who would work for racial healing in his district and in the city at large.

It's not just mobsters and politicians in Cleveland who exhibit that gritty fortitude, though. It's pretty well every Clevelander. They are a steadfast and sturdy people. They brace themselves against the brutal winds of harsh economic times, failing relationships, dying neighborhoods, addiction and other illnesses, losing sports teams, and negative press from around the country the way they shoulder into the frigid squalls that blow in from the lake each winter, blasting them with a million pellets of lake effect snow. Clevelanders down a beer, grit their teeth, and carry on. They are people who have been knocked down but keep getting back up. In fact, you might find it difficult to knock some of them down at all.

A friend of mine was out with a buddy one day. He and his buddy stopped to get gas. A thief approached the car, pulled out a handgun and shot my friend in the side. My friend's buddy drove him to the nearby main campus of the Cleveland Clinic, the proximity of which, he believed, was a sign of God's amazing grace. While he waited for surgery, he telephoned his wife to explain why he was running late and then argued with her for a full ten minutes before surgery because she didn't believe that he had truly been shot. Cleveland. You've got to be tough!

Clevelanders are not just physically tough. They are mentally resolute - unwaveringly badass in their ability to persevere, emotionally, in the face of some of the harshest conditions. Whether it is the jarring winters that bring with them storms like the famous blizzard of 1978 - aptly dubbed the White Hurricane that killed fifty-one people throughout the state - including one woman who, according to the Plain Dealer's John Kroll, froze to death while walking her dog, or any of their numerous sports tragedies, Clevelanders exhibit the unique ability to soldier on. Give them a winter storm and Clevelanders will cheer, "Snow day!" Deliver bad news and they will tell you they've seen worse. Lose a game or season, or even a super-star and they'll shrug it off and start a victory chant.

Just minutes after getting over the shock of LeBron's devastating announcement to leave the city, Clevelanders at the Harry Buffalo sports bar - an East 4th Street favorite near the downtown stadiums - quickly turned their hope away from LeBron James and the Cleveland Cavaliers and toward their losing Browns again with a rousing Browns chant: "Here we go Brownies. Here we go! Woof, Woof!" At the same time, 'the Buffalo' cranked out over its loudspeakers Cleveland's most endearing anthem, Ian Hunter's Cleveland Rocks! Michael Scott could not have called the play any better. The following day he wrote: "Fans at the Harry Buffalo demonstrated Cleveland's necessary short memory and strange, enduring hope."[28]

In Cleveland, I discovered a people who, while suffering greatly from low self-esteem - the Eeyore complex that continues to dog them still to this day, are extremely house-proud. They are as passionate about their city as any man who loves his old clunker of a car, or any kid who is unconditionally proud of his old clunker of an unemployed dad, or any teenager who defends his mother's homemade lunches. They are loyal to their city, for rustbelt-better or frigid-winter worse, to the biting and bitter end.

When I first arrived, someone asked me what I thought of Cleveland so far.

"Great city!" I responded. "But you don't have many trees for a town called 'the Forest City.'" I had just moved from Savannah, after all, an award-winning city for its success and commitment to urban forestation and, ironically, also dubbed "the Forest City." Cleveland, particularly, downtown Cleveland, on the other hand seemed to me to be a city of very few trees, and most of those were fairly recent plantings – sticks, compared to Savannah's lush and moss draped Live Oaks - that offered no tree canopy to cool the city in the summer, or disperse the wind in the winter.

Based on his response, though, you would have thought I just insulted the lunch his mom had made him for school.

"We've got trees!" He snapped. "Open your eyes and take a look around."

As defensive as he was, I liked the idea of living in a place where people were as hardy as they were in Cleveland. Like the plants up on our Friends balcony, Clevelanders showed themselves to be a people

[28] Michael Scott, "Cleveland-Akron fans saddened . . ."

who knew how to suck the life out of the few moments of sunshine they got every few decades or so.

That kind of Cleveland resilience brings with it a rare kind of honesty, too. In rust belt cities like Detroit, Buffalo, and Cleveland, where some days are just too damn cold to linger while waiting for the right words, or to sift through the kind of nuanced comments you might find in places like Savannah, or for someone else to meander to their point, Clevelanders are quick to let you know exactly how they feel about you, or about something you said or did. Whether it is immediately following a sermon you just preached, an article you wrote for the paper, or a comment you made in a local bar, Clevelanders will bless you with an uncalculated honesty, a rare authenticity that, in my experience, you just don't find in many other places. In Cleveland, you never have to go home from the party or work or even church regretting something you said. If people really didn't like it, they will let you know before you leave. Even if they don't, they are not going to harbor resentment or Lord it over you for years to come. As one friend said to me, "Mark, it isn't much of a Cleveland party if someone expects you to call and apologize the next day."

That kind of rough-edged honesty was appealing to me. I just wasn't sure I had it within me to be a part of that kind of world. I was conflicted. On the one hand, I admired Clevelanders for their in-your-face boldness with one another. On the other, I longed for the southern gentility as much as anything I had lost in my move to Cleveland. In Savannah they had similar issues as those in Cleveland - gender discrimination, racial injustice, poverty and crime. It was just that in Savannah they were politer about it.

Clevelanders may affix a bomb to the under-carriage of your car, or to the one parked next to you, as they did with Danny Greene. At least in those last fleeting moments just before you see the flash of the explosion, though, you'll know where you stood with them. Cleveland: You've got to be tough!

2012-2015: ANGER

*"You will not be punished for your anger,
you will be punished by your anger."*
- Buddha

Chapter Nine

Wake Up Call

"The truth will set you free, but first it will piss you off."
Gloria Steinem

WE DON'T CHOOSE a purpose in life. Purpose chooses us.

As a pastor, folks sometimes ask me to help them find their purpose. All I can tell them is that, in my experience, we find our purpose. More often than not, it finds us. We don't select our calling the way we read over a menu and decide what we'll order for dinner. Or the way we bring home paint swatches from the hardware store, hold them up next to the wall or pieces of furniture in search of just the right color.

The author, Frederick Buechner, once wrote that our vocation is found in that place "where our deep gladness meets the world's deep need."[29] For some, this simple definition rings true. What do I love doing? Can I do it in a way that makes the world a better place? Seems like a perfect fit. For others, however, it's not the intersection of our joy and the world's need that awakens purpose within us, rather it's the collision of our awareness of the truth – what is fair, what is just, what is compassionate – and the world's lack of it. It's not necessarily our "deep gladness" but our restless passion for a better world that

---

[29] Frederick Buchner, *Wishful Thinking: A Theological ABC*, Harper & Row, 1973.

urges us toward our purpose. One of the clarifying moments of my ministry in Cleveland found me in this latter way.

•   •   •

By 2012, I had begun singing the praises of Cleveland, especially its emerging downtown community, to anyone who would listen. The heavy lifting of spiritual and civic leadership was paying off. Cleveland was rising and I was happy to spread the good news with the fervor of a born again believer. Hallelujah! I'd been converted by hard work, dedication, and enough small victories to offer testimony to God's love for Cleveland. I had become a hardcore Clevangelist. And like a newcomer to an old church, I squeezed every possible opportunity to serve church and city into my days and nights.

I was elected to a number of economic development boards and volunteered on an advocacy committee that lobbied state legislators to continue offering a record number of important tax credits for more re-development in downtown. Regularly, I met with downtown stakeholders and city planning groups. I attended charrettes and other visioning days for community stakeholders as new design implementations in downtown were explored. Whenever I saw the opportunity, I helped court new retail, and then personally spent too much money at grand openings. I filled almost every conversation with espousals to the growing number of new business opportunities that, I believed, would increase incentives for downtown living, contribute to an increase in much-needed residential density, and ultimately raise the well-being and standard of living for all residents in the city's core. I partnered with the City of Cleveland, the Downtown Cleveland Alliance (DCA), and the Cleveland Division of Police to host monthly safety and security meetings at the church and in the common rooms of downtown apartment buildings. Our individual agendas may have been slightly different, but we held in common the goal of making downtown a safe, violence-free community where people could live, work, and play.

In the church, I was overjoyed to see the congregation's annual Hope for the City symposium gaining traction. We were attracting architects and designers, city planners, public transit CEOs, non-profit and religious leaders, politicians, and a dedicated and faithful following of students from the Maxine Goodman Levin College of Urban Affairs at Cleveland State University, as well as other fellow new urbanists who shared the church's vision for an economically viable, environmentally sustainable, and just city for all. We invited national speakers such as Jeff Speck, the former director of the National Endowment for the Arts and author of Walkable City: How Downtown Can Save America One Step at a Time and the Architectural Digest "Top Ten Innovator" and designer of Mark and Beth's tiny urban terrace, Diana Balmori, who drew crowds sometimes into the hundreds. We were opening people's hearts and minds to a new vision for Cleveland.

Downtown and its phenomenal growth energized me. The residential population was surging. At our first annual meeting of the Downtown Cleveland Residence, during my State of Downtown speech, I envisioned that in the next ten years we could come close to doubling our population from ten to twenty-thousand downtown residents. Following the meeting, one downtowner challenged me for being too pie-in-the-sky aspirational in my forecast. I huffed, "I suppose that goal could seem overly ambitious if it were not for the fact that the downtown population had tripled in the previous ten years!"

Sure, I was cocky. But better days for Cleveland were at hand. Like clouds breaking after a miserable winter storm, bright spots were bringing scattered rays of hope to the city. New high-tech jobs in Northeast Ohio were on the rise. In fact, they were out-pacing most other places in the nation.[30] Even Clevelanders had a hard time believing it. The uptick in the economy had become a part of our coffee

---

[30] Just one week later, Marcia Pledger of the *Plain Dealer/Cleveland.com* would publish the results of an independent study by the non-profit group, *Engine Advocacy* (San Francisco) that showed that while the national average in the same category was languishing at 2.6 percent, "Cleveland-Elyria-Mentor area saw a 9.1 percent increase in high-tech jobs created from 2010 to 2011." https://www.cleveland.com/business/2012/12/northeast_ohio_named_a_tech_h o.html (Updated Jan 12, 2019; Posted Dec 07, 2012, accessed April 19, 2021).

shop chatter and post-work happy hour banter the way a rare win for the Browns could dominate conversations around the city for weeks. "How long do you think it will last?" cried the cynics. Eeyore still lived among us. Still, after years of living under the weighty clouds of a dismal economy, there was finally a flickering light of hope on the horizon.

The mucky construction of the Greater Cleveland Transit Authority's Euclid Corridor Healthline was a thing of the past, as well. Ridership was up. Awards were being won. And new businesses were beginning to pop up along the five-mile route that had recently connected Northeast Ohio's two largest employment districts – downtown and University Circle. Historic tax credits were working, too, incentivizing the repurposing of architecturally outstanding properties from empty office spaces into apartments and even a small handful of condos for the growing young professional population and empty-nesters like Beth and me.

It was hard not to be glassy-eyed about the prospects of a new Cleveland. Big ticket developments in downtown were under way, too, bringing with them thousands of local construction jobs. The three-hundred-and-fifty-million-dollar Horseshoe Casino - now Jack Casino - on Public Square had recently opened, and the four-hundred and sixty-five million dollar public-private partnership Medical Mart - later to be renamed the Global Center for Health Innovation - and the accompanying new Convention Center were well into their construction phases and less than a year away from their grand opening. For me, Cleveland's downtown pastor, a trustee serving on a couple of downtown development organizations, and the organizer of an emerging downtown residents association, it was a busy time of ribbon cuttings, glad-handing, and squeezing in with other dedicated leaders for photo-ops and television appearances. During this time, the mayor even presented me with an award for my "dedication to downtown businesses and residents." It felt good to be doing good.

Cleveland was starting to shine. Literally. The Downtown Safety Ambassadors, the clean and safe workers of the DCA, were making our city so inviting that even Canadian tourists commented on how clean Cleveland was. Crime in downtown was in decline, too, especially if you subtracted from the equation, "smash 'n' grabs" which accounted for the higher-than-necessary statistics. Many drivers had yet to be swayed by the "Put your junk in the trunk" campaigns.

Most encouraging for me, and a lot of other downtowners, was the headway we had made with the wave of violence and vandalism that washed over the downtown Warehouse district from 2010-2011. The City of Cleveland invited Ken Bergeron, a U.S. Department of Justice Community Relations Service mediator from Chicago to lead a variety of stakeholder meetings to see if we could resolve some of the more serious problems facing the district. I volunteered the church hall as the gathering spot for the meetings. Whether they worship in a church or not, folks tend to behave better whenever they're inside one.

A variety of local stakeholders, from Cleveland Police to city councilors, crowded the church hall to participate in the roughly six-month process. I wore two hats – pastor of the Old Stone Church and representative of downtown residents.

The ultimate goal of the Department of Justice meetings was to resolve a variety of conflicts plaguing the Warehouse District and holding back further commercial and residential growth in the city's core, including the booming late night noise from street level clubs that shook the residential apartments and condos above. The crowd-choked streets that made accesses to residences almost impassible on weekend nights were a problem too, as was the early morning trash, especially the sea of shattered glass that littered the streets and nearby parking lots in the wake of party-goers who had gone home to their neighborhoods just hours before dawn. The greatest concern was the violence connected to some of the clubs in the area that was making residents feel unsafe in their own neighborhood.

Things were particularly bad on Thursday, Friday, and Saturday nights when West 6th and West 9th streets, and the main floor clubs and bars that lined them, could swell with up to ten thousand partiers or more. There had been a number of deaths from bar fights as well as afterhours shootings, including one that happened across the street from our home.

A few bullet holes were left in the window of one of Beth's and my favorite lunch stops, John Qs, which was located right next door to the church. It was past time to do something about it.

Some suggested that the desire to bring the bars under tighter control by imposing sound and private policing regulations wasn't about safety or quality of life at all, but was a racially motivated plan to keep African Americans out of downtown, as many of the bars were hip hop and dance clubs that seemed to appeal to a largely, but not exclusively, African American clientele. As I recall, District 10 Ohio House Representative Bill Patmon attended only one of the four meetings held at the church between November 2010 and March 2011, the last one. The mid-sixty-year-old politician entered the room, it seemed to me, appearing farcically out of touch with the rest of the group, especially his own constituents – the new, young professional residents living in downtown who were deeply committed to making their neighborhood safe and more livable for all. Patmon strutted into the room with one pant leg rolled-up to his knee, his ball cap on his head spun sideways. When he got his turn at the mic, Patmon grandstanded, making accusations that he might not be allowed into the clubs because of his skin color or the way he was dressed. I just hung my head, embarrassed for my state representative, wishing he had showed up for all the meetings and praying that his divisive approach wouldn't tank everyone else's sincere efforts.

Thankfully, in the end, we were able to move beyond straw man distractions, craft and sign a meaningful memorandum of understanding[31] that eased the stress in the neighborhood, increased safety, and allowed the Warehouse neighborhood and, later, the nearby Flats East Bank district to thrive. I believe even representative Patmon, a decent man and friend of the people, saw the merit in the plan. Signing the document was my first official act as the president of the newly formed Downtown Cleveland Residents Association

---

[31] Memorandum of Understanding, Preserving the Quality of Life and Safety for the Cleveland Historic Warehouse District and Adjoining Neighborhood, March 4, 2011. Accessed July 3, 2018. http://webapp.cleveland-oh.gov/aspnet/moc/Cleveland%20Warehouse%20District%20MOU%20Final%2003032011.pdf

(DCRA). As it was also for my vice president, Joseph Giuliano – my brother, not by blood, but by faith. We swaggered out of City Hall reveling in our small victory for downtown residents and headed to a nearby watering hole to celebrate. We had codified symbolic but meaningful change for the city and had our very names on an historical document to prove it. Things were looking up.

Gun violence in downtown decreased. Summer of 2012, we had survived a whole summer season of dance clubs and street parties without a single fatality. In fact, it had been almost nine full months since an off-duty police officer killed a recent high school graduate during an arrest at East 9th and Euclid Avenue. That was one too many shootings, of course, and clearly needed thorough investigation. Still, the unified efforts of residents, business owners, civic leaders, politicians, and police looked promising.

•   •   •

There is a story in Cleveland folklore, a well-rehearsed narrative about the time team Cleveland was up 2-1 over the Marlins in game seven of the World Series heading into the bottom of the ninth. So confident were Cleveland's front office owners and upper management, so the story goes, that the victory champagne had been cradled in ice and wheeled into Cleveland's locker room for the post game celebration. Some have argued that the premature icing of the champagne jinxed the win for Cleveland. The bubbly was wheeled right back out of the locker room when José Mesa blew the save allowing the Marlins to tie it up and, ultimately, claim the title in the eleventh.

The thought of something going wrong for our city at this time was certainly conceivable. After all, all around me were longtime Eeyores and naysayers who warned me not to bank on a smooth-lined upward trajectory. Even so, I was riding so high on a wave of optimism that I never anticipated that the tragic turn of events that would come over the next two years, the ones that would stir many of us from our sleep and awaken within me a deepened sense of purpose for my time in Cleveland. I most certainly never saw the horrific killings of

November 30th, 2012 coming. My spirit was too busy putting the champagne on ice and getting ready to celebrate Cleveland's rising.

Early in the evening of Thursday November 29th, Beth and I were getting ourselves ready to go out. Beth was on the board of an organization that worked tirelessly for an end to homelessness in the city. We didn't have far to go. The event was being held next door to our condo at the House of Blues. For a moment, we stood by our windows overlooking the city to watch a fiery red sunset over the Warehouse district. In the crimson glow of the setting sun, the neighborhood looked to me like a charming nineteenth-century European village. I slipped my arm around Beth's waist and sighed with contentment. "It's been a good season, hasn't it? Do you realize that we haven't a single shooting this year?"

The next morning, Friday November 30, my day off, I sat down by the fireplace with a steaming cup of coffee to sip while reading the morning news. The warm morning sun streamed into our charming condo. It filled the room with a peaceful light. With my cup of coffee in my right hand, my tablet on my lap, I clicked on the news. It was time to put the champagne away.

• • •

The morning of Friday November 30, 2012, the headlines on Cleveland.com were teeming with reports of two people who had been shot to death by Cleveland Police officers: "2 dead in shootout after leading Cleveland police on chase through 3 cities,"[32] read one. "Police shoot and kill 2 in East Cleveland after chase,"[33] read another.

---

[32] 2 dead in shootout after leading Cleveland police on chase through 3 cities, Cleveland.com, November 29, 2012, accessed July 5, 2018. https://www.cleveland.com/metro/index.ssf/2012/11/no_one_injured_during_pol ice_c.html

[33] Police shoot and kill 2 in East Cleveland after chase (video and gallery), Cleveland.com, November 30, 2012, accessed July 5, 2018. https://www.cleveland.com/metro/index.ssf/2012/11/2_men_shot_after_chase_e nding.html

Even a third announced, "Police say man and woman were killed in police chase that ended in East Cleveland."[34] Television and radio media were covering the story, as well, blasting out scant details of the incident as they became available. Quickly, we learned that the pursuit that would lead to one of the most historic and horrific police shootings of two unarmed African Americans began in our own downtown neighborhood after police claimed to have heard shots fired from a suspicious looking vehicle.

What was extraordinary, and that which initially caught the attention of many readers, including my own, wasn't that the morning news was reporting an overnight shooting but that there were so many headlines about just one incident. That was odd.

In my capacity as the president of the DCRA, I was also receiving emails from Cleveland Police's Third District Commander, Calvin Williams (now Chief Williams), containing relevant daily crime reports from previous nights' activities. It didn't take long for me to learn that the chase referenced in the news articles began half a block from the church and just across the Square from our condo. It concluded in a massacre miles from downtown.

Initially, it was believed, that dozens of shots were fired. One WEWS News 5 reporter who had been doing a ride-along with the police reported thirty to forty shots, although photographs of the car that appeared alongside news reports made that number seem conspicuously conservative. William Greer, a neighbor to the Heritage Middle School where the victims were cornered and then shot, stated to reporters that he had heard the gunfire. "Pop, pop, pop. Bang, bang, bang. I couldn't believe how much – it must have been more than 50 shots."[35]

---

[34] Police say man and woman were killed in police chase that ended in East Cleveland (video and gallery), Cleveland.com, November 30, 2012, accessed July 5, 2012.
https://www.cleveland.com/metro/index.ssf/2012/11/police_say_man_and_wom an_were.html

[35] Police shoot and kill 2 in East Cleveland after chase (video and gallery), Cleveland.com, November 30, 2012, accessed July 5, 2018.

It seemed sadly ironic to me that Beth and I had snuggled-up in the warm glow of a late autumn sunset and gazed out on our fair city with great satisfaction just the previous evening. We had believed, quite mistakenly, that a new era of well-being for all was emerging for downtown Cleveland.

"Are you seeing this?" I turned to Beth who was on the couch, curled-up with her morning coffee and scrolling through her tablet. The old cold carp of reality had just whacked me over the head. "Had we still been looking out our window," I groaned in disbelief, "we'd have probably heard shots! Seen the whole chase begin!"

For the first time, I began to feel the discomfort of my privilege. It was a Friday morning and the sun was shining. I was cozied up next to my fireplace drinking coffee. And I was most certainly alive and well. Two other Clevelanders were not.

· · ·

As the days passed and details trickled out to the public, Clevelanders learned that there was nothing matter-of-fact about the killing of Timothy Russell and Malissa Williams, the two suspects-turned-victims. It was confirmed that they were unarmed. They had been identified as African American. We were also told that of the thirteen officers involved in the shooting, eight were white, one was Hispanic. Russell and Williams had been pursued by sixty-two police cars and over one hundred officers from the police departments of three different cities, the County Sheriff's Department, and the Ohio State Highway Patrol. At one point, even the transit police got in on the chase that covered twenty miles, lasted a full twenty-three minutes, and involved speeds of up to one hundred and ten miles per hour. In the end, Russell and Williams were cornered in a schoolyard and shot to death, their bodies pulverized by one hundred and thirty-seven shots fired at them, point blank, by thirteen police officers.

Media provided us with the usual background information. Both Russell and Williams were living in shelters at the time. Both had police records. Williams was affected by addiction and mental illness. While both were African American, the majority of officers involved

https://www.cleveland.com/metro/index.ssf/2012/11/2_men_shot_after_chase_ending.html

were white. This tragedy would most certainly exacerbate the tension in a city that too often found itself divided along lines of color.

We also learned that there may have been little need for the hyperbolic pursuit that ended in such cataclysmic catastrophe in the first place. A plainclothes officer had spotted Russell's thirty-three-year-old clunker, a 1979 Chevy Malibu, in an area of downtown known for its drug trade, and ran his license plate. The check came back clean. There was no immediate need to waylay Russell. By law, officers have the right to pull drivers over if there is reasonable suspicion of anything unusual. The legal term is "probable cause." In this case the probable cause, read the report, was Russell's failure to use a turn signal. Many have argued that Russell was, more likely, pulled over because he failed to use his turn signal and because he was DWB: Driving While Black.

The chase that followed was hardly necessary. At the very least, it didn't need to unfold with such dramatic and dangerous excess as it did. It endangered other motorists and pedestrians, expended hundreds of thousands of dollars in tax payer revenue to execute, clean-up, and investigate,[36] not to mention, it cost Russell and Williams their very lives. The Ohio Attorney General blamed the tragedy on "police leadership and communications failures during the chase."[37] The investigation disclosed that during the pursuit Detective Kevin Fairchild had even called out a radio dispatch that clarified that what was originally thought to be a gun in Williams' hand was, in fact, a red pop can.[38] Still, the adrenaline induced chase continued. The rush was already on. No one stopped it.

Though some may have imagined the chase scene to unfold like some dramatic shoot 'em-up flick there was nothing 'Hollywood'

---

[36] Peggy Gallek, "I-team: Prosecutor's office releases costs in investigation, trial of Officer Michael Brelo," *Fox 8 Cleveland*, June 10, 2015, Accessed July 18, 2018. https://fox8.com/2015/06/10/i-team-prosecutors-office-releases-costs-for-investigation-trial-of-officer-michael-brelo/

[37] "Cleveland car chase ends with two dead, 137 shots fired and six police charged," *The Guardian* (from Associated Press), September 20, 2017. Accessed July 10, 2018. https://www.theguardian.com/world/2014/may/31/cleveland-car-chase-russell-williams-police-shooting

[38] Jen Steer, "Officer says passenger was holding pop can, not gun during chase and shooting," *Fox 8 Cleveland*, April 17, 2015. Accessed July 18, 2018. https://fox8.com/2015/04/17/trial-resumes-for-cleveland-officer-charged-in-2012-fatal-chase-and-shooting/

about this tragedy. The suspects-turned-victims being chased would have made the most uninteresting of villains: two self-medicating, mentally ill citizens who lunched at local soup kitchens and slept in our downtown neighborhood shelters. I imagined that they were the sorts of folks we may have seen at the church for Sunday morning worship and the refreshments that were served afterwards, or coming for our Friday food program during the week. At the church we had a deep commitment to work and pray for the well-being of the city. On a regular basis, we saw many of those with great need on our little corner of Public Square and Ontario Street.

Troubled folks like Russell and Williams often left my staff and me feeling emotionally threadbare. Meager resources and the limits of good will are no match for the persistence of need in the city. Even so, we never stopped caring for the least among us. "You'll always have the poor with you," warned Jesus. I suspect he was talking about places like Cleveland where, in 2012, the year Russell and Williams were killed, 34.2 percent of Clevelanders were living in poverty[39] and 21,873 were homeless[40], Russell and Williams among them. I called them the "friends of Jesus" - the ones Jesus would have associated with and, likely, the ones Jesus would love. Whether we knew it or not, or whether they knew it or not, Russell and Williams were friends of Jesus, too.

They most definitely were not the sort of people you needed to hunt down like animals and at speeds exceeding one hundred miles per hour. It wasn't like Russell or Williams were going to flee the country like some sophisticated masterminds from a James Bond suspense thriller. They weren't going anywhere else because they had nowhere else to go.

The police could have easily caught up with them the next day while they stood in line for a free lunch at the Cosgrove Center on

---

[39] Greater Cleveland county poverty rates range from 8 percent to 19 percent: Statistical Snapshot, Cleveland.com, https://www.cleveland.com/datacentral/index.ssf/2012/09/greater_cleveland_county_pover.html, Posted Sep 24, 2012, Updated Sep 24, 2012; accessed February 26, 2019.
[40] North East Ohio Coalition for the Homeless (NEOCH), Poverty and Homelessness statistics, 2012, https://chris-knestrick-ataf.squarespace.com/overall-numbers-2012/, accessed February 26, 2019.

Superior Avenue. They could have found Russell snagging a bed the next night at the men's shelter at 2100 Lakeside. They could have spotted Williams at the Norma Herr Women's Shelter half a mile from that. Better yet, the hired guns could busy themselves with real criminals and, instead, let the social workers and addiction counselors untangle whatever social mess in which Russell and Williams may or may not have been entangled. When you consider that much of Russell's and Williams's small lives were lived within, roughly, a few square miles of downtown Cleveland, you could argue that they were already contained. You certainly do not need to chase them through a maze of city streets like a pack of salivating Dobermans on the leathery tails of a couple of sickly alley cats.

•   •   •

I dug deeper into the tragedy and quickly discovered that those first reports that I had read over my morning coffee were terribly misleading. The media's irresponsibility enraged me. The click-bait headlines were wildly inaccurate and they perpetuated the false narrative of how dangerous "the city" is. They promulgated a cultural misunderstanding of crime in the very downtown in which I was so personally and professionally invested and where countering that false narrative was a daily mission for me. By selecting the word "shootout" for the headline, one of Cleveland's major media outlets, Cleveland.com, romanticized the inhumanity of the shooting. The news source implied that there was a rally of shots fired back and forth between the police and the two suspects. The shoddy headlines shaped images in our minds akin to a Jesse James shootout down at the Northfield Bank, or the famous shootout at the O.K. Corral where everyone was armed, or the even more renown killing of Bonnie and Clyde who had a stash of weaponry ranging from handguns to machine guns in the car with them. To be clear, Russell and Williams were not notorious bank robbers or hardened criminals, nor were they armed.

In fact, though police claimed to have heard shots fired from Russell's car in downtown which led to the chase in the first place, no weapon or bullet casings were ever found to be with Russell or Williams, nor was anything ever located along the highway or roads of the chase route. Even Detective Fairchild tried to call off the dogs with his call to dispatch verifying that what had been thought to be a weapon was nothing more than a red pop can.

Later, investigators concluded that the so-called gunshot sound likely came from the backfiring of Russell's clunky old Malibu. Police Chief, Michael McGrath, confirmed that the investigation also showed, conclusively, that the only bullet holes found in police cruisers following the kill came from weapons fired by the police officers themselves.

A more appropriate term than shootout might have been "shooting gallery." Police fired on Williams and Russell like fish in a barrel. In total, the thirteen officers unleashed one hundred and thirty-seven rounds at Russell and Williams. Forensics revealed that of those one hundred and thirty-seven shots, Russell received twenty-three direct hits and Williams, twenty-four. Bullet entry points included chest and bellies, faces and temples. As if the story could not be more horrifying, we learned later that even after the perceived threat of danger had abated and the blasts from other officers' weapons had completely subsided, one lone officer, Michael Brelo, launched himself up on to the hood of Russell's car and from his haunches fired down through the victim's front windshield. Brelo stopped only to reload and then continued shooting.[41] In total, it was determined that of the one hundred and thirty-seven rounds, Brelo alone fired forty-nine.

To be sure, Russell and Williams were troubled. And often people who are troubled can bring more trouble. However, we should ask ourselves if police were right to be curious about Russell and Williams and the car they were driving, in the first place, simply because a turn signal hadn't been used? The "reasonable suspicion" hand is often overplayed by police in America, particularly when African American

---

[41] "Everything you need to know before the start of the trial for Cleveland police officer Michael Brelo," Ida Lieszkovszky, cleveland.com, April 6, 2015. Accessed July 10, 2018. https://www.cleveland.com/court-justice/index.ssf/2015/04/everything_you_need_to_know_be.html

and Latinx drivers are concerned.[42] University of Arkansas law professor, Blair Woods, states that minor traffic violations are used as a "pretext" to search for criminal activities which would normally require "probable cause."[43] "Traffic stops," says Woods, "are the most frequent interaction between police and civilians today. And because we know traffic enforcement is a common gateway for funneling over-policed and marginalized communities into the criminal justice system, these stops are a persistent source of racial and economic injustice."[44] For this reason, Woods, as well as others, have made compelling arguments that traffic laws should be maintained, not by police at all but, by separate unarmed traffic agencies.[45]

Some might argue that Russell and Williams made the dangerous decision to try and outrun the police, as if being chased and killed was their own fault. However, in both a pre and post- George Floyd world it is clear that African Americans don't trust the police.[46] In fact, as far back as 2016, a Massachusetts high court has stated that an African American suspect may be as:

"motivated by the desire to avoid the recurring indignity of being racially profiled as by the desire to hide criminal activity. Given this reality for black males in the city of Boston, a judge should, in appropriate cases, consider the report's findings in weighing flight as a factor in the reasonable suspicion calculus."[47]

---

[42] "Law Professor Argues for Removing Police From Traffic Enforcement," News, University if Arkansas, April 22, 2021, https://news.uark.edu/articles/56706/law-professor-argues-for-removing-police-from-traffic-enforcement, accessed May 4, 2021.

[43] Ibid.

[44] "Law Professor Argues for Removing Police From Traffic Enforcement," News, University if Arkansas, April 22, 2021, https://news.uark.edu/articles/56706/law-professor-argues-for-removing-police-from-traffic-enforcement, accessed May 4, 2021.

[45] Ibid.

[46] "Two-thirds of black Americans don't trust the police to treat them equally. Most white Americans do," PBS, News Hour, https://www.pbs.org/newshour/politics/two-thirds-of-black-americans-dont-trust-the-police-to-treat-them-equally-most-white-americans-do. Accessed May 4, 2021.

[47] "Black Men May Have Cause To Run From Police, Massachusetts High Court Says," Bill Chappell, The Two Way: NPR, September 21, 2016,

The fact that the police believed there was a need to pursue Russell's vehicle is curious. The over-the-top, bang-bang, shoot 'em-up way police hunted and then gunned down two unarmed citizens, however, makes the case even more troubling. Sadly, not even a day in court would truly settle the matter.

•   •   •

Six officers were fired for the killing of Timothy Russell and Malissa Williams, and only one officer was charged with a crime. Michael Brelo, the Cleveland officer who mounted the hood of Russell's '79 Malibu and fired continuously down through the front windshield was slapped with two counts of voluntary manslaughter, though not convicted of either. Brelo was exonerated of all charges when the judge in the case, Judge O'Donnell borrowed a page out of Justice Antonin Scalia's playbook and stooped to an apathetic non-dispositive homerun analogy which was the equivalent of a child throwing his hands in the air, frustrated by a math problem and claiming that it is just not possible to solve this problem. He stated:

"Consider a baseball game in which the visiting team's leadoff batter hits a home run in the top of the first inning. If the visiting team goes on to win by a score of 1 to 0, every person competent in the English language and familiar with the American pastime would agree that the victory resulted from the home run. This is so because it is natural to say that one event is the outcome or consequence of another when the former would not have occurred but for the latter. It is beside the point that the victory also resulted from a host of other necessary causes, such as skillful pitching, the coach's decision to put the leadoff batter in the lineup, and the league's decision to schedule the game. By contrast, it makes little sense to say that an event resulted from or was the outcome of some earlier action if the action merely played a nonessential contributing role in producing the event. If the visiting team wound up winning 5 to 2 rather than 1 to 0, one would

https://www.npr.org/sections/thetwo-way/2016/09/21/494900984/black-men-may-have-cause-to-run-from-police-massachusetts-high-court-says, accessed May 4, 2021.

be surprised to read in the sports page that the victory resulted from the leadoff batter's early, non-dispositive home run."

·   ·   ·

The Russell and Williams killings have become a "moment that will define Cleveland," said Mayor Frank Jackson. The Russell and Williams police free-for-all, or as it has simply come to be known around Cleveland and by others throughout the nation who work to warm the icy hearts of Americans into trickles of justice for all, the "137 shots," is now part of Cleveland's narrative. We may have been working tirelessly to lift Cleveland, to see it raised – "a city on the rise" we would declare it with folks near and far, but in just twenty-three minutes of the wee, somber hours of November 29, 2012, we were awakened, violently and tragically, to the fact that all was not well in paradise.

"The events of November 29, 2012 are sui generis and not likely to recur," promised Judge O'Donnell at the conclusion of his Brelo verdict. His verdict was incompetently mistaken. Clevelanders, particularly African American Clevelanders, however, knew better. O'Donnell's closing remarks were as misguided as was his verdict. Stress was rising. The racial chasm, widening. More killings of unarmed Clevelanders, particularly African men - even children, by the very ones charged with protecting their very right to life, were yet to come.

Almost two years to the day that Russell and Williams had been gunned down in the Heritage Middle School lot on the city's east side, Cleveland would experience another fatal and, now, infamous police shooting.

·   ·   ·

November 22, 2014 was a chilly day for a twelve-year-old boy to be playing outside in the park near his house, especially when he had a perfectly warm recreation center right next door to the park available to him. This particular Saturday, however, the boy chose to be inside only every now and then, we presume, just to warm up a bit. The rest of the time he preferred to play outside in the park. He had made what he believed was a fair trade that day, a good deal, with another young person at the youth center where the two often played together. Just for the day, the boy swapped his cell phone for the other boy's toy gun, an Airsoft BB gun that, although meant for play and shot only plastic BBs, had an uncanny resemblance to a Colt M1911 semi-automatic handgun. Its orange safety tip had been previously removed making it look even more like the real McCoy. Better to be outside while playing with the BB gun than get caught with it inside the center and have it taken away. "You'll shoot your eye out!" a rec counselor might have tried to dissuade him, like everyone from his teacher to Santa Claus warned little Ralphie in Cleveland's famous Christmas movie, *A Christmas Story*. I wish it had been taken away from him. Removed from his backpack and locked away until the end of the day when it would be returned or, perhaps, when he brought back a parent with him to retrieve it. After all there are no laws in the State of Ohio that prohibit twelve-year-old children from doing what many of them want to do: own a BB gun.[48] I believe every good and tender-hearted Clevelander wishes to God that the BB gun had been removed from the boy's possession. Before he was shot by police while playing with the toy.

Like the slaying of Timothy Russell and Malissa Williams, the killing of Tamir Rice and the subsequent failure of the justice system to bring fair and just resolution to the Rice family, and to the good citizens of Cleveland on the whole, will be fodder for Thanksgiving and Sunday dinner family quarrels for many years to come.

Legal questions were given answers. None seem to satisfy. The death of Tamir Rice, according to the grand jury that chose not to indict Timothy Loehmann - the officer who killed young Tamir, argued that

---

[48] "No laws regulate air rifles, BB guns," Amanda Seitz, Dayton Daily News, October 7, 2014, https://www.daytondailynews.com/news/laws-regulate-air-rifles-guns/a028jQPc5U45W9Ppa5SkdM/#:~:text=Despite%20the%20danger%2C%20Ohio%2C%20along,use%20of%20such%20weapons%2C%20either, accessed May 4, 2021.

his death was less about one individual act than the sum of many mistakes and biases along the way:

Timothy Loehmann, shot too quickly after arriving on the scene. A mere 1.7 seconds by some estimates. Jesse Wobrock, the expert in biomechanics who testified during the grand jury process claimed that Loehmann fired his weapon in less than one second. Loehmann should never have been hired by the Cleveland Division of Police in the first place. He was already on shaky ground when he left his previous department in Cleveland's nearby suburban city of Independence. His personnel file from the Independence Police Department noted his "dangerous loss of composure" on the firing range, among other issues. Loehmann lied about this on his application to the Cleveland Division of Police. Loehmann, a rookie with just over one year on the Cleveland Police force under his belt, and his partner raced up on Tamir too quickly, aggravating what they already believed to be a dangerous situation. Tamir was sitting by himself at a picnic table under a pavilion. There were no other children in Tamir's proximity when the two officers arrived on the scene, skidding through the snow and making a dramatic stop just feet from Tamir. He did not have the toy gun drawn at the time. Loehmann and his partner did not attempt to understand and deescalate the situation and, in fact, they may have aggravated it by racing up on the boy. Loehmann did not leave Tamir, a sixth-grader at Marion-Seltzer Elementary School in Cleveland, much time to understand what was happening or even to raise his hands in the air before the shooting occurred. Can we appreciate what state of mind the twelve-year-old might have been in when the officers descended on him? Was he surprised or in shock? Did Tamir reach for the toy simply to clarify for the officers that what he had was, in fact, just a toy? Even before the policed charged on toward the playground pavilion, the person who had taken the 911 call, Constance Hollinger, had not communicated the fullness of the message to the police dispatcher. The 911 caller had told her that it was, "probably a toy." Hollinger was suspended for just over a week without pay for her mistake but it hardly seemed a fitting punishment considering the tragic consequence of the error. Tamir's mother was stunned. Her lawyer protested, "Eight days for gross negligence resulting in the death of a twelve-year-old boy? How pathetic is that?"[49]

The grand jury, under the guidance of lead prosecutor, Tim McGinty, concluded that there were mistakes made at numerous junctures along the way. Similar to Judge O'Donnell's non-dispositive position in the Brelo verdict, the grand jury rationalized that if many people and departments hold a portion of responsibility for Tamir's death, how can only one individual be held accountable? Loehmann wasn't charged with anything for his killing of Tamir Rice. He was fired, however, but only for lying on his application to the Cleveland Division of Police.

By the time all was said and done, the waters were so muddied that people could not or would not see straight on the matter. Some marched and shouted, "Black lives matter!" Others marched with police, shouting, "Blue lives matter." A Cleveland friend of mine went so far as to make a documentary style movie called, *Bleeding Blue*. It was his admirable attempt at balancing anti-police sentiment by anecdotally lifting up decent police and the dangerous situations they find themselves in each and every day. The film could have gone much further, however. It could have revealed how some of those good cops are entangled in an agency systemically broken. One that regularly allows for the use of excessive force on suspects including the mentally ill, African Americans who are arrested at disproportionately higher rates than white people and, without due justification, too often grants 'no-knock' warrants that have left infants severely wounded and scores of other innocent people, including police officers themselves, dead. The killing of Tamir Rice has given rise to questions about the central role of 911 dispatchers. Not every call needs to be turned over to a police agency. Social services, community watch groups, and others may play a more appropriate role in responding to a situation than calling in the police who view most calls as "something that ought not to be happening and about which someone had better do

---

[49] "911 dispatcher in Tamir Rice case suspended for 8 days," AP News, March 14, 2017, https://apnews.com/article/6c98afc9631f4d4ab6f17f13b37f7d47, accessed May 4, 2021.

something now," states the author and renowned criminologist, Egon Bittner.[50]

Current policies and funding demand that police play the part of social workers, family services, mental illness and addiction counselors, in addition to that of law enforcement. Police are required to work in a variety of social situations without adequate training, funding, or resources. "There is evidence that demands on front-line cops are becoming broader. More than four-fifths of the calls they receive are not related to crime," cites Bittner.[51] Countries such as Canada and Britain have reallocated funds and eased the amount of "policing" required in their respective nations by introducing more support services into the mix. Police shootings in those countries are a fraction compared to those in the United States.[52] [53]

Even so, the conservative writer, David French, argued in a 2018 article, far fewer innocent civilians died in Iraq at the hands of American soldiers than African Americans who die in their own neighborhoods at the hands of police here in the United States. "One may argue that we ask too much of our cops, but I don't think so; younger soldiers perform the same balancing act in more dangerous circumstances for less pay every day"[54] yet, they do not kill at the same alarming rates as do police officers here at home.

Even if Clevelanders didn't march or make movies, following the killing of Tamir Rice, everyone seemed to have opinions. The city was

[50] Egon Bittner, "A blurred blue line for cops," *The Economist*, June 23, 2018, https://www.economist.com/britain/2018/06/21/a-blurred-blue-line-for-cops (accessed July 20, 2021).

[51] Ibid.

[52] Alexi Jones and Wendy Sawyer, "Not just 'a few bad apples': U.S. police kill civilians at much higher rates than other countries," Prison Policy Initiative, June 5, 2020, https://www.prisonpolicy.org/blog/2020/06/05/policekillings/ (accessed April 8, 2021).

[53] "Policing in Canada Vs. Policing in the USA," Wilfred Laurier University Online, March 1, 2019, https://online.wlu.ca/news/2017/01/03/policing-canada-vs-policing-usa (accessed April 8, 2021).

[54] David French, "Shouldn't Police at Home Exhibit at Least as Much Discipline as Soldiers at War?" *National Review*, April 4, 2018, https://www.nationalreview.com/2018/04/stephon-clark-shooting-police-should-show-more-discipline-restraint/ (accessed April 29, 2021)

split. We were divided. Torn asunder. From 2014-2016, it was easy to find yourself at work or in social settings, unwittingly falling off the cliff of civil discourse and down into the bottomless pit of raised-voice arguments about the killing of Tamir Rice.

• • •

I had been encouraged to run for various political offices in Cleveland. Each time, after a period of prayerful discernment and meaningful conversation with good folks much brighter than me and with way more political savvy, I concluded that I already had an influential voice as the pastor of one of the oldest and most recognized institutions in the city. The tragedies of 2012 and 2014, however, confronted me with purpose defining questions: Was I really using my voice effectively to bring about change? The ghosts of Timothy Russell, Malissa Williams, Tamir Rice and others demanded an accounting from me. And, I believed, God did, too.

In the daytime, I could stay busy enough to keep the voices quiet. But at night when I tried to find rest against the noise of conflicts on the street below – the drunkenness and fights, the sirens and shootings, and when I fought the lights of the city gleaming from billion dollar corporations and the towers that housed them peeking through the slits in my curtains, I could hear God whispering to me through the voices of my ancestors: "Take away from me the noise of your [church] songs; I will not listen to the melody of your harps. But let justice roll down like waters, and righteousness like an ever-flowing stream."

I occupied one of the most influential offices in the city – the pulpit of the Old Stone Church. How could I stay silent about the central issues demeaning our city? My silence was complicity.

When I tried to close my eyes at night, I was overwhelmed by terrifying images: the lifeless bullet riddled bodies of Timothy Russell and Malissa Williams who were left in the front seat of Russell's car as it was wrapped in plastic, hoisted onto the back of a flatbed, and hauled off for investigation. These were human beings. Friends of Jesus, whether they knew it or not. In the darkness of my mind, I replayed the footage from the park outside of the Cudell Recreation Center over and over again. I could see the look of surprise on young Tamir's face as a police cruiser rushed up on him in the park and in 1.7 seconds, less than a second by some accounts, one of the officers - charged with protecting Tamir's constitutional right to life – opened fire on the boy. I imagined a look of innocence as, perhaps, Tamir tried to show them that he was just playing with a toy gun.

When I stared myself down in the mirror, what I saw was a man who tended to comfort the afflicted far more than he ever afflicted the comfortable, himself included. I saw a preacher who preached more pastoral sermons than prophetic, who only dabbled in justice when he should have leaned into it. I saw a preacher who spoke a word about liberation rather than preaching a liberating word, an urban interloper who preached eloquently about the truth rather than doing the dangerous work of proclaiming it directly.

It was four years into my time in Cleveland when my purpose for being was refined in the fires of the city's racial inequalities and injustices. With all due respect to Mr. Buechner, it was not my "deep gladness" defining my vocation, but the collision of my conscience crashing into the world's great need. I had no business championing walkable, safe city streets if our streets couldn't be safe for every single Clevelander, particularly the least among us. It was time for me to use my influential voice as a downtown resident, a civic leader, and as the pastor of Cleveland's regarded heart-of-the-city church. I couldn't see it any other way. If I was going to do my small part in making the city of Cleveland a better place, a safer place for all, and a home for Beth and me, then I had no choice. It was time to step out and speak up, or pack up and move on.

Truthfully, I had opportunities to be engaged years before the shootings of Russell, Williams, and Rice. These earlier moments were informative and would provide much needed wisdom going forward. A cause can sometimes find us in a Damascus Road flash of light. Other times, purpose moves in slowly like a spring storm that we've watched inching its way across the lake for hours. Clouds build and the sky darkens over the horizon. A distant rumble can be heard thundering over the water. Perhaps we've been preparing for it for some time, though we are hardly aware of it until the heavy winds start bending trees and kicking up sand, and stones, and road debris.

Three years before the 137 shots, our diverse congregation joined with three prominent African American congregations and, together, planned an event called From King to Obama. Each congregation hosted a gathering which celebrated the civil rights movement in America that, among other important strides, ultimately led to the election of our first African American President. The last of the four events was held at the Word Church, one of Cleveland's impressive empowerment congregations led by the Rev. Dr. R.A. Vernon. Of the three or four hundred attendees, I seem to recall that I was the only white person in the room. Yes, I took note. The gathering ended with the audience submitting questions on little slips of paper and having our distinguished panel which was comprised of media hosts, a judge, and a Vanderbilt Divinity School professor – Rev. Dr. Dale Andrews, attempt meaningful answers. On one of the small sheets of paper someone had scribbled out the question: "Do you think Obama is the anti-Christ?" When the question was read aloud from the stage, you can imagine the look of panic on my face when everyone in the room directed their attention toward me, the only white guy in the room. Thankfully, it was my job to deliver the benediction which meant that I had the last word at the Word Church that day.

"I didn't write that question!" I protested incredulously. Thankfully there was plenty of good willed laughter in response. "In fact, I voted for President Obama," I continued. "And not because he's African American, or because I thought he was the be-all to end-all. No. I voted for him because he seemed to be calling the best out of all of us. We've got to stop electing people we think will fix everything, and start choosing leaders who will challenge and inspire each and every one of us to stand-up and get involved in our local communities!"

The benediction was a great way to end the event. It received lots of Amens from the participants, not to mention it blessed me with an opportunity to clear my name. More importantly, however, it taught me that white folks have to "show up." It doesn't matter if you are the only white guy in room at gatherings meant to explore issues of race, or the only male who shows up to stand in solidarity with women who rally for equality, or the only middle-aged guy who marches with teens to end gun violence and mass murders in our schools.

Cleveland taught me that those who have struggled for justice need those of us with power and privilege to stand with them. They need friends and advocates to be there, even and especially as silent partners in the good work to be done. Or to challenge other folks who hold even bigger power – city councilors, state representative, financial backers with deep pockets and voters to be the change we need to see in the world.

When it was my turn to speak at another gathering for racial justice, I stood before the crowd of two or three hundred, mostly African Americans, and asked the question that was most likely on everyone's mind: "Where are all the white folks tonight?" The response was some laughter mixed with a sea of Amens and right-ons that affirmed my comment. With my simple seven-word speech introduction, I had named the elephant in the room, or better yet, the white elephant that wasn't in the room. Then I heard one woman who was sitting midway back in the audience shout seven words of her own that changed my way of thinking: "You go get 'em!" she yelled. "Bring 'em back!" The crowd cheered her remarks.

She was right, of course. How could I have shown up to this important event alone? I had invited others to join me by way of a couple of announcements in our church's Sunday bulletin but I hadn't telephoned a single person and urged them to join me. The work of justice isn't just about showing up. It's about showing up with others in tow. It's about picking up the phone, sending out a text, or personally tapping a friend or two on the shoulder at church on Sunday morning and saying, "I'm going to the event, and you need to come, too! I'll pick you up." It's inviting your entire committee, study group, or circle of friends who are of like mind - or even of closed mind that just need of some coaxing - to walk, march, and pray with you and others. The work of justice demands a river of many, not simply the slow drip of a few. It may start small but with the invitation and inclusion of others, the river begins to flow. Even when if can't get others to come with you, then it may be time to join others in your community and start conversations of your own

•   •   •

The morning following the 87th Academy Awards - February 23, 2015, was an unusually chilly day for Kristy Capel, the sparkling young white co-anchor on Cleveland's Fox 8 television channel. During the morning show, not only did Ms. Capel stick her foot in her mouth, she stuffed a whole ankle and a calf in there, too.

Capel and co-anchor, Wayne Dawson were chit-chatting pleasantries back and forth about Lady Gaga's powerful tribute to the British singer, Julie Andrews and the score of the *Sound of Music* film at the Oscars the night before. Capel, sounding very much like a sheltered private-school debutant expressed her surprise at Lady Gaga's talent by accidentally using a racial slur: "It's hard to really hear [Lady Gaga's] voice with all the jigaboo music."

Capel's co-anchor, Wayne Dawson, was an older and more experienced anchor, and an African American man. He remained straight-faced as only a well seasoned professional could, though internally his wheels must have been turning. His raised eyebrow seemed to express what we were all asking at that moment: "Did Capel really just say what we think she said?" And as if saying "jigaboo" once wasn't offensive enough, Capel repeated the word. "Yes!" she confirmed for us viewers, "She did say what we all thought she said!"

Video clips of Capel's comment immediately went viral and drew a considerable amount of negative attention to Fox 8 and the city of Cleveland, which was still entangled in the legal aftermath of the notable police shootings of Russell and Williams, and Rice. Cleveland had not been as racially divided, perhaps, as it had been during the time of the Hough Riots and the Glennville shootout. Capel apologized for using the racial slur, claiming that she didn't understand what the word meant, and was temporarily suspended as a morning anchor. The damage, however, had been done. Her use of the derogatory term fanned the flames of tension that already existed throughout the city. From social to mainstream media, there was an outcry that Capel's apology wasn't enough. She was insincere and had to have known exactly what she was saying. NBC published an op-ed immediately after her apology referring to Capel as the "'jigaboo' muttering anchor from Fox Cleveland" [sic] in an aptly titled piece, "The 'Jigaboo' Apology for Gaga Comment is Not Enough."

At the time of Capel's comment, the church and a Cleveland marketing company were sponsoring my program, Power2ools: 2 minute tools for life which appeared on Fox 8 during their mid-morning show, New Day Cleveland. My show wasn't a hit by any stretch of the imagination, but we were watched by close to thirty-thousand viewers each week, and our sponsors were investing a lot of money with Fox 8 for the airtime. It seemed to me that Capel's blooper was a perfect opportunity to flex some of our advertising muscle and for me to use my voice in a more impactful way.

While I stopped short of threats to pull Power2ools from Fox 8, I did call our sales representative and threaten that I could either write an op-ed for the Plain Dealer and Cleveland.com, or Fox 8 could have me on one of its morning shows to talk about race issues in Cleveland. "Trust me, though" I warned, "the op-ed will be a lot harder on Fox 8 than if we can simply sit down and talk openly on air."

I have to hand it to station manager Andy Fishman and Fox 8's commitment to local issues. I was booked to appear on Fox 8 before the end of the week, and for a half decent spot at that. The Saturday morning show has a strong viewership. Folks are up and enjoying a coffee, catching up on local news and getting ready to head off to Home Depot or to mini-van the kids to hockey or basketball games.

Saturday morning anchor, Todd Meany and I sat down on Fox 8's iconic red leather sofa shortly after 8:20 A.M. and went live with the pretense of discussing Power2ools. Primarily, however, we spent our time together discussing the racial divide in Cleveland. It was perfect timing, too. Mayor Frank Jackson, just the day before, had held a press conference to unveil his new "use of force policy" which had evolved out of recommendations from the Federal Department of Justice's investigation (at the Mayor's request) of the shootings of Russell and Williams. Meany was an excellent interviewer and allowed me to talk indirectly about Capel's on-air racist blooper – he simply couched it as part of the "events that have been happening," and, more directly, about how we people of different cultures might start to come together and begin to listen and hear one another. It was hardly an MLK moment for me, and I still can't get over the fact that the two people on the couch talking about race in Cleveland were both white. Even so, Cleveland was helping me find new ways to use my voice and to invite others into deeper thinking about one of the most important issues confronting Cleveland, and the nation as a whole.

In 2016, I was able to bring other voices into the conversation in a very intentional way by inviting a number of national speakers to the church - "Visiting Scholars" who would help us explore some of the race issues confronting America as Cleveland prepared to host the Republican National Convention (RNC). One of those speakers was, once again, my old friend, the Rev. Dr. Dale Andrews from the Vanderbilt School of Divinity. The title alone for Dale's lecture was daunting to say the least: Prophetic Praxis: Wrestling with the Moral Injury of Anti-Racism.

In Dale's second open forum, we knew from the start that we were going to be thrown into a storm before the clouds of misunderstanding could part. Dale began by calling every single one of us racists.

You could have heard a pin drop once the collective gasp in the room had subsided. Some folks squirmed. Others turned toward me and glared with laser beams of animosity shooting out of their eyes as if to say, "Dr. Mark, who is this guy and why the heck did you invite him here?" But Dale won us over. He helped us explore our own prejudice, our silence when we should be speaking, our speaking when we should be listening, and our complicity in the systemic racism holding our city back from being a safe and equitable home for everyone - whether you're a person dealing with mental illness and addiction, a kid playing with a toy gun in the park, or a new urbanist living in downtown and investing in the revival of the city.

We followed up Dale's presentation with a short Q and A and a panel discussion that included a couple of city councilors, another pastor, Dale, and myself seated at a long table that stretched across the front of the room in the church's art gallery. The discussion was moderated by the regarded local television anchor, Leon Bibb. Mr. Bibb is not only a solid journalist and news anchor, he is also a man deeply committed to his faith and an incredible civic leader who loves the city of Cleveland dearly. I knew Mr. Bibb from some of the times he had interviewed me about the Old Stone Church, or chatting with him at one of his many speaking engagements. I knew he would be the perfect person to moderate our panel.

Right out of the gate, though, Mr. Bibb caught me by surprise by directing his first question to me: "Dr. Giuliano, could you please tell us what white privilege means to you?"

Ugh! I wish he had started with someone else. I blew it. I mumbled and bumbled trying to find the right words for what should have been a simple and thoughtful response but I'm sure came out sounding tone deaf to the racial injustices in my own community. I wished I had a do-over so I could have said something pithy like, "White privilege means that I get to be sitting here on this panel for no other reason than the wealthy, predominantly white church that I serve is hosting this event."

In Cleveland, I would learn about my white privilege and how and when to use it, as best I could, to bring about positive change for our great city, to make it a better place to call home for all,

Though the deaths of Timothy Russell, Malissa Williams, Tamir Rice, and countless other African Americans who are disproportionately killed by police in Cleveland and throughout America, forced me to confront my own participation, or lack thereof, in the very society that allowed for those killings, I discovered that I wasn't helpless. One thing Cleveland seemed to have more than any other city I've lived in was opportunity. Opportunity to get connected. To be involved. And to make a difference. The more I got engaged with different groups, civic partners, and individuals striving to build a better city for all, the less daunted I was by the headlines about police shootings, crime in the neighborhoods, or even the kind of poverty I saw in downtown Cleveland and at the church on a daily basis.

Perhaps one of the most famous Northeast Ohioans, LeBron James, said it best during the pandemic when he spoke online and on television to millions of safe-sheltered 2020 high school graduates about commitment to the local community. James was passionate, eloquent, and absolutely right:

"The community needs you. And when I say the community, I mean your rec league, your church, your youth group, and most of all, your school. They need you. Most importantly, building your community is how you change the world . . . Education, violence, racism, they must be solved in the street. Class of 2020, I know the last thing you want to hear right now is stay home. That's not my message to you. My message is stay close to home. Maybe not physically, but in every other way possible. Pursue every ambition, go as far as you possibly can dream, and be the first generation to embrace a new responsibility, a responsibility to rebuild your community. Class of 2020, the world has changed. You will determine how we rebuild, and I ask that you make your community your priority."

I continued to make my community of Cleveland, Ohio, and in particular its growing downtown my priority. At the church, we continued to host a variety of speaker forums, film director's nights as part of the Cleveland International Film Fest, and art shows in the church's gallery that helped us revision life in our city. One of the most powerful exhibits we hosted was called Shooting without Bullets. It was a moving show initiated by an exceptional up and coming Cleveland lawyer-turned-artist-activist named Amanda King. King both challenged and empowered young people to go into their own neighborhoods, not with guns, but cameras and sketch pads, paints and paintbrushes and show us what their communities looked like to them. King's show was as haunting as it was inspirational for those who experienced it, and as energizing as it was empowering for those whose works appeared in it.

Our congregation also began sponsoring a variety of organizations that shared our vision for a safer and more just community, including the important Cleveland advocacy group, God Before Guns. I continued to speak from our pulpit as well as out and about in the community at large. In October 2015, I was invited to give the invocational address to a national community health conference focused on ending gun violence. The goal was to rename gun crime in our communities for what it was – a health crisis. I was blessed to be invited. The more I used my voice the less dispirited and more empowered I became.

My Canadian family would see the news coming out of the United States – school shootings, police shootings, corporate and political corruption, peaceful protests turning violent and ask, "When are you moving back to Canada?" My answer was always the same, "There's too much work to be done here. I feel like I'm making a difference. Besides, isn't that privileged, too? To be able to pack up and move to Canada when so many others have to stay and figure things out?"

The greatest enemy to urban revival isn't lack of money, or opportunity. It's the lack of spirit. What holds us back is the misguided belief that things are beyond our own influence or control, or that the only way to end the violence in our cities is to apply more of what has already been proven ineffective: hiring more police, or adding more racially biased and, therefore dehumanizing policies such as "stop and frisk" into systems already broken, or even sending federal policing agencies into our neighborhoods to tamp down on protest and unrest with the heavy boot of law and order.

"Blessed are the poor in spirit," preached Jesus. Sadness, disappointment, growing distrust of our police, our neighbors, anxiety about safety and security in some of our most challenged neighborhoods, these are the things that wear on us day in and day out. They are the things that keep us spiritually impoverished. Cleveland blessed me with hope. It gave me opportunities to step up and step out with others who were already busy fighting the good fight.

To be sure, I was met with resistance along the way. Sometimes standing up to injustice in the city meant, first, scuffling with the leadership within the congregation. "Not in our house" was often the response when I tried to bring in outside organizations and action groups. "You're getting too political," I was warned. I came to understand that when folks in the church say that preachers are too political what they really mean is that they disagree with the preacher's politics, or even the politics of the gospel. Very few grumble when you lift up issues with which they are already in agreement. Other times people just don't want to expend the energy or deal with the messiness that the work of confronting tough issues brings with it. Even so, on Sunday mornings, from the pulpit, I got more courageous and often reminded people that Jesus himself engaged at a political level numerous times – from his peaceful Palm Sunday march on Jerusalem to his symbolic destruction of property at the temple. In the end, Jesus was tried and convicted of a political crime. I liked to remind folks, too, that our very nation was formed by political revolt – the American Revolution, which, in England, was often called the "Presbyterian Rebellion." It was Scots and Irish Presbyterian pastors and members driving the revolution. We're Protestants, for crying out loud! It's in our theological and denominational DNA to protest.

"Work and pray for the well-being of the city," said the prophet Jeremiah, "for in it you will find your own well-being." It was in the work for the well-being of the city, in my labors for a safer and more just community, that I was discovering the home I had longed for since my move from Savannah. For me, home was where the cause was.

• • •

On March 31, 2017, I was blessed to meet Samaria Rice, Tamir's mother. Our congregation's newly formed Peace and Justice subcommittee was acting as a "community partner" for the film, Dispatches from Cleveland which had its world premiere at the 45th Cleveland International Film Fest. Dispatches is an exceptional film in that it weaves together numerous social issues confronting the city of Cleveland – extreme poverty, violence toward transgender people, and the outdated and excessive use of force policies employed by the Cleveland Division of Police as named by the U.S. Department of Justice. The most compelling part of the film is that it tells the story of what happens when otherwise disparate social action groups find common ground and unite in common causes - like voting out Cuyahoga County Prosecutor Tim McGinty, who had failed the Rice family in the Timothy Loehmann grand jury process.

At the film's premiere, I was to bring opening remarks before the movie started, and so had an opportunity to speak with Tamir's mother who was part of a post-film panel. I was immediately impressed by both Samaria's strength and sincerity. The suffering she had experienced from the devastating death of her child is unimaginable. Online comments following Tamir's death were brutal. Tamir was unfairly called a "thug" and blamed for his own death. Samaria was accused of being a "gold digger" for taking legal action to receive justice for the wrongful death of her son. Yet, from somewhere within, or perhaps, beyond, she found both the grace and resolve to use her voice, her power, and her son's tragic death to empower youth from some of Cleveland's toughest neighborhoods, and to make Cleveland a safer and more prosperous city for so many who, without her investment in it, would otherwise lose hope.

After the event had concluded, I had a unique opportunity to speak to her personally. When I thanked her for her good work that she was doing in the city and on behalf of every single one of us, she said to me, "Pastor, I didn't choose this path. The day my son was shot and killed, it chose me."

I regret that I wasn't quick enough on my toes that evening to tell her that, in some ways, it chose me, too.

Chapter Ten

What's Love Got to Do with It

"Who needs a heart, when a hear can be broken?"
Tina Turner (written by Terry Britten, Graham Lyle, and Graham Hamilton Lyle)

THERE IS A MYTH that younger generations just aren't interested in the church any more. In my experience, however, that narrative hasn't always lived up to the negative hype. During my tenure at the Old Stone Church, for example, we received into membership over two hundred and twenty-five new members – many of them under the age of forty. What has become apparent to me, however, is that unless leadership and other opportunities are shared with new members, and unless an organization is open to the innovative ideas and interests that come with those new members, many younger folks will simply walk away. At Old Stone, some did. They were just as disheartened as I was by the institutional resistance and slowness to adapt to twenty-first century models for the church. "Dr. Mark, I just don't know how you ever get anything in the church accomplished," one frustrated thirty-something member and highly successful business entrepreneur said to me over coffee one morning. "If we operated this way in my company, we'd have to shutter our doors within a year," he added, just before he told me that he was leaving the church.

By 2014, a decades-old conflict between the church's two boards was becoming more pronounced. One board – a board of "elders," called "the Session," was elected annually by the congregation and, therefore, believed that it represented the church and its mission. That's not surprising given that in most Presbyterian Churches throughout the United States, the session has the final say on all church matters. However, at Old Stone there was a second board - a board of 'directors' - which was elected by an entirely separate entity called a "Society." In fact, a person does not even have to be a member of the church to be elected to the society or its board of directors. The 'society' managed the majority of the church's physical and financial resources and believed that it "owned the church." The second board – the society - often overrode the efforts of the first board – the session. Consequently, moving things forward such as programs, outreach, the installation of a sculpture in front of the church, and adding twenty-first century updates to the facilities required an increasing amount energy at a time when the discord was beginning, again, to wear people thin - myself included.

I wasn't the first pastor to get entangled in the conflict, of course. Letters dating all the way back to the early 1950s revealed that pastors often felt caught in the middle between the two boards. The tenth and eleventh senior pastors, the two that had preceded me, had both resigned their positions – the latter after less than four years of ministry with the church, amidst frustrations similar to those that were bubbling up during in my time.

I needed a survival plan, and so began reflecting in earnest on a powerful principle I had gleaned from an older and much wiser gentleman than me named Cal. I met Cal when I was serving one of my very first congregations. The sun was beginning to set on his journey in ministry, and just beginning to rise on mine. Cal was a colleague, twenty-five years my elder. He graciously offered me some advice so potently vital that it not only saved my nascent career from complete wreckage, more importantly, it awakened me to the unnecessary sacrifices I was imposing on my marriage, my family, and myself. Although I was a fledgling pastor at the time, Cal's thoughtful input helped me navigate my steps ever since.

Not only was Cal super smart – a professor with double doctorate degrees in ministry and psychology, he understood all too well what

I was going through back in those early days of ministry long before I had ever known about Cleveland or the Old Stone Church. Back then, I was being sucked ever more deeply into a swirling eddy of disappointment, burnout, and depression. Like a lot of clergy, I wanted nothing more than to please my congregation. I was eager to serve well, so I worked tirelessly, day and night, doing everything I thought I could possibly do to strengthen and grow the church. In the imagination of my heart, I believed that the good people of my congregation would be shouting hallelujah's and singing the praises of their new pastor for bringing in all sorts of new young families. "Well done, good and faithful servant" they might say some Sunday morning during the announcements for my having done my part in the good efforts to save their church from a slow death by decline, the dull but fatal stroll into obscurity.

It seemed the harder I worked, however, the harder the work became. I suppose one might call that irony. To my surprise there were no official accolades or personal praises from the board, or even the personnel committee to accompany the success or the increased responsibilities. There were gracious comments here and there from friends in the congregation, but nothing from the ones who decided on annual raises, or put their signature on my weekly paycheck. Instead, it became disappointingly apparent that just the opposite was happening: the more the young church grew, the more the people grumbled. I guess you could call that irony, too.

There were a series of soul sucking events that gnawed at my spirit like a dog on a bone. There was continual growling about the scuff marks all these new kids in the church were leaving on the gym floor. There was the day I stormed out of a worship committee meeting after older members grumbled for an hour about the behavior of all the new teens coming to worship. "You don't want young people in your church," I barked. "You want young people who act like old people!" I was ashamed for having lost my cool.

There seemed to be an endless run of evening home visits to chase down newcomers and potential new members, as well. One night I met in the home of a family who had recently visited the church. They had asked me over to their home to pray for their little girl who was facing surgery. In the living room, I gathered everyone in a circle – mom and dad, grandpa and grandpa who were visiting, and the eight and ten-year-old kids, one of which was the daughter. We joined hands and prayed. During the prayer the family mutt hopped down off the living room sofa and mounted my leg. It was hilarious. Really. Even so, I remained dignified as I tried to flick that little dog off my shin while choking back my laughter. As you can imagine, I wrapped up the prayer in record time. When our little circle of prayer was broken, I joked, "Was it just me or did anyone else feel the Holy Spirit moving in that prayer?" The family just stared at me deadpanned. They didn't have a clue what the family pooch had been up to while our heads were bowed and our eyes were closed. Even so, when I said good night to them, I'm pretty sure I saw that dog lift his head from the couch where he was sleeping again, turn and give me a wink and a smile just before they closed the door.

The congregation was booming. I was calling on people non-stop and hadn't had a break in a while. I couldn't understand why there were so few pats on the back from the church.

Apparently, my exhaustion was beginning to show. One afternoon, after our clergy study group meeting broke up, Cal offered to give me a lift home. He parked his little blue pick-up truck on the street in front of my house and let me pour out my guts to him. I confessed my anger. My shame at feeling anger. My sense of failure.

Like a priest, Cal listened generously, interrupting only to ask a question or two for clarification. When I finished, he leaned back in his driver's seat, drew in a slow, deep breath as he paused to run diagnostics the way an orthopedist might stand back and hum and haw over an x-ray, or a cardiologist might scan her eyes back and forth over the results of an ECG, analyzing and interpreting the results. After a thoughtful moment, Cal looked me squarely in the eyes and offered me a prescription that I swallowed easily that day: "Mark, don't ever try to love something or someone who can't love you back"

• • •

There have been times throughout my ministry, particularly in Cleveland, that I have found great relief in Cal's axiom. Withholding love from those who could not love me back protected me from investing so deeply that I lost myself. As best I could, I attempted to keep a healthy personal distance from those with great needs. I started to practice, in earnest, what up until that time I had only preached: throw a life line if you can, but never swim out to a drowning victim lest they grab hold of you and pull you under. I augmented Cal's axiom with a mantra of my own: "There is a God, and I'm not it." It became my life's refrain as I tried to keep a meaningful work-life balance. Or is that life-work balance? Either way, I hope Cal would be proud.

Still, there were other times that I argued in my head with Cal. Isn't loving those who can't love you back exactly what Jesus did? He loved people with a selfless love, fully and completely. He loved them when they were chewing him up like a pack of slithering Bobbit worms, eating him alive with their unreasonable demands for help and healing and even power and privilege. "Grant us to sit, one at your right hand and one at your left, in your glory," lobbied Mr. Zebedee's petulant sons, James and John. Most impressive, Jesus loved those who couldn't love him back even when he hung dying on the cross. Gasping for breath, through the grit teeth of pain, he found it within himself to ask God to forgive those who were persecuting him.

For a pastor to withhold anything from those with great need, especially love, seemed downright contrary to the teachings of Jesus. Jesus was the one, after all, who said that the son of man came to serve not to be served, and any who wanted to be followers needed to get on board with that new upside-down hierarchy and be right quick about it!

I especially debated the merits of Cal's axiom in Cleveland. Hadn't I come to Cleveland, after all, to love a church and a city that quite possibly would never love me back. Or precisely because neither could love me back?

One crisp but dull October day in 2015, I was sitting at my desk, a big banker's special, gazing across the expanse of my palatial office toward my tufted leather chesterfield. I was having a bit of an argument with myself. Or was it God? I believed that I was trying to love worthily in Cleveland. Sometimes I was successful. Sometimes I was not.

"The mere fact that Beth and I chose in 2008 to move to Cleveland in the first place could be considered an act of selfless love. No?" Cleveland was in bad shape back then.

Besides, when I visited the city that year for my first meeting with the pastor search committee, I was already on my way to "preach for a call" – the final step in the hiring process with another congregation. A church located on the doorstep to Manhattan, arguably one of the wealthiest, most dynamic and powerful cities on the planet. Beth confessed after the fact that she let me stop in to Cleveland on our way to New York just to humor me. She was sure I'd change my mind about Cleveland as soon as I saw it. She had quite the point: downtown Cleveland looked like a frigid, post-apocalyptic wasteland, a ghost town compared to the vibrancy and grace of Savannah's downtown streets like Broughton or Bull Street or the wonderfully touristy cobblestone River Street, or the promise of the charming New England-styled town with Manhattan in its view.

In that crushing year of 2008, Cleveland was starved for even a hint of Rockwellian charm. Its streets were empty. It's sidewalks barren. There was absolutely zero public activity on downtown's frozen avenues because there was absolutely zero public to be found. Period! The only warmth we spotted on the salt-and-ice-topped streets was the steam rising from the iron grates in the concrete. Waiting to meet the Old Stone Church interview committee inside the lush lobby of the Renaissance Hotel, we gazed out onto Public Square and wondered aloud about the whereabouts of people in the city.

"The rapture has happened and we've been left behind!" I joked. The only activity we saw were a few homeless folks huddled under newspapers, and a couple of pigeons pecking away at what appeared to be the remnants of a pizza crust.

At the very same time, I was sure Beth was thinking about the New York church but chose not to invite conversation on the matter. In fact, I was just days away from accepting the offer from the New York congregation which included a charming Victorian house, a huge salary compared to what Cleveland was offering, and an opportunity to serve a young, active congregation only a stone's throw from downtown Manhattan. Like the folks from Old Stone's interview committee, the New Yorkers were good and decent folks who chuckled easily at my sense of humor, even when I joked that their pulpit with its swinging door reminded me of a penalty box. I warned them that my sermons were much longer than a two-minute penalty and they laughed right along with me. Or at least they pretended to. Either way, I was good with it. Still, something nagged me about Cleveland. I was uneasy about going for the goodies in New York when there was a church and a city in Northeastern Ohio with a much more apparent cause, at least in my imagination.

Still, the suburban New York City church had an offer on the table, while Cleveland's Old Stone Church was still many months away from even selecting and interviewing its final candidates, so I went ahead and accepted the call to go and be with the good Presbyterians in the suburbs of New York City. Beth and I had already begun eyeing eight year's worth of accumulated junk around our big house on Wilmington Island. We were eager to pare down and get a For Sale sign planted on the front lawn. In spite of my doubts, we were all set to make the move further up the East Coast when, during a telephone conversation with the interim pastor in New York, a lever within me was flipped and the Cleveland light came back on.

The interim pastor affirmed for me that I was being called to serve an exciting and dynamic congregation. One with hundreds of kids and families. Lots of money. Lots of energy. And then, with one simple unassuming statement, he tripped the switch. If I had thought to look at the clock, I would have marked the date and time. It was one of those remarkable moments when one simple sentence can change the course of events for our lives forever. He said, "Mark, this is a church that most pastors would die for."

It was in the precise moment of his utterance that the static of my doubts cleared like the clouds after an afternoon summer storm. Clarity alighted and chirped a quiet, almost whispering truth in my ear: "But I wouldn't. I wouldn't die for it." It was in that one moment when the falsehoods of the self, my ambitious personal and professional pursuit of ladder climbing success fell to the ground like the empty rag that it was.

The New York church was filled with top traders and partners in major Manhattan law firms, they had hundreds of children and youth, and devoted parents and families in their membership. They may have wanted me to be their pastor, but I wasn't sure that they needed me to be their pastor. They didn't need me to die for them. But Cleveland? That was a different story.

I finished up the call with New York, came back into the living room looking, as Beth would tell me later, a sickly-grey. "I told them that I couldn't come. I wasn't their next pastor." Still to this day, it was one of the most difficult decisions I have ever made.

"Cleveland and it's Old Stone Church need a pastor who's willing to come and die for them." I reasoned with Beth to help her understand the epiphany I had just experienced in my telephone conversation. "I can't go to New York. It's not right." In my heart of hearts, I knew from the beginning that Cleveland was where I was being called. I was so confident that Cleveland was where God wanted me that even when the Old Stone Church was still months away from calling its next pastor, I turned down the New York church just for the possibility of coming to Cleveland. I set free the bird in my hand for the two pigeons on the sidewalk.

Our Cleveland years cost Beth and I our meager life savings. We took a beating on our house. At various points, we both experienced heart-twisting, chest-tightening tension and sheer exhaustion. When I asked the on-duty doctor at the new Cleveland Clinic walk-in facility across the street from my apartment what had caused my shingles, she asked if I had been experiencing any stress recently. I burst out in laughter but felt like crying. It couldn't have been more cathartic. I was up to my ears in stress. No one could accuse me, however, of not trying to love something or someone who couldn't love me back. I loved Cleveland and I loved the good people of the Old Stone Church, even when my city and my church could not love me back.

•   •   •

Somewhere near year five of my ministry in Cleveland, I came to understand the Old Stone story – the good, the bad, and the ugly much better. I had been scraping away at the upper crust veneer of the congregation for quite some time now. Like an archeologist carefully brushing away lamina of various eras, I had sifted my way down through the church's many layers until the connective tissue of a much larger story of systemic division and distrust revealed itself. Ironically, this great congregation - with a history as rich as its multimillion-dollar investments - suffered from what I perceived as a great, two-fold poverty of spirit: a worry about scarcity, on the one hand and, on the other, a belief that its better days were buried deep in its past.

I should have seen it from the start but, quite frankly, it would take me more than a decade to comprehend fully that at an institutional level the congregation suffered from a subtle yet misguided belief that it had outlived its glory days and, therefore, needed to be managed and managed conservatively in order to protect its dwindling prominence in the city. Unwittingly, supporting narratives and operative institutional dogma had evolved over the church's two centuries. Being loved and, especially being loved in a way that it might, in turn, love others and serve freely, joyfully with an audacious faith - the way the revered ancestors did - too often, seemed just out of reach. More often than not, we spent inordinate amounts of time and energy navigating the systemic sludge with which the church was also heavily endowed.

To be fair, Old Stone is not alone with its review mirror-focused vision. As the Christian church in North America hemorrhages members, downsizes operations, and adjusts post-institutional ways of doing business, there is widespread anxiety among congregations at denominational institutional levels, as well. Congregations, regional bodies, and national assemblies are courageously rethinking outdated nineteenth and twentieth century ways of being the church. Old Stone is going through what the mainline churches throughout North America are experiencing. It's just that Old Stone has more, or had more, resources than many: decent membership levels by national comparisons, a physical, historical, and psychological place of prominence in the city, and more money than God. Well, at least more money than most other congregations in the United States. It frustrated me that a church with so much could do so little, or at least couldn't do things with more expediency. The church was hamstrung by its own conflicted system of governance. Consequently, outreach and growth moved slowly and with less daring than it could have.

Early on in my ministry, just three years into my new work at Old Stone, the church had already revealed something of an identity crisis. I found myself caught in a conflict between who the church said that it wanted to be and who it really was, or was willing to become. We developed and adopted a ten-year mission plan, a recapitulation of a mission study the congregation had completed a year or so before my arrival. But just getting approval for the document proved to be a contentious process. People blamed and argued with one another claiming that the plan was too vague. Others stated that it was too detailed, or financially unfeasible, and asked that we slow it down a bit. Others attempted to thwart the whole effort by demanding to know just where I had obtained the information for the plan (from their own mission study among other places), as if the work that went into it and the articulation of the plan was mine and mine alone and not the group effort that it had been. No one, including myself, could spot the efforts of sabotage for what they were: a confluence of systemic resistance to change, anxiety about resources, and plain old self-doubts.

Admittedly, we may have just had a differing perspective on who and what the church in our day should and could be. It is entirely possible that what the church really needed most of all was a leader who wouldn't love them but rather one who would simply, well, lead them ("an innovative pastor with fresh vision" who would inspire the church to "remain exactly the same"). I didn't know how to do that. Leading without loving isn't in my DNA. I believe that deeply woven into the fabric of the Christian tapestry, perhaps the very first anchoring knot on our Christian loom, is a new commandment to love one another.

By 2015, I had swept away most of the dirt and dust of the church's prominent status. Underneath, I discovered the fragments, shards from an early time which, when pieced together, formed a heavy vessel that contained a theologically peculiar belief. It was a belief not unlike the one that lurked beneath the city's own doleful spirit: "Our value is based not on who are, but on who we were." Like the city itself, the church often celebrated its past – who it used to be with as much or even more fervor and devotion than it did its present or even its future. I often preached messages that reminded people that we were loved by God no matter what, but institutional memory didn't always agree with me.

What made the city stand apart from the church, at least in recent years, was a burgeoning hope for the future. It was that hope that excited me and, I believe, many of the congregation's individual members. Cleveland was shaking the rust from its steel toed boots and walking a new path. Cleveland was moving forward with or without the church. Its labor-based economy, for example, was dramatically shifting toward high tech industries and medicine. More people today - healthcare professionals, doctors, nurses, specialists, technicians and the like are employed by the Cleveland Clinic than ever worked in the steel plants of Northeast Ohio. The dynamic of the city core was changing rapidly, too, as young professionals and empty-nesters, like Beth and me, chose to live downtown or near downtown over the distant suburbs surrounding the city. People were choosing walkable, bikeable, and sustainable neighborhoods over the car dependent ones of their parent's generation.

That meant that the neighborhood surrounding the church was in growth mode. In fact, from 2005 to 2018, and perhaps even to this day, downtown Cleveland was the fastest growing neighborhood in the city, yet the church, as institution, dug in its heels on simple updates to campus, staff, and programs that would make it more attractive and welcoming to the very demographic that was missing from the life of the church. Initially, the leadership put up great resistance to social media and other online opportunities, too. I heard more protests than your Primitive Baptist grandmother when the champagne was uncorked at midnight on New Year's Eve.

I came home from Grand Rapids to Cleveland following an invigorating 2013 national meeting of CEOs for Cities feeling supercharged by a number of top tier speakers that included the late Tony Hsieh, former CEO of Zappos, Philadelphia Mayor Michael Nutter, Bruce Katz of The Brookings Institution, and Anil Menon, president of Cisco's Smart+Connected Communities initiative. You probably already know that Cisco is one of the largest information technology and networking companies in the world. According to

Steven Nickolas, writing for Investopedia, "As of November 1, 2019, Cisco had a market cap of $199.59 billion and was the largest company in the networking and communications devices industry."[55] At our meeting, it was Cisco's Menon who made the most convincing case that over the next ten years the world would not only be exponentially more connected via internet, it would be doing so primarily on video-based platforms. The next generation of internet communication, he posited, would be more than simply sending files of print or even favorite photos of your kitty cat, it would be in motion, and talking and, often, in real time. It would virtually remove borders and, in the world of medicine, for example, it would allow physicians in first world nations to guide the hands of surgeons, human or even robotic, through complicated surgeries in developing nations, or do assessments and recommend treatments for those suffering physical ailments.

Video-based internet would allow engineers and planners in different parts of the world to participate in real time global charrettes and planning exercises that could help solve real world challenges such as a lack of water, energy, or mobility. The global pandemic of 2020-2021 has made it even more clear to most just how important video-based technology is to our rapidly changing world. Zoom conferencing and Skype meetings with business partners around the world are common place today. Even my daughter, who lives in England, teaches private cello instruction to students in America.

What an exciting day and age we live in, I mused throughout the five hour drive home from Grand Rapids through some of the most impressive rustbelt cities making comebacks of their own – from Grand Rapids, itself, Lansing, Ann Arbor, Detroit and Toledo, before making my final entry into Cleveland. How can Cleveland - a city on the rise, I wondered, make use of this burgeoning technology to build up our own city? Or benefit from the trade on information from our

---

[55] Steven Nickolas, "Top 5 Companies Owned by Cisco", Investopedia, Updated Nov 28, 2019, https://www.investopedia.com/articles/company-insights/090716/top-5-companies-owned-cisco-csco.asp, accessed January 3, 2020.

one-hundred-and-fifty-year reserve of expert industrial know-how? And how could we as the church – what should be a change-making, headlight congregation – step up our game to communicate the gospel to a much broader audience, and to serve the city in even more meaningful ways than we had been doing in recent years?

There are good reasons we encourage leaders to take along board members or constituents when they attend conferences these days, not least of which is that too often, lone CEOs are energized with new ideas but end up being lone voices upon their return. Such was my experience after Grand Rapids. When I returned, I floated a few simple ideas to the corporate decisionmakers in the church. In truth, my ideas were low hanging fruit such as streaming services, or an online show I had been developing even before the move to Cleveland called, Power2ools: 2 Minute Tools for Life. I was greeted with rolling eyes of derision and harrumphs of cynicism. I had seen resistance to new models and approaches in other congregations. It was nothing new. In fact, high-risk aversion and low tolerance for change throughout the North American church may, in part, help explain significant portion of its decline.

In spite of initial resistance, over a year later, I was able to garner enough support from a handful of leaders just adventurous enough to give me support to launch a few concepts including my show, Power2ools. The church elders, along with a Cleveland-based company, AMG Marketing, agreed to sponsor the show which allowed us to purchase airtime on television, and more importantly, online.

Our humble foray into Menon's video-based world was a huge success, at least by church standards. In just twenty weeks we engaged far more people on television and online than we ever could have simply by having people come to us for Sunday morning services. According to ratings, an average of twenty-three thousand viewers between the age of twenty-five and fifty-four were watching us every week on Fox 8's morning show, New Day Cleveland. Additionally, almost double the number who gathered on Sunday mornings were now viewing videos online. I was being kept extra busy responding to hundreds of online conversations with viewers who might never darken the door to a church. There were lots of trolls – people whose sole online purpose was to create conflict or ugliness, of course, but there were also those with real need, including some who had a desperate desire to talk about concerns ranging from depression and suicide, to murder and forgiveness.

Our worship numbers were climbing as a result of the show, too. In 2006, only three hundred and sixty people attended Old Stone's Christmas Eve candlelight worship - four hundred and twenty if you counted the family service which happened earlier in the evening. In 2016, just two years after we launched Power2ools, along with video rebroadcasts of sermons on our YouTube channel, the number more than doubled to well over one thousand worshipers between the two services. In 2017 we offered a third service to accommodate the growing numbers.

Alas, all good things must come to an end; and so it was for Power2ools. The spirit filling my sails and as well as others within the congregation fizzled to a dead calm after enough discontent and pettiness among the vocal minority - particularly those who held seats of power or influence among the organization's governance sullied the joy that should have abounded. Though it wasn't making money, some folks argued over issues of copyright and who actually owned the Power2ools concept, or who got the money if the program ever did make money. Others saw the staggeringly positive viewing results and grumbled that online viewers weren't giving any money to the church. It seemed to them a waste to sponsor a show that simply took the hope of the gospel beyond the doors of the church but didn't generate enough income to sustain itself. Never mind the fact that nothing the church does sustains itself. Everything the church does relies heavily on gifts from the membership, and from the church mothers and fathers who, before moving on to glory, first endowed the church with millions of dollars in reserve to care for itself in perpetuity and continue contemporary ministries within the church and beyond.

My discouragement was my own fault, though. I was operating under the misguided notion that the church really could or would at least try to step out in faith and become a true twenty-first century game-changer both for the city and for the denomination throughout the country. I believe, one day, it still just might.

Admittedly, I suffer from a dangerously high level of tolerance for both change and risk. I saw our little Savannah congregation triple, its Sunday attendance quadruple, and the congregation unite to undertake a three-quarters of a million-dollar expansion without a penny in the bank – one that was paid off in less than six years. I was eager and, believed that I was now equipped to help lead a city center church into the twenty first century with excitement and love, and the congregational resources to back the vision.

One dear friend and Old Stone institutional agent, however, laid it on the line with me with a "read my lips, no new taxes" kind of certainty one day when I privately shared with him my growing frustration with the church's lack of interest in moving forward: "Dr. Mark, you can do whatever the hell you want after we [the leadership] are all dead and gone. But in the meantime, I'm telling you, nothing is going to happen here." He is a good man, and a dear friend. I know that his comment was intended to help me stop banging my head against the old stone wall of intransigence and free me up to enjoy the Old Stone ride of affluence and privilege. After all, I could have easily accepted what was a fairly comfortable living for a pastor. I could have flown effortlessly beneath the radar of true societal need and injustice and, instead of expecting much from those to whom much had been given, including myself, puttered along listlessly until retirement. But I hadn't come to Cleveland, to the Old Stone Church, simply to cruise. I came to help tear down and, with others who were beginning to believe in their city once again, raise up. To lead and to love those engaged in that kind of fearless, prophetic ministry of compassion and justice, outreach and growth from the heart of one of the poorest cities in the nation.

In hindsight, I see that I could have been so much easier on myself, and probably on the good folks of the church. I could have spent less energy by simply preaching solid sermons on Sundays and helping the congregation heal from its most recent decade of conflict. I could have made my ministry about quietly loving folks who struggled to believe that their better days were not behind them.

Within me, a different spirit was moving. I wanted, and continue to want more for the church in the twenty-first century. I can still see in my mind's eye, Cal shaking his head in disappointment and groaning, "Mark, Mark, Mark. Quit trying to love something that can't love you back."

Please, make no mistake about it. I'm not talking about who these folks were as individuals, or as families and friends. Individually, the people of the Old Stone Church were as good and decent as you will ever meet, even courageous and faithful at times. Individually, many were saints who befriended Beth and me. They invited us into their homes, welcomed us at their table, included us in their family traditions. I considered it nothing short of a privilege to have been permitted to walk with them in some of their most vulnerable times: when they allowed me to visit them in hospital and pray with them at their bedsides as they tugged on paper thin gowns to protect their dignity, often with extreme pain and discomfort; or hold their hands as doctors delivered staggering prognoses; or when the child of a loved one had been murdered and I was asked to go view the body because mom and dad just couldn't bear to do it for themselves. I was given access to a very private and precious world where the authentic faith of parishioners was graciously, tenderly, honestly shared with me. I am forever in debt to the abundance of grace that, individually, the members of the congregation revealed to me.

Apart from the conflicted structures of the church, the majority of individuals sustained us with their prayers. They sent us cards of encouragement when our parents – my father and both Beth's parents were sick and dying all within a three-year period. There were even individuals from the congregation who made the eight-hour journey along icy roads, and through one of the worst Great Lake storms in decades to be faithful witnesses to me and to my family at the time of my father's death. I will cherish that act of kindness forever.

Those who abandon the church or, worse, their Christian faith because they see Christians behaving badly clearly don't get it. What some see as the epic failure of organized religion - so called hypocritical Christians, I see from an entirely different point of view. To me, there are sinful people in the world and there are sinful people in the church. But if you can come in and spend some time with the ones in the church, roll up your sleeves and work alongside them as they swing their hammers for Habitat for Humanity, or walk beside them in a walkathon to promote mental health awareness, hold each other up in times of loss, you would be as moved to tears as I have been when those same people do good and decent things. One of the most impressive things about the church to me is that you get to see a bunch of folks who could go either way. They can hurt you or each other – and sometimes they do both. But from time to time, church folks will also do some of the most extraordinary things you'll ever be blessed to behold – in spite of the corporate structures of the institution. Their faithful courage bears witness to a God for whom all things are possible. Even amidst the brokenness of our worldly systems and institutions - of which I count the church, people of faith will still surprise you with thoughtful words, kind gestures, and ironic acts of goodness.

Old Stone was filled with individuals living out their faith in and through the church. Without them I would not, could not, have served as long as I did. Even those who were simultaneously serving on boards that institutionally pressed the brake when we tried to move things forward, or sunk the congregation and its leaders in the mud of the church's systemic culture of "no" had a way of inspiring me. They helped me keep at it. To give more. To love more. Their actions were to me like those of a boxing coach who splashes cool water in the face of a fighter, towels him off and then sends him back into the ring to battle it out for another round.

One Sunday morning, as the peace was being passed among worshippers, I saw something that I pray will never leave me. When the liturgist invited people to extend God's peace to those around them, a petit, elderly woman moved out of her pew and across the aisle to physically embrace a tall and scruffy member of the church who had just been released from prison, for the second time in his-her life.

The elderly woman was an upper middleclass church woman, privileged in every way – white, educated, affluent, and enjoying status within a high society church and the broader community. There was a time in her life when, on week nights, she hosted church groups among the lovely floral-patterned settees and ottomans of her grand suburban home.

Marion, the one who received the elderly woman's hug, was a transitioning person. A person who had served twenty-six years in prison for armed robbery and then, following eight years among us, an additional nine months for drawing the SWAT team, Beth and me, and another member of the church to his home where he waved a toy gun about hoping to coax the police to shoot him. He was depressed, of course. Thankfully, the police were thoughtful, experienced, and already knew Marion. They understood and refused to play along. Still, Marion had to go back to prison and do more time. Were it not for a wrap-around team from the church – another group of highly dedicated and loving individuals, I suspect that Marion would still be there.

Marion's first Sunday back with us, the slight suburban woman slid from her pew – her usual spot - and across the aisle to greet Marion back in Marion's usual spot. She reached her arms around Marion's broad torso and, as she squeezed Marion tightly, I overheard her say, "Don't you ever leave us again!"

In a religious world that seeks to divide us up into sheep and goats, and a political one even more vehement in its attempt to encamp us as conservatives and liberals, alt-right and alt-left, Republican and Democrat, or even African American and white, here was an unabashed and unfathomable act of compassionate love happening right under my nose. It was a remarkable step toward a kind of holiness that can be glimpsed only in the church, one that wouldn't play well on either Fox News or CNN. To me, her divine act of kindness was pure, and it rose far above the vitriol which spews forth from the sewage pipe of popular culture. Her generosity of spirit was a brilliant light. It revealed an amazing God whose audacious word proclaims in our own day as surely as it did in the first century: in God there is no more "Jew nor Gentile, neither slave nor free, nor is there male and female, for you are all one in Christ Jesus." Ask me to show you where I see the reconciling word of God at work in this, too often, bent and broken world, and I will tell you the story of the plucky lady who brought unconditional welcome to the transgender ex-con in the pew across the aisle from her. Her radical hospitality, and Marion's warm reception of it, revealed nothing shy of the radiant glory of God beaming before my world-weary eyes, and within our conflict-weary congregation.

In his book, A Passion for the Possible: A Message to U.S. Churches, one of my former professors, William Sloane Coffin, famously wrote: "You can't think straight with a heart full of fear, for fear seeks safety, not truth . . . A heart full of love, on the other hand, has a limbering effect on the mind." When we acted as an institution, we didn't always think straight. We thought more about protecting a system of church governance created almost two centuries earlier, even if it meant sacrificing the well-being of the congregation and its important ministries of outreach to the city beyond its doors. With all apologies to my friend, Cal, I believed that what was needed was not less, but more love - something that might have a limbering effect on our minds. More love from me for them. More love from them for each other. More radical, liberating love to help them untangle the language of their oppressive historic documents and free every last one of them to exhibit more love for those in our city who were hungry for good news and faithful leadership from the congregation at the heart of the city.

Maybe Cal was right, though. I couldn't keep loving something that wasn't loving me back. At least not for much longer. In time, my heart began to seize up.

•   •   •

I like to think that love doesn't keep score, or at least it shouldn't. After five or six years of fighting, what I believed was, the good fight, however, my spirit was weary. Keeping score is just what I caught myself doing every now and then. For years, I tried to ignore that little itemized ledger sheet in my mind that accounted for all the times the institution said "no" to one proposal or another: "No" to a green roof. "No" to a ten-thousand-dollar grant we were offered to do a development study. "No" to a proper security door for the children's wing to keep the children safe - even after the leadership had been presented the case of First Presbyterian in Plymouth, Michigan where a pedophile wandered in off the street and sexually assaulted a child. "No" to welcoming the Greater Cleveland Congregations in preparation for their march to the Justice Center after the not-guilty verdict in the trial Michael Brelo was read. After a while, there were too few yeses and far too many noes on my ledger sheet for me to keep my frustration hidden. Besides, I knew the score card wasn't healthy for me and it wasn't fair to those I had come to love. Each no felt like a little rock that added up to a greater weight that pressed down on my spirit until the burden became more and more difficult to bear.

One of the hardest things for me to accept was the "no" the institutional gate keepers gave to holding a rally following the Stoneman Douglas High School shooting in Parkland, Florida. I was given an often-cited excuse: it was too political, and the one organizing it, former Congressman Dennis Kucinich, was too controversial. I cited the number of school shootings in an email and my number was off by one. A mass email was sent out to church leaders and others accusing me of spreading "fake news" and that we should resist this kind of political agenda in the church.

This time I refused to be out of step with my personal values and beliefs. I rented space in a local hotel for the event. I spoke at the rally and gave my most impassioned and enthusiastic "enough is enough" speech which turned into a great call and response with the crowd, although apparently Dennis must have thought my speech was going on too long. I got the tap. Dennis's toe discretely nudged mine under the lectern as if to say, "Mark, enough is enough!" Dennis certainly knows how run an event.

With every school shooting that happens, I share in the collective national grief that washes over the hearts and minds of all Americans. Along with millions of other people, I ache with a deep sadness and utter disbelief at the inability of our law makers to create legislation similar to laws in other advanced nations who have overcome political lobbyists and partisan divisions to create legislation that truly says, "enough was enough." With every killing, I feel more homeless.

Isolated. Disheartened and alone. And not just in the city in which I live, but in America on the whole.

I experience a unique flash of anger burn within me when I consider the number of churches throughout our nation - especially those that hold in reserve a great wealth of power, privilege, and historic influence, yet continue to hunker down in silence on the matter, cowering in fear that too strong of a voice and they just might lose even more members than they already have. Ironically, it may be that the very demographic for which the church in the twenty-first century pines – those under the age of thirty-five, may be very eager to learn what the gospel of Jesus Christ has to say about our American lust for weapons that are used to kill children in our schools. They might want to know about this one who, for two millennia now, has called people of faith to be peacemakers in the world. I imagine, that the young people the church seeks to attract also experience a sense homelessness when they encounter our silence on the matter. "Thoughts and prayers are not enough," they cry out after every mass shooting. Are we listening? Fifteen thousand young people and supporters gathered just beyond the church's front doors on Public Square on a Saturday morning following the Parkland school massacre. The church's doors were locked up tight. How mind-boggling it was for me to hear from longtime members of the church on Sunday mornings asking why we couldn't attract more millennials. The poetic words of the Georgia-based singer-songwriter duo, the Indigo Girls seem to speak to the church in our day and generation. To paraphrase: 'We wrapped our fear around us like a blanket. We sailed our ship of safety until we sank it."[56] Lord, have mercy.

In time, I began living into the Old "Stone" name. Systemic resistance in the church was exacerbating my longing for place while turning my heart to stone, petrifying it into a rock just as brittle as the exterior of the church's Berea sandstone edifice.

There were days that I felt very much like Sisyphus, the Greek god and King of Corinth who, for his sin, was condemned to an eternity of a having to heave a boulder up a steep hill every day only to witness

---

[56] From *Closer to Fine*, E. Saliers, The Indigo Girls, Godhap Music.

the futility of his grunting efforts each evening as the boulder tumbled back to base. The rock I shouldered in Cleveland was my own stony heart. Like Sisyphus, I was paying for my sin: the sin of loving an institution that would not, could not love me back.

Still, I loved.

Sorry, Cal.

2014-2016: Bargaining

"If you can't walk away from a negotiation, then you aren't negotiating. You're just working out the terms of your slavery."
– James Altucher

Chapter Eleven

Doubling Down on Cleveland

"You've got to know when to hold 'em
Know when to fold 'em
Know when to walk away
And know when to run"
Kenny Rogers, *The Gambler*

IT IS IRONIC, at least to me, that my Cleveland home - a crumbling condo whose physical problems and unrelenting legal battles were bleeding me dry - was situated directly across the street from a casino. Like a gambler whose endorphins are fired up just playing the game - win, lose, or draw, I was hooked on Cleveland. No matter how bad things got, I found it almost impossible to fold.

The constant conflicts in my work, the unbridled crime, police shootings, and the incessant wear and tear of the gritty streets of downtown, the never-ending lawsuit that our condo association board had with our developer, the inability to sell our condo while in litigation and move to some other place in the city with more healing points of grace were all flattening my spirit. Even so, there were enough wins for Cleveland, albeit small and often short lived, to keep me at the table playing the game long after I should have walked away. Like Giles Corey, the only person on American soil to be executed by crushing, I taunted, "more weight." With every win, no matter how miniscule the payout, I found myself doubling down on Cleveland.

Elizabeth Kubler Ross would accuse me of bargaining. Every day was a constant negotiation. My life had a new soundtrack - the hit song by the 1980s British punk band The Clash: Should I stay or should I go now? I even opted to go at one point, submitting my resignation to the board – the one elected by the church. I was desperate for relief. The majority of the church's members, I believe, were unaware of just how bad the internal conflicts had become. How much they were paralyzing the church and its mission. The elders held meetings and then coaxed me back while promising to help untangle the conflict between the two boards so we could get the church moving forward. I rescinded my resignation.

One afternoon, I invited a retired pastor to join me for lunch in exchange for some wise counsel. Let's call him Cameron to protect his innocence, or lack thereof. Cameron was a crusty old sod to a lot of folks who preferred their pastors docile. He was a gravelly Scotsman who didn't suffer phonies easily, and who loved just as hard as he fought. He was also a no BS kind of friend to me.

Cameron finished his scotch and slammed his empty tumbler on the table. Reminding me of an old pirate – cracked face and grey beard, he closed one eye and stared at me with the other. He leaned over the table to make sure I heard him when he growled, "Kid" (I was in my fifties), "The thing you have to understand is that the church is like a twenty-dollar whore. Just when she thinks you're leaving, she'll give you a little tickle to keep you around a little longer." Cameron was right. Every time I thought I had an exit strategy worked out, something would pull me back in again. But it wasn't the church that attracted me as much as the city. I loved Cleveland.

I loved the restaurant scene in downtown Cleveland. In my humble opinion, there are very few cities in North America that can match it. "Cleveland doesn't get a lot of culinary love, and that is a shame," wrote Lenore Newman in her 2019 book, Lost Feast: Culinary Extinction and the Future of Food. I agree. Cleveland is carousel of international delights. Each neighborhood offers something unique and wonderful, from Cleveland's Polish Village to Little Italy to

AsiaTown. While filming a 2007 episode of his culinary show, No Reservations, Anthony Bourdain said, "I like Cleveland. Always did. I find the much-maligned town beautiful. A stark reality up against a unique sense of humor and resignation, a surprisingly hopeful place for food if you only bother to look." Beth and I bothered to look!

Likely, the most notable spot during my time in Cleveland was Iron Chef, Michael Symon's East 4th bistro, Lola. With all apologies to the vegetarians in the room, one didn't go without ordering at least one serving of the beef cheek pierogi. Lola, thanks to the pandemic of 2020-2021, is now closed. My go to spot, though, was across the street, Ristorante Chinato. Beth and I often didn't get out of the office until after 7:00 P.M. Too tired to think of something decent to make at home, we would drag our weary souls over to Zach Bruell's restaurant for its excellent Italian wine selection and fried baby artichokes. We joked that the servers must have groaned when they saw us coming because we usually closed the place.

During its first year of operation, at a time when downtown was still struggling, Beth and I went to dinner with the brother and sister-in-law of one of Ohio's former Governors and U.S. Senator. It was a desolate Tuesday evening but still, we were asked if we had reservations. We didn't. The host whispered to us that even though the place looked deserted there was a 'special party' coming in that evening. We talked our way into a booth in the bar area and later watched as a number of the members of the Rolling Stones paraded into the restaurant. I posted on Facebook the next day, "Out with the former governor's brother and his wife at Chinato. Rolling Stones popped by. Typical Tuesday evening in downtown Cleveland." Sadly, Chinato shut its doors permanently in 2019 when, according to Cleveland.com, Bruell and his landlord, MRN Ltd, after months of negotiation couldn't reach a lease renewal agreement.

There were so many great places to eat in downtown and throughout Cleveland that one night when we were walking home from a Lebanese feast over at Taza on East 6th, I asked Beth, "Do you think this city makes me look fat?"

Theater kept us in Cleveland for a long time, too. We were season ticket holders, first to the Broadway series, and then to the much more intimate Cleveland Playhouse series. We loved being able to walk from our condo to the theater district, grabbing a quick dinner before a play or a bite after a show. We knew all too well that we were, in many ways, living a charmed life.

I loved the city's great needs, too, and my ability to do something about them. In Cleveland, I had a purpose.

Cleveland played the little guy card well. I have a passionate belief in the underdog. In fact, "I'm a sucker for the underdog," I wrote in my very first article for the Plain Dealer. "I love to see God upend the powers and principalities who try to keep good cities down. Believing in Cleveland is a little like believing in the Browns; one day they are going to knock those Steelers on their behinds and the Dawgs will have their day."[57] I believed it then. I believe it today, and with even more fervor.

My belief in the underdog, however, is also my kryptonite. It's my one true weakness. Well, one among many weaknesses, I suppose. Championing the underdog is what kept me from accepting better jobs in better cities throughout the years. I even sabotaged offers and opportunities from other churches when they came my way just so that I could stay with Cleveland a little longer. Wired within me is a compulsive hope that one day losers will be winners, that the little guy will knock the bully on his boney ass just like little Ralphie did to Skut Farkus in A Christmas Story. It's my deepest desire that one day the dead will be raised and that I will be there to witness it. I want to rub my world-weary eyes and behold the bright light of God's great and redemptive plan for the downcast and lowly unfolding in my very midst. I was blessed to witness those redemptive moments often in Cleveland.

I was convicted by the belief that one of the greatest American stories was the one I was living. The story of a city on the rise. For a long time, it didn't matter how toxic my job was, or how much street dung from life in the city, or our falling down condo, I had to scrape

---

[57] New pastor at Old Stone Church: God called me to Cleveland, March 5, 2009, updated January 13, 2019, https://www.cleveland.com/religion/2009/03/new_pastor_at_old_stone_church.html, accessed July 29, 2020.

from the bottom of my urban walkers, I was participating in one of the greatest comebacks ever.

It was a dramatic narrative in which I played one of the protagonists, a champion of the city. For me, Cleveland was the Little Engine that Could, or the Ugly Duckling. It was the story of the city once mocked and scorned but now being revealed as a beautiful, soaring bird gloriously taking flight among the swans. Okay, maybe not a swan. Maybe a swooping seagull. At the very least, it was becoming a city far greater than what the four-term Mayor Frank G. Jackson recently claimed was perceived as the "butt-hole of the world."

Being part of that story energized me. It convicted me. It convinced me that choosing to make my home in Cleveland was a meaningful part of the city's resurgence. I wasn't the only one, of course. There were a lot of good folks investing their hearts and souls in the restoration of the city, particularly of its downtown. It takes a village to raise a village. Making it my home seemed less of a choice as time rolled on. It was my calling.

I recognize that when I sing Cleveland's praises, I can be as annoying as a holy-rolling, born again Bapticostal during summer revival week but, I can't help it, I am a true Clevangelist. I'm up on my feet, throwing my hands in the air shouting hallelujahs because I saw that the good things happening in the city weren't just individual moments of success, but were part of a much greater moment: the resurrection of Cleveland. I continue to Clevangelize even to this day. Once a Clevangelical, always a Clevangelical.

Admittedly, sometimes we can be the most vocal proponents of a person, place, or thing – a president, a city, or even a religion because we harbor deep seeded doubts about that person, place, or thing. Our faith is fragile. Our charismatic case-making may be little more than a fervent attempt to strengthen it. If I can convince you then maybe I can convince myself.

My belief in the great city of Cleveland was and continues to be real yet it was also fragile, and for very good reason. With every small win, there were often great losses. As soon as new apartment and condo conversions were constructed, the facades of other buildings were crumbling, like the one I was living in, or like the National City

Bank building on East 6th where, in April 2015, a sizeable portion of brick and mortar from the west facing wall plummeted nine stories and crushed a minivan parked in the street below. Thank God there wasn't someone in the van at the time, or walking on the sidewalk beside it. Cleveland would clean up the sins of one or two corrupt politicians like Jimmy Dimora and Frank Russo, sending them off to prison, and others would rush in to take their place. As recently as February 2021, City Councilman Kenneth Johnson was indicted for swindling close to one hundred and thirty thousand dollars from city coffers. In all, Johnson was charged with fifteen counts including, "two counts of conspiracy to commit theft from a federal program, aiding and assisting in the preparation of false tax returns, tampering with a witness and falsifying records during a federal investigation."[58]

With every three steps forward, Cleveland often slides back two. I believed Cleveland needed folks who would herald the good news. People who would excitedly, passionately preach the gospel truth: if we're taking three steps forward and sliding back two, then at least we're averaging one step to the good!

It was deep winter 2015. A friend and I had met for coffee. I couldn't understand why he complained so much about the city that morning. We had our cold hands wrapped around hot lattes. It was my treat. We were in one of our favorite downtown cafes, Phoenix Coffee on East 9th at Superior. Even so, he was in a funk. Languishing. We had each other's generally good company. Heck, even our eyeglasses had finished defogging after coming in from the cold. Still, like Eeyore, he was resolutely focused on the gloom and, on this particular day, wasn't holding back:

"I hate this f***ing city!" He griped about the bitter cold that whipped off the frozen lake and jetted between the skyscrapers that created Cleveland's East 9th wind tunnel that he had to battle to get to the coffee shop. He groused about the roller coaster economy and the apparent lack of opportunity for him. He grumbled about the

---

[58] Cleveland Councilman Kenneth Johnson indicted on federal conspiracy charges involving reimbursements from city, Cleveland.com, February 23, 2021. https://www.cleveland.com/cityhall/2021/02/cleveland-councilman-kenneth-johnson-indicted-on-federal-conspiracy-charges-involving-reimbursements-from-city.html (accessed May 3, 2021).

countless potholes – one of which had popped one of his tires the week before, and the City's lack of interest in repairing them. He had to file a complaint and make his case to access the fund that is set aside just for that purpose. Mostly, he absolutely despised the people who seemed to accept things the way they were. Clearly, he was having a bad morning. In Cleveland, it happens.

I don't know if it was the caffeine coursing through my veins or just the warm glow of being inside and away from the arctic blast coming off the lake but I recognized that I was returning his grumbles with a joyful volley of all the great things that Cleveland offered: the city's somewhat affordable downtown and near downtown housing stock with great walk scores (my building boasted an impressive 94 on the walk scale!), its second-only-to-New York City performing arts district, its world renowned orchestra, its museums, not to mention the prettiest grocery store in the world just down the street that had just opened weeks earlier. "Cleveland's hard to beat," I preached.

It was in that moment, though, that I saw something in myself that I had never seen before. A little curtain in my mind was drawn back and I caught a glimpse of awareness: what I was most passionate about and felt the strongest need to help him see wasn't just the good things about Cleveland. It was the overall revitalization that was taking place in the city. Its redemption. For me, there was an old Cleveland, one that had been in decline for decades. And there was a new Cleveland, one that was on the rise. His spirit belonged to the old Cleveland. Mine belonged to the new.

• • •

In Savannah, I often felt like I was living life on the sidelines. Even though I was a pastor in a region that still respects its religious leaders to a certain degree, and even though I was a professor in one of the most prestigious art schools in the country – the Savannah College of Art and Design, I was unable to break into the tightly closed deep South circles that made things happen in the historic city, or kept them from happening. In Cleveland, however, I found myself blessed with opportunities to be involved. Certainly, being the Senior Pastor of one of the most renowned churches is the city didn't hurt. Having the strength of the Old Stone Church name behind me helped open many doors. Within the first three weeks I was already a guest on one of the local television network's morning shows, along with Dr. Rajmohan Gandhi, historian, political activist and grandson of Mahatma Gandhi. From the very start I had a sense that I was going to be traveling in some important and open circles as the city sought to reinvent itself. I also recognized quickly that I had better be prepared to live up to the opportunity, to give back to my new hometown wherever, whenever I could. To whom much is given, much is expected. Carpe Cleveland.

I started seizing the day in late 2009 after reading an article in Crain's Cleveland, a go-to magazine for business types, that discussed three potential new television shows that Hollywood's TV Land network was entertaining for its first original series. One of the shows being considered was a sitcom called, Hot in Cleveland. It would star Betty White and Valerie Bertinelli among other popular actors. A little light went on in my head: if they produce that show, someone from Cleveland should purchase the HotinCleveland.com Uniform Resource Locator (URL). It could be a great way to promote the city at a time when it was receiving a lot of bad press.

I set my copy of Crain's down on my desk and quickly researched the URL. Sure enough, no one had claimed it yet! I whipped out my credit card and bought the dot com address for less than twenty dollars. For a few days I celebrated the novelty of my purchase with some family and friends and then almost forgot about it altogether.

One church member - let's just call him Dick, an elected leader in the congregation who learned of my Hot in Cleveland URL purchase showed up at my office red-faced. Steam was rising from Dick's head. He tried to act cool about my recent acquisition but his controlled breathing and flared nostrils betrayed him. I'm not sure if he was angry at himself for not thinking of it first, or if he was jealous, or anxious that it might turn into a money maker for his pastor. Dick's measured conversation was confusing and left me feeling as if I had done something wrong, which I hadn't. My intention to use the site, should the show be finalized, was fully devoted to the promotion of the city. I also hoped to bring positive attention to the congregation which, in recent years, had become invisible to the world around it. "Is that a museum?" some people asked about the church when I had first arrived in the city.

"If you sell that site, you have to give the money to the church," Dick warned me. "You were on church property when you bought that URL. You might have used your own credit card but you used your office computer to buy that site."

Dick may or may not have been correct. I was too stunned to argue with him. Besides, he was totally missing the point. This was a great opportunity to bring a little attention to Cleveland's then sleepy church on the Square and, more importantly, lift up the city to a national audience that would be eager to explore all that was hot in Cleveland. In my humble opinion, it was an innovative way for the church to "work and pray for the well-being of the city" as the prophet Jeremiah had charged us to do.

Instead, Dick's concern revealed to me the first of many signs of church pettiness that, over the years, would eventually wear away at my reserves so badly that I would find myself sliding into a muddy funk of discouragement. I tend to live with a spirit of abundance; Dick reflected to me one of scarcity.

A week before Hot in Cleveland premiered on national television, I launched a rudimentary website to celebrate all things Cleveland. HotinCleveland.com was basic. Crude, really. I had huddled over my desk (in my own study at home, for the record) late into the night over many evenings to build my homespun site from a template resting on the WordPress platform. Even so, just forty-eight hours before the show's launch, the website visitor counter was ticking up numbers faster than a car's odometer in a Fast and Furious flick.

Every two seconds someone from around the country, possibly around the world, visited HotinCleveland.com. Thirty people every minute clicked on to the site. As soon as the first episode concluded the visitor counter reeled like a jet's altimeter at takeoff. Over one hundred thousand people had clicked on to the site.

Thousands more continued to visit HotinCleveland.com throughout the show's six season run. Most of them were looking for information about the show, of course, or Betty White. What they got were a lot of pretty pictures and introductory information about the city. Things that I believed were truly hot in Cleveland – the Rock & Roll Hall of Fame, the CAVS, the Westside Market, Little Italy, and a whole host of other places and opportunities that I thought might be of interest to potential tourists and future job hunters. I had also added a lot of "hot links" that took seekers to other articles and stories about Cleveland's great comeback. It was hilarious for me to receive emails from viewers asking if I could "Please give Betty White a message" or if I could "Please ask the producers to shoot an episode" in a certain part of the city, not understanding that the show wasn't actually filmed in Cleveland and that I had absolutely nothing to do with the show. I usually responded to requests with, "I'll see what I can do."

Local media took notice, too. ABC NewsNet 5's Alicia Scicolone did a great piece with me that connected my venture with the show's debut, suggesting that my part might "give the city a huge comeback." I don't think my contribution was particularly noteworthy, but it did make me feel as if my work would become part of the new Cleveland that was unfolding in my midst, not to mention it might help lift up Cleveland's city center church an institution of entrepreneurial savvy and creativity.

HotinCleveland.com is still floating around out there on the web, but it's long since been forgotten by most people – especially by me. The site still gets visitors because Betty White is a superstar and because the show, though cancelled after the sixth season, still lives on in reruns. Just in case anyone is wondering, especially Dick, no one has ever offered to purchase the URL, not even TV Land, but if you've a good idea for its use, something that will help promote what is truly hot in Cleveland these days, please feel free to send me an email. You don't need to be a Dick.

· · ·

Cleveland was overflowing with opportunities for me to be a part of its story. To be a change agent. The fact that I was a pastor who had chosen to make his home in downtown – on Public Square, no less, was a novelty that drew a great deal of attention. It had been years since downtown had any residential population to speak of let alone someone whose home overlooked the Square. A hundred years or more had passed since someone had lived right on the Square. Most longtime Clevelanders remembered our home in the Park Building at the corner of Ontario and Euclid from the days when the wonderful aroma of roasting nuts wafted out of Morrow's Nut House, and when the building also housed the offices of lawyers, architects, and even a dentist. Now the historic nine-story office building was home to three daring new couples including the Senior Pastor of the Old Stone Church and his spouse. I did a lot of interviews with media. Wrote a lot of articles. Spoke to a lot of groups and organizations about life in our new and growing downtown. People were curious.

By 2013, the church was back in to the city's view, too. People no longer asked if it was a museum. We were hosting a variety of prominent events and gatherings, meetings for the city and outside organizations, television crews were showing up to feature us in a variety of news stories. News 5 Cleveland's Academic Challenge show - where high school students compete in knowledge-based categories, often dropped by to film me asking a question about Cleveland history for a video challenge question which delighted me. Usually anything that got me away from my desk and connecting with the broader Cleveland community interested me. The congregation was growing again and most importantly, it was alive and engaged in the work and life of the city, as well as drawing people to services in person and online throughout Northeast Ohio.

In 2014, the church sponsored the International Gay Games when Cleveland won the bid to host the games. We opened our doors as a daily rehearsal space for the three-hundred-member Gay Games Choir. I invited a friend and colleague of mine, Rev. Ray Bagnolo to speak from our pulpit on the Sunday morning of the games. At the time, Ray was the director of a national organization called That All May Freely Serve which supports LGBTQ people who are wrestling with a call to ministry. Ray was a dynamic speaker – warm, accessible, full of love, and easily endeared himself to the congregation. During his visit, Ray met with one of our boards individually to speak about the ordination of gay and lesbian pastors in the Presbyterian Church

(USA), as well as explore the subject of same sex marriage. He helped us move the needle just a little bit closer to making the congregation fully inclusive. Less than a year later, ahead of the Supreme Court's ruling on same sex marriage, I asked the congregation's ruling board, the session, if we were going to wait for the Supreme Court to tell us what we could or couldn't do? Though not unanimous in its decision, the board voted overwhelmingly in favor of opening its doors for all couples to be married in the historic church. It was one of the proudest moments in my entire work in the church and the city.

Individually, both Beth and I had received accolades from the mayor. Beth was presented with a "Woman of Distinction" award for her work in the city toward ending homelessness for women, human trafficking, her speaking engagements, and her work in New York with the United Nations - first as a delegate for the Presbyterian Church (USA), and then in subsequent years as the Ohio representative of the national non-governmental organization, Women's Intercultural Network (WIN). The Mayor presented me with an award for my "Human Kindness and Dedicated Support to Residents and Businesses in Downtown Cleveland." Beth and I were investing much of time and energy, our hearts and souls into both the life of the church and the city. What a delight it was to be acknowledged for those things for which we were most passionate.

While I was the twelfth Senior Pastor of the Old Stone Church, a title I wore proudly, at times I felt like I was also Cleveland's pastor. I could hardly walk down the street without someone stopping me to offer an encouraging word about my inspirational television shows, Power2ools: 2 Minute tools for life or 30 Second Sermons, or about the church's online outreach, or one of my recent speaking engagements. One of the most meaningful speaking invitations came from the Take 5 Jazz Club. One of the two owners asked if I would be a part of its grand opening by offering a dedication blessing. I must admit, it was not only a unique kind of opportunity but, given my love of jazz and blues, it was a joy. I wrote and offered a spoken word Jazz and Blues blessing.[59]

---

[59] **Jazz and Blues Bar Blessing by Mark Giuliano:** "Duke Ellington, 'Sir Duke' himself, once said that jazz 'is like the kind of man you wouldn't want your

Other times I was asked to bring invocation prayers and speeches where I was privileged to share the platforms with the Governor, Senator, Congressman, and Mayor and other leaders, or to dedicate a section of Public Square as "Jesse Owens Way" along with other leaders and the famous Shaw High School Marching Band. When I finished my brief remarks on the steps of the county courthouse where we had gathered for the celebration of the bicentennial of the War of 1812, I turned to one politician and joked, "I wonder if the event coordinators remembered that I grew up in Canada?" Canadians are fond of celebrating that victory over the United States. Another time, I had been asked to speak in front of the Moses Cleaveland statue on Public Square to help celebrate the settling of Cleveland. I honored the settlers, of course, some of whom were founding members of the Old

---

daughter to associate with.' So what is the Pastor of the Old Stone Church on Public Square doing in a jazz club, bringing blessing to this fine new establishment? Let me tell you:

For me, Jazz embodies the Eternal rhythms of our lives: conflict and resolution, confrontation and revolution, bitter discordance and sweet denouement.

If God had a favorite genre, don't you think it would be Jazz, maybe the blues. Who knows suffering and healing more??? Who more than God, loves it when God's people gather to celebrate God's great blessings.

And didn't King David call us to put the band together: 'Praise him with trumpet sound; praise him with lute and harp! Praise him with tambourine and dance; praise him with strings and pipe! Praise him with sounding cymbals; praise him with loud clashing cymbals! Let everything that has breath praise the LORD!' (Psalm 150:1-6)

'Jazz is open-ended music created for open-minded people!' May *Take 5* bless us, and bless God, not just with space, but also with holy and sacred time that we might be the open-minded people Cleveland needs right now. Let this place be a place of bridge building, road paving, and peace making through music-making for all people (21 years and over!). May old friendships find healing in the soothing balm of live music. May new friendships be forged in the heat of dance and song. May our spirits and our bodies be fed in the breaking of the bread around these tables and at this bar. In the Holy name of the Eternal One, the author of all song, and the lover of all people; Amen."

Mark Giuliano, Dedication of Take 5 Jazz and Blues Bar in downtown Cleveland, Ohio - March 20, 2013

Stone Church, but I also gave mention to those whose land had been settled. I was blessed and I was "privileged" to be in a position to help shape a message for the city well beyond the doors of the church. It was in my heart to be a public pastor in and for the great city of Cleveland.

There were enough cookies - good things happening for me both personally and professionally - that I was easily able to overlook, or contend with the challenges for years. I truly felt like I had arrived when the Republican Congressman, Jim Renacci and his team invited Beth and me to attend a bipartisan event at the U.S. Capitol in Washington D.C. Congressional leaders from both parties, state representatives, mayors and business leaders from all over the state of Ohio were invited to network and be empowered to bring important information about the D.C. happenings back to their various districts.

Beth and I booked a little apartment on Airbnb not too far from the Capitol. Donning our best professional evening attire, we headed out toward the Capitol on foot. As Beth and I hurried up Pennsylvania Avenue not wanting to be late, we held hands and felt very much like the ministry team God had formed in the heart of our marriage. I found myself just a little overwhelmed by how far our lives had come. Just before the steps to the Capitol, I stopped, turned to Beth and marveled, "Who would have ever imagined that little old us - a couple who met way back in high school in little old Windsor, Ontario, would be walking up the steps to the U.S. Capitol as invited guests to a gathering of prominent leaders?" I was in awe.

When the evening was over, we ducked around a velvet cord and followed what we thought was a short cut out of the building. Instead we navigated our way through a seemingly endless maze of dead ends and empty hallways down in the basement of the U.S. Capitol, giggling to ourselves every step of the way. We were completely and utterly lost. We agreed that it was a great metaphor for our nation and its leaders as they attempted to lead during our uncertain times, navigating a series of paths that seemed endless and went nowhere.

• • •

Nowhere did I have more hope that I would see the underdog rise up than on the streets of downtown Cleveland. It was there that I was able to witness, on a daily basis, our abhorrent societal failures to adequately care for the mentally ill and addicted. But it was also the place I saw the redemptive power of God at work. On rare occasions, like the city itself, I saw homeless and hurting people raised. Like Michael who was HIV positive and living on the street when I first met him. Michael welcomed the spirit of God into his life and experienced a faith conversion. I hadn't seen him since the day, years earlier, when we sat together in the sanctuary of the church and prayed. Then one Wednesday afternoon in the spring of 2015, out of the blue, Michael came strolling in through the open front doors of the church and asked if we could talk.

"Do you remember me?" he teased.

"Of course, I do, Michael." I braced myself, worried that he might be there to ask for money. I was delightfully surprised to discover he had just come to say "thank you."

"Pastor Giuliani," he mispronounced my name. A lot of folks do. "You were one of the few people that treated me with any kind of respect in those days. You actually held my hand when we prayed. And you knew I was sick!" I was moved when I saw that, after our simple prayer, Michael had been able, by the grace of God, to turn his life in a new direction. He had found a job. Found a home. And, for the first time in more than a decade, found a way to love himself enough to take care of himself. "I gotta run," he said. "I'm just on my way to work and I wanted to stop in to say, "thank you!"

Indeed, there were blessings happening all around me that lightened the load of living and working in downtown Cleveland. We did a funeral for one of our homeless worshippers - a friend of Jesus named Tom who had self-medicated himself into an early death. When Tom's small family from a distant suburb arrived for the service they were overwhelmed with joy to see that Tom had found a pastor - the Senior Pastor of a prominent downtown church, no less - who knew him well enough to deliver a heartfelt eulogy. They were greatly relieved to know that in his final years, Tom had found a church, or that the church had found Tom, and had been able to love Tom even after he had worn his own family down past the point of their being able to care for him. God had not forgotten Tom.

Some managed to stay sober. Others didn't. Either way, they continued to greet me when they saw me walking along the street. They asked nothing more of me than maybe a friendly "hello" from someone who knew their name. Even when we feel helpless to respond to the outstretched hand of poverty, a simple greeting or "God bless you" as we pass by can make the difference between a stark and lonely day and one where humanity is being restored – for them and for ourselves. Often, I'd stop and have a visit or offer a prayer. It was as good for my soul as it was for theirs. Always, I'd ask, "When you are going to come over to the church and let Jesus work some miracles in your life?" Sometimes, some did come. And on some days, they found a home in God, too, like Michael who had moved onward and upward with his life after he understood that he had been seen, and known, and loved by God. After a lifetime of being shamed for his sexual orientation, and after years of being made to feel dirty because of his disease, he felt human again. Some remained part of the life of the church. They were an ever-present reminder to me and to others that with God all things are possible. It was exhausting work. There weren't a lot of miracles, but there were enough to keep me at the table. I banked the days of victory to sustain me on days of loss. Even Agnes, the scruffy shouter who sold the homeless newspaper in front of my condo building ("Hi! Wanna help the homeless?") found a home among us. She became a full voting member of the church. One year for Christmas, she purchased simple Christmas presents for everyone in the congregation. Like one of Santa's special elves or better yet, one of the Magi bringing gifts to Jesus, Agnes went from table to table at coffee hour blessing church members with her gifts. She gave me a jigsaw puzzle of the Ohio Stadium, home of the renowned Ohio State University Buckeyes football team. I treasure her gift as I treasured her presence in the life of the congregation. Who else but our mischievous God, that scamp of life-restoring miracles, could have brought this special woman into the body of Christ. God had brought into my view, the shouting woman below my condo window who had me pulling my heart out with frustration. All her realness. Her humanity. Her gracious heart and generosity of spirit. These folks and their stories of healing and redemption were the sacramental bread which fed my soul. They were the holy wine that quenched my spiritual thirst.

In my head and in my heart, I often renegotiated the terms of my personal commitment to Cleveland and its Old Stone Church. There were systemic struggles within each. Gossip. Infighting. Power struggles. Stasis versus innovation. For a long time, I was able to shrug these things off. They were nothing new for church or secular politics. More importantly, I felt blessed to be engaged, to have a purpose, and to be working in ways that, I believed, were truly making a difference in the city and in people's lives. And when I saw a major windfall about happen for the city, I doubled down on Cleveland. Like most Clevelanders, I was betting on 2016.

Chapter Twelve

"2016"

"Hope smiles from the threshold of the year to come, whispering, 'It will appear happier.'"
Alfred Lord Tennyson

———————————

FOR CLEVELAND, the year 2016 deserves a chapter to itself. I imagine that some will write entire books or, perhaps, shoot entire documentary films about the year 2016 and what it meant for Northeast Ohio's great city by the lake. When future generations search American history books for information describing this era, they might find in the index under the subject heading of 2016, "please see Cleveland." When they enter 2016 into a search engine, it will respond: "Did you mean 'Cleveland'?" Cleveland owned 2016.

For Cleveland, though, 2016 began in 2014. Like many of the life's most monumental events or experiences, when we trace our fingers backwards along the chronological line that brought us to them, we often discover that there was one single a point of origin, a root cause, or precise moment which set the whole sequence of events that followed in motion. We have all known that couple who never would have met, started dating, and eventually got married if both of them, individually and after much arm-twisting from friends, hadn't gone to that party years earlier. Or the person who would never have got their dream job had they not rescheduled a flight for an earlier hour and ended up sitting next to the very person who years later would sit on the other side of the desk conducting the interview. Sometimes the love, the joy, the success we seek is already in motion though we cannot yet see it.

Two important things happened for Cleveland in the year 2014 that allowed for 2016 to unfold in the triumphal way that it did. In fact, the occurrence of these two events – concurrent cosmic phenomena? - revealed themselves mere days apart from one another. Some might even go so far as to say that these two, seemingly unrelated events must have had to occur in 2014 in order for 2016 to unfold in the victorious way that it did.

First, as Cleveland charged toward summer of 2014, we dolled up the city, wore our best pearly-toothed smiles, and laid out a fresh new welcome mat for the Republican National Committee's Site Selection Committee which had placed Cleveland on a list of potential cities to host the 2016 National Convention. The competition was stiff, and even included one other Ohio city: Cincinnati. The GOP was eager to win a swing state. Hosting its convention in one of those states was critical if it was to secure a victory in the upcoming presidential election.

One particular morning, I received a phone call from a friend. He was an insider who traveled in the right circles. Like an informant on the other end of the line, he urged me to make sure the that front doors to our historic church were swung open as wide as possible, and to make sure that we had one or two of our top docents on hand to offer a gracious welcome to the RNC site committee. "They're in town now. If you see a Lolly the Trolley tour bus pull up in front of the church, be ready!" he charged me, as if to set 'Operation Persuasion' into motion.

At the church, we scheduled our secret weapon that day: Bob Reid. Bob was a true ambassador for the church and the city. It wasn't unusual for me to receive a "thank you" from visitors from around the globe who appreciated the work and welcome of the church and would mention a particular greeter – "I think his name was Bob," who had extended to them a very generous "Hi-Diddily-Ho neighborino" with Ned Flanders enthusiasm as well as expert information about what to see and do in Cleveland. If you have ever visited the Old Stone Church on a Sunday morning or during its midweek 'Open Doors' hours and found yourself regaled by a gentle and avid Old

Stone/Cleveland booster with a pleasant smile and an enthusiastic welcome, it was probably Bob.

In many ways, Bob is representative of some of Cleveland's finest self-declared ambassadors and other Clevangelists who are naturally inclined to celebrate with anyone who will listen, helpful information and fun facts and stories about the city they love. On the day of the GOP site selection committee's visit, they were out in full force at every possible gathering and amenity between the Rock Hall down at the Lake to the Soldiers and Sailors Monument and the Old Stone Church on Public Square.

Two months had passed since the day we rolled out our welcome mat. We were due for an announcement any day. Throughout the first week of July, I was on the edge of my seat hoping, praying - yes, praying, that the news we were waiting for would come quickly and in our favor. Cleveland was desperate for a win.

Beth and I had left town for a week to cottage with our extended family up in Central Ontario. We were just a three or so hour drive north of Toronto, but our thoughts and our hearts were seven or eight hours back in our hometown, Cleveland.

Cell service in the remote location was maddening. To get service you had to walk down to the dock on the lake to get clear of the trees or, if you didn't want to drive everyone in the surrounding cottages batty with you loud talking on the cell phone, up the hill and out on to the highway where you could wave your phone around in the air as if you were trying to flag down a rescue plane or, perhaps, communicate intergalactically.

Sometime in the morning of July 8th, I excused myself from the family-sized breakfast table and walked outside to try and pull in a signal. Sure enough, I began getting news reports and texts from friends: Reince Priebus, then Chair of the Republican National Committee, announced that Cleveland had beat out Dallas, the other final contender, as the host city for the political party's 2016 convention. Priebus praised Cleveland, calling it a "city on the rise." He was speaking my kind of language.

I floated back into the kitchen where family members – aunts, uncles, my brother and his wife, my mother, and Beth were gathered around the table engaged in "let's all talk at once" family free for all. It's how our family rolls.

"Guess what, everyone!" I bogarted my way into the buzzing conversation. One or two stopped talking, which is a lot for my family. I could barely breathe, let alone talk, I was so overwhelmed with joy at the good news. I choked back my tears of joy and announced, "We won! The GOP is coming to Cleveland!" Cleveland's bubbling midwestern hospitality hadn't been missed by the RNC.

My family looked at me and responded with an underwhelming, "Oh" and then went back to whatever it was they were talking about.

It didn't matter to me whether they understood it or not, though. Beth and I, and about a million and half other Northeast Ohioans understood just how exceptionally good the news was for Cleveland. The city that had been known as second poorest in the nation, fastest dying, the mistake by the lake, the city of the burning river, would now have the opportunity to unroll the red carpet, welcome the world, and showcase a new Cleveland. A city on the rise.

Beth and I spent the rest of the morning huddled together drinking coffee and making plans for our part in what would be become one of the biggest parties the city had hosted in decades. Sometime in the afternoon, we packed up our planning calendars and schematic drawings and switched to wine so that we could simply bask in what was truly great and glorious news for our beloved, Cleveland. So many had worked so hard, ourselves included, to lift up the city's true greatness – all those things that made us proud to call Cleveland home. It was time to celebrate.

Of course, at this point, no one knew that the party's guest of honor would be a contentious character who would bring with him stress and anxiety to our city, and unrest to the nation: presumptive Republican presidential nominee, Donald J. Trump.

•   •   •

Just three days on the heels of the GOP's announcement, the second piece of the puzzle fell into place. July 11th of 2014, almost four years to the date of his famous televised dumping of Cleveland for the chance to win championships with his new love, Miami, King LeBron announced a second coming. He was coming home to Cleveland. In an interview with Sports Illustrated, LeBron said that he was coming back to resolve unfinished business: "My goal is still to win as many titles as possible, no question. But what's most important for me is bringing one trophy back to Northeast Ohio." And just as quickly as fans had torched their LeBron jerseys outside Harry Buffalo's restaurant in downtown Cleveland in 2010 after his cruel broadcast break-up, the city forgave him and then joined arms and began singing in the streets. Reunited and it feels so good!

And just like that, two years ahead of the great summer of 2016, the cosmic tumblers that would unlock Cleveland's destiny as a city of champions, were already falling into a fortuitous, one-two combination.

•   •   •

2016 didn't simply arrive. There was no simply 'passing Go' and heading directly to the events that would eventually nudge Cleveland's self-image out of from under the dark clouds of loss and self-loathing. The effort and energy we invested into courting the GOP was just a drop in the rusty bucket compared to what was needed to host a major political convention. Previous host cities both promised and warned us that hosting a political convention would be the equivalent of hosting a Super Bowl in our city every day for five days straight. City leaders rubbed their sweaty palms together with glee as they envisioned a river of revenue flowing into the city coffers like water from the annual spring runoff into Lake Erie. Hotel rooms sold out more quickly than online tickets to a Rolling Stones farewell concert. Everybody and their uncle planned for a cash grab by converting everything from basements to garden sheds into "luxurious and close to the city" Airbnb rentals. The home owners in our condo building, which was smack dab in the heart of one of the main convention gathering sites – the speaker's platform on Public Square, voted to allow short term rentals just for the two weeks surrounding the convention. The promise of lucrative leasing opportunities were just too tempting to pass up, although, in the end, not one owner ever rented out their unit.

True to form, within the church there was initial disagreement. Some of the powers-that-be were wary of allowing the church to remain open during the convention. One or two even floated the idea of boarding up the grand dame's ten multi-million-dollar stained glass windows and hiring security to patrol the perimeter of the church campus throughout the week of the convention. Leaders of the society – the self-elected and self-proclaimed owners of the church, rubbed their chins as they hummed and hawed about whether to grant the congregation and its board of elders permission to keep the building open. Our two boards were at odds. One was eager to fling wide the doors of hospitality by offering programs and tours throughout the convention. The other was battening down the hatches, still needing to be convinced that the building be could safe and secured. I found myself somewhere in the middle, as was often the case, wanting the church to open up as much as possible but also trying to love even those who remained unconvinced.

Outside the church, in addition to my regular pastoral ministry, I was tearing off to event planning meetings, host committee meetings, security meetings, Public Square stakeholders redevelopment meetings, Downtown Alliance and Downtown Resident meetings. My days were packed with meetings and gatherings more tightly than dad's old Chevy the night before summer vacation. The busyness energized me. We were building toward something positive for the church and the city so I allowed the frenetic pace to fill my sails as we whirred toward the crescendo of the big event.

The coming convention energized the city and gave us an excuse to repair, construct, or purchase just about everything on everyone's ten year wish list. If ever there was a reason to fix up the old house, getting ready to welcome the projected fifty-thousand guests who were coming to visit for a week was it. Public-private partnerships were forged and the city took on a fifty-million-dollar Public Square redesign project, the construction of a shiny new thirty-story, two-hundred-and-seventy-two-million-dollar hotel to connect to our freshly minted four-hundred-and-sixty-five-million-dollar downtown convention center and medical mart - the Global Center for Health Innovation. Beth and I, along with hundreds of other business leaders, civic partners, and law enforcement agencies aligned our efforts and zeroed in on making Cleveland a safe and friendly showcase city for the world.

The church anted up enough to fix our aging façade while the construction of the Square outside of our front doors was underway, and committed other significant amounts to host, promote, and secure a variety of programs and tours on our campus. Our Director of Operations, Beth Giuliano, was taking the lead with Homeland Security, FBI, and local police agencies. It was truly impressive how she was able to convince them to comply with our needs. Beth had a way with people and could negotiate easily with the city, the department of police, general contractors, and anybody else who might have had a stake in the projects or events that happened on the Square or on the city blocks surrounding the church. She convinced the city to surrender whole sections of Cleveland's busy Ontario Street, as well as the transit authority to divert bus routes so that the church could have parking opportunities on Sunday mornings, or for weddings, funerals and other programs that needed to happen during that year. Beth, more than anyone, protected our first amendment right to peaceably assemble in the same location where we had been worshiping for almost two full centuries.

Cleveland wasn't all RNC focused in spring 2016, though. We had our sports to keep us pleasantly distracted, particularly our American Hockey League (AHL) team, the Lake Erie Monsters (now the Cleveland Monsters), and our basketball team, the Cleveland Cavaliers or as they are affectionately known, the CAVS. Both teams played at the Quicken Loans Arena in downtown, now the Rocket Mortgage Field House. And in 2016, both teams were flaming hot with wins. It could not have been a better year for Mr. Gilbert and for our great city. For the first time since moving to Cleveland, I saw people across the board speaking, without pause, about how proud they were to be Clevelanders. Heads were raised with pride.

On June 11, 2016, before a sellout crowd of 19,665 victory hungry fans, Beth and I among them, the Monsters triumphed over the opposing team from Pennsylvania, the Hershey Bears. After three full periods of regulation play, neither team had scored a single goal and the game was sent into sudden death overtime. With just 1.9 seconds remaining in the first overtime period, the Monsters scored their winning goal. Never before had I worried that such a new stadium might utterly collapse. I was sure that beneath the deafening roar of the crowd, I felt the ground tremble under my feet. As I look back on it now, I know that would have been impossible. My feet weren't on the ground. With almost twenty thousand other Cleveland fans, I was in the air. As we joined together in singing a raucous rendition of We Are the Champions a tear rolled down my cheek. I surveyed the thousands of cheering fans throughout the stadium and whispered a prayer that the father who had once taught his son to get comfortable with losing – "we're Clevelanders," was in the crowd with his son to celebrate this moment of victory.

Just five nights later, in the very same arena, the mighty Cleveland Cavaliers had come back from a 3-1 game loss deficit to tie their series with the Golden State Warriors at three games apiece. The win for Cleveland would send LeBron James and the CAVS back to Oakland's Oracle Arena for a Sunday evening NBA final showdown.

Game seven in Oakland was truly a nail biting, hair pulling, spectacular event. Never before in NBA history had a team come back from a three-games-to-one deficit to win a final. The CAVS were very much like their hometown: a team worth cheering for but clearly the underdogs. The fact that they had made it this far in the series was truly remarkable. At the beginning of the final series, a friend of mine who lives in Oakland even offered to make what he and every other basketball fan in the country saw as an easy bet on the Warriors. If the CAVS won, he promised to send me a case of California wine. I joked that since the Warriors were clearly favored to win, he should, instead, send me a case of Italian wine. If the Warriors won, I promised to ship him two cases of Great Lakes Brewery's popular lager, Dortmunder Gold. With every Cleveland loss, my friend zipped out a text goading me to abandon the shame, declare defeat and give-up now. With every other Clevelander that year, I dug in and refused to wave the white flag of surrender. The CAVS didn't disappoint.

I attended worship with my mother in Canada on June 19th, the day of the final game. The pastor surprised the congregation by concluding the service with a benediction that included the cheer, "Go Warriors!" My jaw hit the floor. Had he not seen me there in the pews throughout the service? Had he not understood my devotion to my hometown? To its resurrection? I couldn't contain myself and so stood up and blasted back, "No! Go CAVS!" All heads in the sanctuary turned toward the loud American shouting in their pews. Polite Canadians unaccustomed to outward displays of emotion in worship wore looks of incredulity. "Go Cleveland!" I hollered. I didn't care if one of the elderly ushers had to drag me out of that sanctuary kicking and screaming. I was a Clevangelist and now, apparently, speaking in tongues! Besides, I couldn't understand how any pastor who preached the gospel of the underdog – "the least of these," could be encouraging a win for the advantaged Warriors, even if he was a big time Steph Curry fan. I imagined it to be nothing more than a bad bushel of sour grapes from the Canadian preacher since year after year the CAVS erased any hopes the Toronto Raptors had of making it to the finals. Raptors would have their day, it just wouldn't be in the year 2016.

With just three and a half minutes left in regulation time, CAVS and home team Warriors were tied at 89 points apiece. In those remaining two hundred and ten seconds, three critical and dramatically heart thumping things happened to give Cleveland the win: Steph Curry failed to make a number of three-point attempts, LeBron James put up a now famous block against an attempted shot from Warrior, Andre Iguodala, and with fifty-three seconds left in the game, Kyrie Irving swished a three-pointer. LeBron James sealed the deal at 10.6 seconds left in the game by scoring one of two free throws that made the final score 89-93.

After fifty-two years, Cleveland's curse had been broken. Shattered. Shadoobie!

"Cleveland!" LeBron howled through tears in an on court postgame interview. "This is for you!" You have never seen so many tears pour forth from a grown man. And here, I am referring to my own.

The very second of triumph – when the buzzer ended game seven and we knew the championship was ours, was the cathartic moment that crystalized the whole of what so many of us had been hoping for, praying for, laboring away in the life of the city for. It's why I came to Cleveland. Why I made it my home. It's why I stayed even when the rocks of disappointment kept piling up in my life and pressing down on my spirit. Time and time again, I felt like turning out the lights and bolting down the highway to better opportunities. But I stayed. For this.

The CAVS victory testified to what all Clevelanders knew in their hearts to be true: Cleveland was no longer the mistake on the lake. We were a city of champions! A city on the rise. Cleveland was home.

For the second Sunday in a row, I encouraged our church organist to play and the congregation to sing along to Queen's We Are the Champions. Quite truthfully, no one needed coaxing. Just a few days later, over a million people, almost three times the population of the city proper, flooded the streets of downtown for a victory parade. It was our moment.

.   .   .

Just a few weeks later, we had another moment. 44,000 visitors descended on Cleveland for a week of politics and protests, hobnobbing and networking for the Republican National Convention. RNC delegates, reporters and broadcasters, politicians and protesters, as well as added security forces from various cities in neighboring states crowded hotel rooms, downtown parks and city streets.

For Beth and me, the morning of the convention began with two practically dressed FBI agents sitting on our living room couch drinking coffee. There wasn't any of the urgency or authoritative badgering that you might see in the movies, but the agents were reasonably curious about protesters from outside the city who, the week previous, had reached out to the church seeking a place from which they could organize before marching in demonstrations or find a place to mend should protests turn violent.

As we spoke, I kept watch out our front windows as thousands of people gathered on Public Square, some of them civilians with semi-automatic rifles strapped over their bodies or hand guns holstered to their hips. Most of them were the various individuals and organizations getting ready to take their scheduled turn at the mic on the speaker's platform to pitch one issue or another. Others made up a sea of local looky-loos who had come to see what all the fuss might be about. Beth and I agreed to share some information with the agents but not all. We answered questions about the types of requests that came to the church which may have helped the FBI understand what kind of protests for which they might need to prepare. We also exchanged direct numbers and promised to keep each other informed as necessary. We weren't willing to reveal names unless things got out of hand. We were still a church after all. Protecting confidentiality from the state, among others, still matters.

For me, the energy of the convention was like a drug. I was a junkie rushing from one high level event to the other to get my next fix: a late-night dinner on a West 6th patio where New Jersey's larger than life Governor Chris Christie showed up, a gathering on the forty-ninth floor of the Key Tower with Speaker of the House, Paul Ryan. I was overjoyed to celebrate all things Cleveland with whomever was willing to listen so did a number of interviews with Bloomberg TV, Belt, and others.

A lot of my time was spent with our dedicated volunteers who greeted thousands of visitors from near and far, so long as they were unarmed – we had posted our gun free zone policy. Our historic church, outside of whose front doors Lincoln's body was once held in state, was a popular place for visitors, especially for those belonging to the party of Lincoln.

In the quiet of one early evening, as we prepared to close up the front doors to the church, our faithful greeters were accosted by gaggle of squawking protesters. Members of the Westboro Baptist Church read on our church sign that we were part of the liberal-leaning Presbyterian Church (USA) denomination of Christians. They locked in on the sidewalk just a dozen feet or so from us and began a rapid fire of well rehearsed and blatantly homophobic profanity. I was aware of the antagonistic group and their protests at military and civilian funerals from recent media reports, but had never had the, uhm, "pleasure" of meeting any of their members. I tried my best to shut my ears as soon I heard them referring to us "ass f----ers" and "anal ripping queers." My grandfather was a Baptist minister. I'm positive that he never used words like that.

Sensing that we were being goaded into a shouting match with a group of raging homophobes for whom we just didn't have time or energy, our thoughtful, well-prepared greeters and docents - God love them - responded in precisely the way in which they had been prepared: they remained in smiling, Buddha-like silence. It's not surprising to me that documentarians, Louis Theroux and Geoffrey O'Connor titled their film about the Westboro group, "The Most Hated Church in America." After the group marched on, I turned to our group of volunteers and proclaimed victory: "Consider it a compliment, a badge of honor!" I declared. "We were just protested by the Westboro Baptist Church. We must be doing something right!"

The evening that presidential nominee Donald Trump was to speak over at the Quicken Loans Arena, I was invited by the convention's lead planner to join him for a full convention and stage tour. Guitar superstar and former Saturday Night Live music director, G.E. Smith warmed up to my left. RNC Chair, Reince Priebus, took family photos to my right. I stepped between them to take my place at the lectern where Donald Trump would take the stage in just a few short hours. I inhaled a deep centering breath and gazed out on the cavernous stadium. Brightly lit red "Make America Great Again" banners were draped throughout the very stadium where I had seen the Lake Erie Monsters win the Calder Cup, and where LeBron James and the Cleveland Cavaliers had done battle against the Golden State Warriors, just a month earlier. I offered a silent prayer. My Democratic friends still tease me to this day that God must not have been listening since Donald Trump won the election anyway. The truth is, however, that among the many important things on my prayer list that evening – our nation, our leaders, our people, I prayed most earnestly for the continued success and wellbeing of my hometown, Cleveland, as we showcased our city to the world. We had worked so hard to get there; I prayed that our labors would not have been in vain. Perhaps God might bless us by helping the world see our city the way we saw it. Indeed, that was a prayer that God answered many times over.

Cleveland came off looking like a media darling, the practically perfect host city that it was. Dan Zack of the Washington Post described the GOP gathering in Cleveland best when, on the last day of the convention, he wrote, "We were promised a riot. In Cleveland, we got a block party instead."

• • •

Summer of 2016 was such a roaring success for Cleveland that, quite truthfully, many of us were in utter shock when our, still-to-be-renamed, Indians didn't win the World Series that fall. We were dumbfounded that the Chicago Cubs, who hadn't won the World Series since 1908, were able to claw their way back from a three-games-to-one deficit and even make it to game seven in hometown Cleveland at all. Of course, we were well aware that our CAVS had done it to the Warriors just a few months earlier. We had grown so comfortable with our new championship persona that we just didn't believe that another team could do it to us. How quickly we forget.

We had been losing most of the night of game seven before we finally saw a flashing moment of possibility. Cleveland centerfielder, Rajai Davis knocked a two-run homer out of the park to tie the game in the eighth. The crowd of 38,104 – mostly deep-pocketed Chicago fans who could afford the inflated price of the tickets were silenced, and millions more around the country were on their feet. In Cleveland, we were breathless in anticipation of another victory. I was almost sure of it. The gods were smiling on us. This was Cleveland's year: hockey, basketball, politics. We were in the national spotlight and doing everything right. How could we lose? The gods were smiling upon us!

And then that all too familiar lugubrious cloud of loss rolled in over the city. Officials did what had never been done before in a World Series seventh game. As they were heading into the tenth they called a seventeen-minute rain delay amid what appeared to be nothing more than a light mist, a few sprinkles. The necessity of the delay will be a topic of great debate among fans for years to come. At least it should be! Most Clevelanders, including myself, will argue that the delay robbed our team of their momentum and cost them the game.

For Cleveland, 2016 ended with a heart wrenching loss. The Indians had blown a World Series that was theirs to lose, the second time in twenty years. Then, as if to rub salt in the wound, the Browns had their worst year in franchise history by winning only one game out of sixteen. On an up note, with that one win the Browns did manage to end their seventeen game losing streak, but with a final game loss to arch rivals, Pittsburgh Steelers, they began another equally long drought.

For me, the baseball and football losses of 2016 were no match for the joy we experienced in Cleveland that year. 2016 was the climactic culmination of my own eight-year blood, sweat and tear investment in the city, as I am sure it was for hundreds of thousands of other proud Clevelanders. I was so caught up in Cleveland's yearlong block party, however, that I hardly noticed the wear and tear that was beginning to show in my body and my spirit. I was too busy riding the celestial high of triumph, inhaling the ethereal air at victory's peak. I was still humming with a radiant buzz of Cleveland pride.

Neil Young once sang that "Every junkie is like the setting sun." Somewhere beyond the horizon of 2016, I was slipping. I was about to crash. And I never saw it coming.

2017-2019: Depression

*"Before you diagnose yourself with depression,
first make sure that you are not, in fact,
just surrounding yourself with assholes."*[60]

---

[60] This quote has been misattributed to many, including Sigmund Freud as well as the American-Canadian speculative science fiction writer William Gibson (who has stated that quote is not his). Quote Investigator attributes the origins of this quote to a Tweet by Notorious d.e.b. (@debihope), Timestamp: 12:23 PM – 24 Jan 2010, https://quoteinvestigator.com/2014/10/25/diagnose/ (accessed April 8, 2021).

Chapter Thirteen

Cleveland Rocks

"Everybody's got a box of rocks, heavy with regret
Angry words and jealousy might hold me down and yet
I believe. Yes I believe.
Gonna break these chains, Gonna let 'em fall
'til nothin' remains, But love that's all"
Tia McGraff/Tommy Parham, *Break These Chains* (written in my
office at the Old Stone Church, Cleveland)

YEARS AGO, our congregation went for a family hike in the woods. For an hour or so, we scrambled over the roots and rocks that jutted out from the stony path. Half way through the walk, a little tyke in the group started fussing about how heavy his back pack was starting to feel. "How much further? I'm tired?" he whined like a mosquito in his father's ear. "My pack's too heavy! Daddy, will you please carry my back pack for me?"

"No, son. You need to carry whatever you brought with you," the kid's wise old dad had drawn the line.

"But Daddy, this bag is waaay too heavy for me. Pleeeeeaaase!" he wailed with dramatic effect. The little boy plopped down on a big boulder and surrendered. "I can't go any further!"

Dad turned around and saw his son stewing on the rock. He softened, but only with conditions. "Okay. I'll carry your pack for a little while but just to give you a bit of a break. And then you have to carry it yourself again. Deal?"

"Deal." the kid agreed.

After a few minutes though it was now Dad who strained under the weight of his child's pack. "What do you have in here, kid? Rocks?" Dad gasped out the words through his huffing and puffing.

"Yes," the little one confessed. "I've been collecting them along the path.

If you ever feel inexplicably tired, or if your neck and shoulders are experiencing pain, you might ask yourself if, perhaps, you have been dragging around some rocks that you have unwittingly picked up somewhere along your path. You might even ask if those rocks were even yours to carry in the first place.

It was Christmas Eve 2018 when I first sensed that I had been lugging around a sack full of my own rocks. My Cleveland rocks. I had unknowingly been gathering them throughout my time in the city. Just three days past winter solstice, the midafternoon sky had already turned a drowsy grey. The weight of the sky pressed down on me as I ran next door to the Cuyahoga County Jail to visit a man in lock-up on charges of drinking and driving. His third time. We visited. Prayed. And then I wished him a Merry Christmas, if you can have such a thing in jail.

As I heaved open the heavy glass doors and stepped outside on to the concrete plaza in front of the Justice Center, I inhaled a sharp blast of crisp December air. It awakened a strange thought within me: "If people can learn to live in jail, or even prison for extended periods of time then I should be able to figure out how to live in Cleveland for just a few more years. If not until retirement, at least until the church's bicentennial in 2020."

I rolled the thought over in my head the way I turned a piece of Ugli fruit over in my hands in the produce section of the grocery store. First touching it. Then holding it out and away from my face. I was curious but didn't want to get too close! "What the heck is that?" But I knew. I knew all too well where the question was coming from. It was rooted in a feeling that had been weighing down on me for quite some time but I had been unwilling, too busy, or otherwise distracted, to admit. It wasn't exactly depression. More like depression's first cousin: burnout. And with that burnout, I found myself less and less recognizable when I looked into the proverbial mirror. I was as hardscaped as the city streets around me. I was losing my tender-hearted, champion-of-the-underdog self. I found it more and more difficult to act with a sense of godly compassion - for myself or others in my life.

Like many downtowners, Beth and I knew by name lots of the friends of Jesus who lived on our city streets or in nearby shelters. Kenny, who was gentle and polite. Sardine Tom, the one who liked for us to buy him sardines when we passed him in the early evening on our way to Heinen's for groceries and who enjoyed pleasant conversation when he was sober but was flirty with Beth and rather aggressive when he was drunk. Darryl, who I sometimes took for coffee and a sandwich if it was early enough in the day and he hadn't yet become drunk and belligerent. There was James Craig, with his binomial two first names who preferred me to buy him a Pepsi but would be gracious enough not to snub his nose at a Coke if that's all that was available. I believed that there might even be room for "Crazy Jim" in our lives and, perhaps, in the life of the church until he became obsessed with Beth. He started sending her dark and troubling letters in the mail every other day, and then signed her up for a free first year's subscription to Guns and Ammo magazine.

For a longtime there had been great joy for me in befriending these ones who were mostly invisible to others. "For as much as you have done it for the least of these," said Jesus, "you have done it for me." I felt like I was doing the work of the gospel.

By 2018, however, more often than not I tried to avoid the panhandlers and beggars who shouted at me, "Hey pastor!" whenever I stepped outside of my front door, or pawed at me with their worn-out pitches for cash. My spirit was threadbare from keeping an eye on the sex-offenders and pedophiles who showed up at church on Sundays for the free lunch, or the disheveled thirty-year-old who confessed to me that he appreciated being allowed to come into the church mid-week to warm up because the Public Library had kicked him out when they caught him masturbating in front of one of their computers. I could no longer shake his hand, even when we prayed together. An 'elbow bump' for him and most others was as far as I could go after a decade of working with these special folks.

Eventually, word spread on the street that the church offered a magnificent coffee hour on Sundays which often included casseroles, meatballs, sandwiches, hotdogs on baseball home game days, and always a plethora of wonderful cookies and pastries. It was just too appealing. The hungry didn't want to miss out and so more and more people crawled in for worship and coffee hour, many who were battered and bruised from spending a night in one of our dangerous city shelters, or under a bush in a nearby park, or behind a bin in an alleyway. Some had dried blood often crusting over unshaven cheeks or caked to ripped jackets or torn shirts. Others came reeking of beer or cheap wine or both. Neither I nor our mostly-aging congregation were equipped to deal with the growing challenges - disruptions in the sanctuary, hoarding of food in the fellowship hall. Sometimes, church members were shocked to walk into public bathrooms and discover a homeless man or woman stripped bare and bathing in a sink.

While some saw this as an emerging ministry for the church, not all agreed. I was dispirited by the congregation's growing resistance, and by its misplaced expectation that I could somehow resolve the issues. Longtime members wanted time for themselves with their pastor on Sunday mornings, but they also wanted their pastor to 'fix' the growing problems that the homeless brought with them.

"It's fine if 'they' come to the church, Dr. Mark. But can't we have 'them' come on some other day than Sunday?" good folks pleaded with me. Little did they know that the friends of Jesus were already coming to the church midweek - for the Friday food program, the Wednesday lunch program when it was still running, and on other weekdays when they tried to get one of our kindhearted staff to buzz them through the locked side entrance into the church so they could plead their case for money or a bus ticket, or just about anything they might be able to flip for cash on the street. More importantly, however, I never saw it as an us-and-them problem. I believed we were just an us kind of community that needed to figure out how it was going to move forward as a whole.

As I stepped on to the elevator one Sunday after coffee hour, one well-meaning member expressed his concern that the growing number of poor people showing for church would chase away the longtime members. He reasoned at me with his pointed finger like it was a loaded gun: "Remember, you need to take care of your constituents first!" The elevator door closed just in time to save me from firing off an angry retort: "We're Christians; I thought the poor were our constituents."

Sometimes, I joke that Jesus only had to stick around and do his ministry for three years, I've been at it for almost thirty! I have a great deal of empathy for the good folks of the Old Stone Church, and other urban congregations that are visited regularly by those with great need. There are no easy answers. And it takes a great deal of community energy and effort. My own, however, was diminishing. I couldn't carry those rocks any more.

•   •   •

It wasn't just the friends of Jesus at the church, though, or the church's unhappiness with them that felt like heavy stones in my heart. Cleveland's active homeless population in downtown itself was beginning to feel out of control. I was tired of seeing drunks urinate on our condo building's parking garage door and, even more so, the self-entitled white kid who came downtown from the suburbs to party during the CAVS victory parade and then defecated in the front entrance door of our building. Apparently, he couldn't be bothered to walk across the street to one of the city's temporary blue porta-potties, or perhaps he was just too in his cups to notice them. His girlfriend, who was standing watch for her boyfriend, turned and screamed at Beth and me as we tried to gain access to our building, "Don't even talk to us. This has been the worst day ever. We came down here [downtown] and immediately my cell phone died!" Yes, I wanted to say, and to make your first-world problems even worse, you are dating the young man peeing on my front door in front of hundreds of incredulous onlookers.

I was desensitized to the violence in the city, too. I no longer woke up when people shot each other beneath my window in the middle of the night. I felt less compassionate and more irked the afternoon that I heard gun shots outside my home - also on the day of the CAVS victory parade. I had just stepped around the teenaged boy peeing in my front door and over a puddle of his piss to gain access to my condo. I was done. I had lain down on the couch to watch the rest of the festivities on television in my socks - my shoes were left in the hallway, of course. I heard three quick pops that I knew immediately were gun shots. "Was that a gun?" I grumbled to Beth as if I was responding to the irritating noise of a doorbell or a telephone solicitor calling on the phone and not the sound of someone being shot outside of our home. I slid off the couch and walked over to the window to see hundreds of people in the street tripping over each other as they scrambled for safety.

The gun had been fired into the crowd by a fifteen-year-old boy and randomly struck thirteen-year-old girl in what was rumored to be a gang initiation rite. The fifteen-year-old pulled out the handgun from the waistband of his jeans and then simply blasted away into the sea of people. Thankfully the boy had bad aim and only hit the girl in the leg. She lives to tell the story but, no doubt, has been traumatized for years to come.

That same year, I experienced something akin to short term post-traumatic stress after the day I was almost shot in the alley way that led to our garage. Were it not for my neighbor shouting from the fire escape outside of his window to distract the young man, I might not have been able to get away. With each incident, I could feel the rocks piling up.

•　　•　　•

The relentless legal battle between the condo owners and the developer, by this point two or three years old, was crushing down on my spirit, too. Month after month, I dragged myself off to more meetings with lawyers and legal advisors to get updates to report back to homeowners, plan strategies, and cobble together more resources than we ever had at any given moment just to keep the water in the building running, the property insured, and the structure itself standing upright. All indicators pointed to a future assessment for every owner of close to one hundred thousand dollars. An amount many in our building just didn't have, including Beth and me. Walking away wasn't an option, though. Without the miracle of a cash buyer, no one could sell their unit. Like the rabbit whose paw was clamped in the trap, I often wondered how long it would be before I had to chew off my own foot, taking on the bloodletting loss of personal bankruptcy in my fifties, just to break free.

We posted our place on the real estate market for half a year or so, listing it with the agent who helped us find it over ten years earlier. Lots of looky-loos came by to take a gander. Still, we succeeded only in awakening curiosity, and gossip within our congregation. With no mortgage company in its right mind willing to lend money to purchase a condo that was tangled up in litigation, potential buyers walked away saying, "Hey, we love your place. Please give us a call whenever the court case finishes up." It seemed like it never would. Cash buyers, no matter how low we dropped the asking price just weren't out there. Eventually, we got tired of the showings for the snoopers and looky-loos who knew full well that they couldn't make a cash offer so we abandoned hope of a sale and removed our home from the market again.

Across the Square, over at the church, I was struggling under the weight of a six-month long social media attack that was waged against the church. An InfoWars reporter had shown up for the rally of speeches we hosted following the 2019 Women's Day March. The reporter seemed less interested in reporting the news than she was in generating it. She goaded one of our associates and captured a regrettable comment on camera. While still at the church, she cropped together a video and posted it with a click-bait headline that went viral overnight. Her campaign forced us to shut down our Facebook account for forty-eight hours and flattened our impressive Google review rating from 4.8 to 1.7 stars in a matter of weeks. We welcomed the support of the local police and their cyber security squad, as well as the FBI when threats or threat-like comments emerged from around the country. Even more crushing than threats, though, was the barrage of ugliness, hate, and outright ignorance from self-professing Christians far too lazy or opinionated to check their facts. They had seen a snippet of a video online, believed what the accompanying headlines had spoon fed them, and assumed they knew the whole truth and nothing but the truth. Stones were hurled at us every day in the form of emails and overnight phone messages, nasty comments on our Facebook and YouTube channel. Even self-righteous snail mail brought us its own special kind of hate.

"Christians are to love God not only with their hearts but also their minds," I growled to staff and lay leaders. "Why on earth do so many check their brains at the door whenever they scroll through the river of hearsay, fake news, conspiracy theories and outright lies that flood online feeds?" Many times a day, and for weeks on end, we witnessed behavior from so-called Christians that was simply bitter and cruel, disheartening and antithetical to the good work of the gospel that the church had been doing for almost two hundred years. As far as I am aware, pastors are not given defensive training to respond to this sort of twenty-first century electronic melee. I would urge seminaries who prepare clergy for ministry in the age of social media to take a hard look at how we empower pastors and other church leaders. At the very least, we ought to have training on how protect ourselves from the social media storms and disinformation campaigns that have already arrived.

I continued picking up rocks for my sack full of stones until I knew that I couldn't carry them any longer. The burden of life in Cleveland was getting heavier. Emotionally, it was crushing. Physically, I experienced very real neck and shoulder pain. I couldn't carry the load any longer so went to see my medical massage therapist - who was the therapist for the Cleveland Cavaliers, my chiropractor - who was the Cleveland Brown's chiropractor, and my doctor - who was the team doc for the Cleveland Indians. At one point I said to each of them, "If Cleveland's 'A' team can't fix me up, I'm in real trouble." Each blessed me with confidence by assuring me that if I stuck with the program for healing, I would eventually get better, which I did. It would just take time. The root of the problem, however, still existed: I needed to set down some of those stones that I was never meant to carry, nor was I capable of carrying, at least not on my own, lest I get pancaked under their weight.

I started driving more, even when I could have easily walked, just to avoid some of the frenetic midway activity of the street outside our doors. Beth and started looking for new a place to live beyond the hardscaped environment of downtown, possibly even outside of the city proper. Beth and I fantasized about having a screened porch or back yard, a private space where we could just sit outside and heal without being hounded by people on the street. We longed for "points of grace" in our lives. Maybe finding renters for our place downtown, we reasoned, we could cover the cost of a second mortgage somewhere else in the city, somewhere with a few more grace points. We would still have the stress of the ongoing condo issues, but at least we wouldn't have to come home to it every night. Just the thought of getting some private, outdoor space made my load feel a little lighter.

I took my first sabbatical in thirty years of ministry – three months to begin writing about my Cleveland experience, to walk the Camino de Santiago in northern Spain and, most importantly, to catch my breath. When I came home I had adopted a new mantra that I had developed along the Camino – "Go slow and enjoy the show." I stopped working seven days a week, and started taking my full allotted vacation time for the first time in over a decade, even though some in leadership grumbled that I was away for too long at a time. It's something I should have done from the start. It would have helped set healthier boundaries for myself with the church from the beginning. If I was going to keep loving those who could not, or would not, love me back, I needed to start taking better care of myself.

I called on some outside help where I needed it, too. I consulted with a media strategist who had worked with a major politician for over a decade. Who better to understand the social media crisis in the church than someone who deals with voter hate and vitriol directed at politicians on daily basis? He was compassionate, understanding, and affirmed that we were responding in all the right ways, but cautioned us to try to avoid entering into conversations online with those who are just sounding off. Many of them were just trolls. Having our strategy affirmed helped me to set down a few more stones. The weight was lifting and I was beginning to breathe a little more easily.

Perhaps the weightiest stone that I had been dragging around, whether I was ready to admit it or not, was my work itself. It was becoming clearer to me by the day that I was being asked to be someone that I was not. Had something changed within me? Since I had taken a sabbatical, I was consciously making healthier decisions, I believed, about how much love to share with those who weren't loving me back. Had something shifted within the church? The church had lots of new members who hadn't been there when I began my ministry among them, and it had said goodbye to many good and faithful servants along the way. Had I out-lived my ministry in the church and the city? Perhaps the answer to all three was "yes."

By summer of 2019, new leadership within the church was looking for me to do more institutional church work than my spirit could take. My butt was sore from sitting in endless meetings, or writing and reviewing documents - personnel policies and procedures, operational manuals, and bylaws to support the new corporation of the First Presbyterian Church in Cleveland which had been formed as a means to delineate power and legal identity for those elected by the church apart from the self-electing First Presbyterian Society that continued to assert its ownership of the church and the church's resources. Either way, I was beginning to see, perhaps for the first time, that the historic conflict wasn't my battle to be fought, nor did I have any interest in having my good spirit eaten up any more than it already had been. The devil destroys us not so much with fire and brimstone but also with the tedium of bureaucracy.

What God had brought together, the church continued to tear asunder. Itself. I saw the division, the same seventy-year conflict that kept bubbling up, decade after decade, was starting to tear strips out of good people on all sides. People I loved and for whom I cared deeply. It was tearing me up, too. And with the division, came multi-million-dollar internal battles. Which board had the right and fiduciary responsibility to lay claim to certain funds and annual payouts on shared gifts and endowments – the one that was elected by the congregation or the self-electing one that claimed to be the rightful, legal owners of the church? To whom did the church truly belong? The correct answer, of course, though not the legal one, is God. It should always be God. Still, some folks argued that the congregation was a tenant occupying space in a building owned by an historic society.

In the Presbyterian Church, we say that "Jesus Christ is the head of the church," but at the Old Stone Church, however, fewer and fewer seemed to be acting that way. At one point, the Session – the church's board was told by the Society that it needed to seek the Society's permission if it wanted to attach anything to the building. A television screen, a plaque, a picture. I could smell a potential law suit and the 'lawyering-up' between the two groups brewing in the air. While I wasn't sure who would strike the first blow, I knew full well that stopping it was well beyond my limited experience and capability. There is a God and, I was well aware, I wasn't it. I was just as certain that I did not want to get tangled up in yet another law suit like the one across the street between our condo association and its developer, one likely to define the last ten or twelve remaining years of my ministry.

At the same time, I found myself becoming the lightning rod for both groups' unease and determination. I was micromanaged, coached, and asked to do ministry with more of a focus on administration. It was an approach that seemed to reflect more of a 'corporate America' culture than one of the first century gospel movement of Jesus Christ. One group sought to leverage me, or at least my position as the pastor of the church, over the other. I felt pitted against the very people I needed to love and for whom I cared deeply. I had less time to be a pastor, too, to care for those who I knew were suffering, grieving, or simply longing for the church to be in its life in new and meaningful ways. There were fewer hours in the day for me to meet seekers and questioners in coffee shops, or downtown residents in pubs for happy hour. I had less time for being at the hospital in early morning prayer with good folks as they awaited life or death surgeries. Less time to be with folks as they journeyed with cancer and other illnesses. Less time to develop meaningful relationships with the hundreds of couples who continued to come to the church seeking to be married. Less time to speak publicly, write op-eds, or do interviews about the things that make the city fair and just for all. I felt as if I was squandering my creative energy and enthusiasm for ministry fixing up an old ship that had no intention of ever leaving dry dock. The church was a vessel that longed for smooth sailing with very little interest in setting out on the choppy seas of the twenty-first century that called to the adventurer in me. Work was getting in the way of my vocation. I didn't see it at the time, but already I was getting ready to drop the rock, to set down the biggest stone of them all - my ministry and my time in Cleveland.

At the end of the summer 2019, I received a confidential five-page, single spaced letter from a senior church leader that unloaded on both Beth and me with double barrel spray of frustration about pretty well every failure that the letter's author believed we had made over the previous two years. I was crestfallen. It felt like I had just been punched in the face. And worse, I was being asked to keep the letter and, therefore, my anguish a secret. I needed support, or at the very least some sort of feedback from others in leadership. Did everyone feel this way about my work performance or just the letter's author? I needed to find stable ground but was asked not to talk about the letter or its contents with others. What was I to do?

One evening, without breaking confidence, I chose to enter into an honest and, for me, tearful discussion about the letter during a closed personnel meeting. I don't think folks knew what to do with my personal expressions of pain. Some admitted having already known about the letter but mostly remained silent about its accusations. Had I placed too much on the table for them to process, I wondered. I still do. Had I shared more, and expected more from people than they were prepared to deal with? Perhaps. For me, ministry has never been about a job. It has been about relationships, about sharing our mutual affection in and for Christ with each other. It has been about our shared vision for ministry in the church and the world. The take away for me that night was simple: the congregation had changed, or at least its leadership had. Right under my nose. Not better. Not worse. It was just different. It happens. It seemed to me that leaders were looking for a different kind of minister than the one they already had.

I had come to Cleveland to help humanize an institution, to soften its corporate shape and structure, to love something even if it couldn't love me back. I had come to take the church and its message of hope into the city. And for a time, that's who we were and that's what we did. We were a messy, less-formed fellowship. We were less 'establishment,' and more of a living, breathing, phenomenon. Not just a historic building, but a light on the Square shining brightly from the heart of the city. Sometimes we knocked heads but we never threw punches.

"You either play on the court or you're upstairs in management," a friend once advised me. "LeBron doesn't set the budget, or manage the staff. He does one thing. And he does that one thing very well. He plays basketball. What's your one thing, Mark?" It felt to me like, for the first time, the church wanted me to be upstairs in the corporate office more than down on the court doing what I did best: preaching, teaching, befriending long-timers and newcomers, and being the public face, the human face of the corporate body that was the church.

I had only another dozen or so years of ministry left in me. I knew that my "one thing" wasn't going to be trying to be someone or something that I knew full well I could not be.

After the personnel meeting wrapped up, I stepped out of the church into the balm of a mid-September evening. Ignoring the 'Don't Walk' signal at empty intersection of Rockwell and Ontario, I strolled into Public Square. The setting sun blanketed me in a warm amber glow. Absorbing the magnificence of the towering city around me and the eleven-acre city park at its heart, I released a great sigh, an expression of both satisfaction and disappointment. As the twelfth Senior Pastor of the Old Stone Church, I was blessed to have brought leadership to both an amazing city on the rise, and to a church filled with good and faithful souls that I will carry in my heart forever. Along with other civic leaders, right there on the church's front lawn, we had created a new public heart for the city. A place for people to gather, where families could picnic and children could splash in a spraying fountain. Beth and I had shared a glass of wine and watched

Shakespeare in the Park in the Square a short time earlier – something almost unimaginable in Public Square just a few years earlier.

I strolled between a couple of young people and a frolicking dog that was chasing the whirling Frisbee they spun back and forth to each other. I had been presented with an award for Downtown Resident of the year on that grassy section of the Square just weeks earlier. It was a great place – Cleveland, the new Public Square, the growing, thriving downtown community. I just wasn't sure that it could be my place anymore.

I turned my gaze southward, past the statue of old Moses Cleaveland watching over the Square. I lifted my head toward our three-bedroom corner unit on the fourth floor of the Park Building. Our home was the backdrop to our new city-center park, it's bubbling fountain - a skating rink in winter that I was privileged to bless on live television each year. Like the church on the northside of the Square, our home on the southside, had a unique vantage point on pretty well every major event that unfolded in downtown Cleveland between 2008 and 2019. Women's Day Marches. Black Lives Matter protests. High school student's March for Our Lives anti-gun rallies. Occupy Cleveland. Founders Day celebrations. Christmas Story Runs, Rite Aid Marathons, and Rock and Roll Marathons, too. Cleveland Orchestra Concerts and enough fireworks displays to satiate, for a lifetime, any desire within me to see things blow up ever again. The block party we threw in 2016 for the Republican National Convention. The filming of The Avengers movie and an episode of American Ninja Warriors. The CAVS victory celebration parties, and same day shooting of a young, teenage girl. The speeches I made alongside the Mayor, Congressmen and Congresswomen, and Governor at the Soldiers and Sailors Monument. The day Congressman Kucinich, our Clerk of Session, and I released a dozen white doves from the steps of the Old Stone Church and quickly turned to one another mindful of the razor-sharp talons of the family of peregrine falcons living atop the Terminal Tower on the other side of the Square.

As I got closer to my home, I looked up at our condo building. The hideous scaffolding that had once wrapped our home had been removed but the never-ending lawsuit over the building's façade remained. As did the brutal fissures that raced up and down the old brown brick work. As did the steel staples that traced up the full height of each of the building's corners. The antiquated structure resembled something more akin to Doctor Frankenstein's monster than the high end "luxury" home that it was billed as when Beth and I bought into the project more than a decade earlier. I glanced down to the far end of the building and spotted a familiar sight: a drunken man, a friend of Jesus, peeing on the brick façade.

"Hmm." I wondered. "He may be right," I mused to no one but myself. "Piss on it," I laughed. Not so much in anger but more in surrender.

I reached for the door handle and dropped the one remaining pebble from my palm. I let it fall to the ground and stepped through the doors. I was ready to be done.

•   •   •

When I ambled into our unit, Unit 400, my phone was buzzing. It was from an area code I recognized well: 912. Savannah, Georgia.

"Hello?" I answered.

"Hi Dr. Mark. This is Susan from Savannah." I would have recognized the sweet sound of Susan's delightful southern accent anywhere. Susan was a key figure in the church I had served before moving to Cleveland eleven years earlier.

"Hey Susan? What's going on?" We hadn't talked in quite some time.

"Well," she rolled the word out slowly as if bracing herself to share something big, or maybe bracing me to hear. "I'm sitting here with our pastor search committee tonight. I think you know that we don't have a pastor right now. How would you like to come home to Savannah and be our pastor again?"

I took a calming breath. Smiled at the remarkableness of God's perfect timing. Without hesitation, I responded, "Susan, I think I'd like that very much."

•   •   •

For two weeks, I wrestled with the invitation to return to Savannah. Can I really go back? They are not the same people. I am not the same person. How can we leave when we can't even get out from the albatross of our condo? I felt like Jacob wrestling the angel down by the Jabbok river before he returned to his homeland to make peace with his brother.

Then in late September, as if God was trying to make my decision clearer, I received another phone call. It was our former realtor.

"Hey, Mark. Are you and Beth still interested in selling your place? I've got a cash buyer who's ready to make a purchase. Do you think you could be out of your place in thirty days?"

2020: Acceptance and Meaning

"To regret one's own experiences is to arrest one's own development. To deny one's own experiences is to put a lie into the lips of one's own life. It is no less than a denial of the soul."

- Oscar Wilde, *De Profundis*

Chapter Fourteen

Home is Where the Cause Is

_____

"Do you regret leaving Cleveland?" I'm sometimes asked. "You loved Cleveland," my family often reminds me as if I could ever forget. No. I don't regret leaving Cleveland. Nor will I ever regret loving it either. I don't think I will ever get Cleveland out of my heart nor would I want to. It has left an imprint there. A soft and tender place. It has also left some scars.

"So why did you leave?" you may ask, that is if you have skipped the last few chapters and jumped to the end. I think the better question, though, is the one I struggle to answer these days: Why did I choose Cleveland in the first place? Or why did it choose me? After all, I could have easily stayed in Savannah, or moved just about anywhere else on God's good and green earth. Cleveland wasn't the only city with whom I had been flirting. There were others. I turned them all down. For Cleveland!

You might even ask why I stayed in Cleveland as long as I did. Sure, there were great victories to be won. Lots accolades and achievements for the city to be celebrated. There were even a few for me personally. I received awards from the mayor and other prestigious groups. A couple of national church publications were starting to take notice of the kind of new urbanist ministry happening at the Old Stone Church in Cleveland, working with city planners and developers to build a successful and just city, to raise the standard of living for all Clevelanders. We even helped the city move up a notch or two from the second poorest city in America to sixth.

By that time, however, I had lost so much steam that the accolades felt like little more than slight puffs of air. They were hardly enough to fill my sails and keep me moving forward through the choppy waters of Cleveland. They certainly weren't enough to sustain me against the even more turbulent currents of the conflicted institutional structures of the church. Those had begun swamping me in their toxic pool of infighting, accusations, and my own sense of personal frustration and disappointment. The achievements started to feel like little more than the rare, seductive wins that keep a person at the roulette table believing, falsely, that with the next spin of the wheel their luck would improve. For me, it never did. Not in the end. Those wins were short lived and very much like my crusty old colleague's metaphorical "twenty-dollar whore" who gives you a tickle in just the right place to keep you around a little longer.

Why Cleveland? It is a question I've wrestled with for more than a decade. The simple answer is this: It's complicated.

It's complicated because Cleveland is both a predictable and, at the same time, unlikely place for me to have tried to make my home. It is predictable, I suppose, because Cleveland is quite similar to the blue-collar city where I grew up - Windsor, Ontario. Windsor is Canada's much cleaner, baby version of Detroit. Like Cleveland and Detroit and a dozen other rustbelt cities, Windsor has a proud history of building the stuff that once drove the North American economy. In fact, it built the very things that Americans drove - cars. Unfortunately, these days, that powerhouse history too often blurs reality for the future, deflates hope, and causes good folks to suffer badly from a flattened sense of self-worth.

I have a soft spot for cities, rustbelt cities in particular. Places that have become like the old sun-cracked Firestone tire keeled over and laying among the broken glass, rotting mattresses, and the single shoe abandoned along the shoulder of the I-90 that cuts across Cleveland, or the I-75 in Detroit, or the I-190 in Buffalo. "How lonely sits the city that once was full of people!" says the scriptures, "How like a widow she has become, she that was great among the nations! She that was a princess among the provinces has become a vassal. She weeps bitterly in the night, with tears on her cheeks; among all her lovers she has no one to comfort her; all her friends have dealt treacherously with her, they have become her enemies" (Lamentations 1:1-2). As a potential home, Cleveland had a familiar industrial smell to it - a sweet memory of onetime greatness that kept it hungry for it once again. Cleveland reminded me of a place I once called home. And so I tried my industrial heartland best to make it my new home.

On the other hand, Cleveland is also an unlikely home for me. After I finished college and ran away. Like my pants were ablaze! I ran from the factories and diminishing shiftwork opportunities, unions, strikes and layoffs, and the irregular rhythms of the boom and bust automotive-driven economy – in recent years, mostly bust - to which Windsorites proudly clung. I swore up and down that I'd never be back. And for over twenty years, until my last kid had moved from home and I experienced a brief moment of midlife disorientation, I had managed to keep far afield of my rusty roots. "We were out! We were out!" My beloved had cried as we thumped and bumped, thudded and banged our way off of the I-77 and on to Ontario Street, dodging the crater sized potholes, faults and fissures that jagged across our pathway into downtown Cleveland over a decade ago.

My decision to move to Cleveland is complicated in the way people will persist, against all reason, in falling in love with the wrong kinds of men or women, or the way your otherwise rational friend stands firm in his irrational yet unwavering assertion that the Electric Light Orchestra was the best rock band ever. Family and friends will implore you take a look in the mirror, give your head a shake, or get off the drugs and think again, but to no avail. It's complicated.

The motivations informing my decision to move to Cleveland (and it was mostly that, my desire that brought us there. Beth would remind us both of this, and usually when we were walking down Euclid Avenue, struggling face-first into a blinding February blizzard) and to stay for almost a dozen years were complicated. They emanated from that deep longing for home which, for me, I have learned, likely means something entirely different than it does for many others.

Home isn't simply where the heart is. For me, home is where the cause is. It is the place where passion is ignited and steadily burns. It is the place where my vocational itch to serve God and country, particularly the least among us, gets scratched. Home is the place, like Cleveland, where those who have been knocked down keep getting back up, where those who have lost their way keep searching and finding it again. It's the place where those who have struggled under the dead-weight of a tired and démodé industrial era for far too long and are so fed up that they're now giving birth to new ideas and entrepreneurial opportunities that will reshape new urban and even new world economies. For me, home is the place where the dark horse charges relentlessly toward a last-minute comeback. It's the place where the consummate loser still dreams of a national title. I longed for a place where I might experience urban resurrection. I longed for a Cleveland.

Mark Twain noted that we choose "heaven for climate, hell for company."[61] Savannah was certainly heaven-like in that it offered me a downright spectacular climate, not to mention, some gracious, lifelong friends, but I chose Cleveland for the same reason some folks, apparently, will choose hell: the company. The tough as nails, never say "die" Clevelanders – both in the church and throughout the city as a whole, blessed me with grace and hope, and who will be forever family to me now. No matter where I happen to be in the world.

I had the greatest opportunity of finding home, or allowing home to find me, among Clevelanders who knew what it was to be bully-bruised by steel-mill layoffs, downsizing, and permanent factory closures, crushed under the weight of bad mortgages and home foreclosures. I believed that I could find a home or, at least, make one among a good people who had been serrated by the brittle winds of the Great Lake, that once default toxic reservoir gnawing on its doorstep and remains, to this day, a scornful body of brown water that every spring, winter, and fall chaffs your face and leathers your soul.

I was overwhelmed by a strange compulsion to walk alongside this rustbelt underdog. I suppose it could have been Detroit, or

---

[61] Mark Twain's *Notebooks and Journals, vol. 3* found on http://www.twainquotes.com/Hell.html, accessed April 15, 2018.

Pittsburgh, or Buffalo, or Indianapolis, or St. Louis, or any one of the dozens of other great American cities that got buried, if only temporarily, under the debris of the great American Industrial Empire's crushing collapse but are rediscovering, deep within the well of their heartland histories, the trinitarian spirit of entrepreneurialism, dignity, and sheer friggin' will. "Go where you're needed most, Dad," my son had advised me. "That's where you're most happy." And so I did. I went to Cleveland where the cause was real, and the city's need was aching. In the words of the singer-songwriter, Jackson Browne, I longed for a "Cleveland heart. They're made to take a bashing. And never lose their passion."

There was a kid in my grade school. Glenn. You never wanted to mess with Glenn. My friends and I had seen him fight before. You couldn't win. No one could. And not because he was the biggest, or the strongest, but because Glenn just never quit. He would have his nose bloodied, his cheeks red and scuffed. He would be down on the ground, his opposer sitting on him and grinding poor little Glenn into the dirt. And just when you thought it was all over, Glenn would be back up on his feet, charging at his enemy like a snorting bull, his fists ablaze in a furious flurry of fire. We never knew where Glenn's resolve came from but very few who knew him ever dared to challenge it. Having grown-up in Windsor-Detroit, I knew rust belt cities. They are a lot like Glenn. Rustbelters never say die.

I believed that it was only by living among those who truly knew what it was to be down, and almost out, that I might experience what it was to be raised back up again. I believed, and still believe, that if God could raise Jesus from the dead on the very first Easter, then God could raise cities like Cleveland, Detroit, Flint and Buffalo. That is resurrection. And I, very badly, wanted to be a part of it.

For Clevelanders, the daily grind seems more magnified than in other parts of the United States. It grinds on them, and within them. It grinds them up and grinds them down. Yet, in Cleveland, I came to know and love a people cut from a hearty Midwestern stock. They're good folks who manage those scathing winter winds and the blinding lake effect snows with rough-edged humor and sheer grit. Clevelanders are blessed with a kind of salt of the earth character that if it were ever to be bottled and shared could easily change the world. They know how to persevere because they have had to do it for decades, generations even. They never give up. Ever. And from the grounds of the grind, the remains of the dust and the rust of yesterday's prosperity, Clevelanders are building an incredible, vibrant, championship city.

Travelling feels like falling in love, wrote Thériault.[62] I was ready to fall in love with Cleveland. And I did. And for a while, I loved Cleveland with all my heart and mind, my strength and my soul. I loved it fully and completely until I couldn't love anymore.

I didn't come to Cleveland just for a visit. I came looking for a home. I chose Cleveland because I had been rooting and uprooting all of my life, moving from place to place compelled by a desire to see how the rest of the world lived and maybe, just maybe, find a home among a good people in a remarkable city or, at the very least, find a home among those who shared a common cause. I moved to Cleveland because I was looking for the purpose driven city.

It only stopped being my home, when I lost my purpose for being there. Even so, I wasn't sure that it was ever going to let me leave. Home is like that. Even when you're ready to move on, home may not be quite ready to let you go.

I still laugh incredulously when I think about how we almost didn't get out. How the cosmic tumblers had to align perfectly in order for us to break free from whatever mysterious force was holding us there. The phone call from the search committee in Savannah that came the very night I had set down the last of my Cleveland rocks – my ministry among the good folks of the Old Stone Church. The one and only cash buyer who appeared out of nowhere to purchase our condo. It hadn't even been listed on the real estate market in almost a year. Heck. The day before the movers arrived our building even caught fire! As five fire trucks pulled up out front on Public Square, the entire building was evacuated. The south and east sides of the

---

[62] Anne Thériault, "Geel, Belgium has a radical approach to mental illness" Broadview Magazine, September 5, 2019 https://broadview.org/geel-belgium-mental-health/ accessed 2019 09 06.

building had experienced extensive damage. I was convinced that our building was related to Stephen King's haunted hotel room 1408 – it was an evil friggin' place and would never let us go. I turned to Beth as we huddled with the other residents out on the street, our soggy winter coats dripping with wet snow wrapped around ourselves, and sang that famous line from the Eagle's song, Hotel California: "You can check anytime you like, but you can never leave!" She failed to see my humor and confessed, only after the fact, that she was sure we were going to be stuck in Cleveland until hell froze over. I reminded her that it had. Every winter in Cleveland.

Miraculously, our side of the Park Building was untouched. As scheduled, the movers came the next day. Packed us up. And by the end of November 2019, we were gone.

Goodbye, Cleveland.

Epilogue

Memory and Longing

"The continuance of your longing is the continuance of your prayer."
Saint Augustine

———————————

IT IS MID-AUGUST, 2020. I am at Tybee Beach just outside of the city of Savannah proper. In the pandemic era, if you get to the beach early enough in the day before the crowds start setting up their chairs and umbrellas, the beach is a good place to practice some physical distancing. It is also a great place to do some serious self-reflection. Twelve full years have tumbled by since that summer Beth and I leaped toward Cleveland in search of a home.

I am standing at the water's edge now. I have just come out from swimming. The ocean's water drips down my hair and face and body. I savor the sultry southern winds as they race up the coast and airdry me almost instantly. The air is warm. It is close. Cleveland is distant. Far away. It has been less than a year since I left. Nine months. Enough time for baby to have been born, I suppose. Even so, Cleveland is long away and long ago. I feel like I have awakened from a strange eleven-year dream – my parallel life in Cleveland. But I am awake now. I am awake, and I am at home again. In Savannah.

The light of the midmorning sun shimmers along the surface of the Atlantic's rolling waters. Its warmth soothes my face and, like a velvety blanket enwraps my entire body. Within its embrace, the

Cleveland hardness within me melts like wax. I am being restored. My spirit is at rest. It is well with my soul.

The waters of the rising tide gently wash over my feet and I am aware of the shifting sand beneath them. As much as I try, I am unable to stand in one place for long. The waves are persistent. They roll in and, as they do, swish the sand out from beneath the soles of my feet. I make a game of it. How long can I remain in one place before losing my balance in these ancient and shifting grains of sand? I catch myself before falling over and step up to one side and then another and start all over again. It is an easy game to play, but not to win. The sand is always moving beneath my feet.

I close my eyes and search the imaginary screen in my mind for the Madeleine L'Engle quote that my mother in Canada has sent to me in one of her recent emails: "We are all strangers in a strange land, longing for home, but not quite knowing what or where home is. We glimpse it sometimes in our dreams, or as we turn a corner, and suddenly there is a strange, sweet familiarity that vanishes almost as soon as it comes."[63]

Maybe that's what home is, I wonder. Not a place, or even a people. But a glimpse. Some sweet familiarity that is recognized only in the ebb and flow of our spirit's restlessness. In our desire for it. Home is a glint. Like the flashing light on each rolling wave before me. It's not something to be grasped, or even held on to for any length of time. Home is more temporal to us than we are to this earth. Home is a momentary flicker of brilliant peace, and beauty, that rides a wave that soon crashes along the shifting sands beneath our feet. The image of home imprints on our hearts the way a sunspot rides the waves and then, as we gaze upon it, forms on the retina. It stays with us, but only for a moment. Then it fades almost as quickly as it came, leaving us with only a notion of what home is and where home might be or where home might have been. Home is a memory. And home is a longing.

---

[63] Madeleine L'Engle, *The Rock That is Higher: Story as Truth*, 1993.

Gratitude

No book writes itself. It is with gratitude and appreciation that I acknowledge the following who helped Making it Home come together in the way that it did: Janice Shay, my agent and friend, who championed this project from the beginning. My beta readers who contributed unique, honest, and helpful input that helped shape the final draft: Mark Lammon, Executive Director of the Campus District, Cleveland; Sarah Grace Ross, Director of Justice, Chiefs of Ontario, Toronto; Julia Stone, Principal, Stone Marketing and Public Relations, Savannah; Tom Williams, Ph.D., Owner, Williams & Company, Book Publishers, Savannah; Betty Giuliano, my mom and best proof reader anywhere; and Beth Giuliano who read, tweaked, challenged, shredded, encouraged, and loved me and my writing with scathing honesty.

I would also like to acknowledge the amazing people of the Old Stone Church who took a chance on me back in 2008 and blessed me with the most challenging and rewarding years of ministry . . . so far; and the very good and resilient people of Cleveland, Ohio – a city of champions, who taught me that we are never so far down that we can't get back up again. They taught me, too, that when we do, we should get up swinging! Lastly, I want to offer my deepest gratitude and affection for the genuine folks of the Montgomery Presbyterian Church in Savannah, Georgia who not only took a chance on me once, but had the audacity and faithful courage to do it twice. They loved me back into wholeness in the early 2000s, and in 2019, they proved to me that maybe, just maybe, a person can go back home.

About the Author

Mark Giuliano has dozens of published articles and media appearances focused on faith and the city. He is a Presbyterian (USA) pastor, former professor at the Savannah College of Art and Design, and hosts a podcast called, *Rags of Light: Ordinary people's extraordinary stories that help light our way.* He has received numerous awards and accolades for his work, and in 2019 he was especially moved to have been elected Cleveland's "Downtown Resident of the Year."

Note from the Author

Word-of-mouth is crucial for any author to succeed. If you enjoyed *Making It Home*, please leave a review online — anywhere you are able. Even if it's just a sentence or two. It would make all the difference and would be very much appreciated.

Thanks!
R. Mark Giuliano

We hope you enjoyed reading this title from:

www.blackrosewriting.com

Subscribe to our mailing list – *The Rosevine* – and receive
FREE books, daily deals, and stay current with news about
upcoming releases and our hottest authors.
Scan the QR code below to sign up.

Already a subscriber? Please accept a sincere thank you for
being a fan of Black Rose Writing authors.

View other Black Rose Writing titles at
www.blackrosewriting.com/books and use promo code
PRINT to receive a **20% discount** when purchasing.